REVOLUTIONARIES AND REFORMERS

REVOLUTIONARIES AND REFORMERS

CONTEMPORARY ISLAMIST MOVEMENTS
IN THE MIDDLE EAST

Edited by

Barry Rubin

STATE UNIVERSITY OF NEW YORK PRESS

Published by
State University of New York Press, Albany

© 2003 State University of New York

For information, address
State University of New York Press,
90 State Street, Suite 700, Albany, NY 12207

Production, Laurie Searl
Marketing, Michael Campochiaro

Library of Congress Cataloging-in-Publication Data

Revolutionaries and reformers : contemporary Islamist movements in the Middle East /
Barry Rubin, editor.
      p. cm.
   Includes bibliographical references and index.
   ISBN 0-7914-5617-X (alk. paper)—ISBN 0-7914-5618-8 (pbk. : alk. paper)
      1. Islamic renewal—Middle East. 2. Islam—Middle East—20th century. 3.
   Islam and state—Middle East. 4. Islam and politics—Middle East. 5. Middle
   East—Politics and government. I. Rubin, Barry M.

BP60 .R46 2003
322.4'0917'671—dc21   2002075876

10 9 8 7 6 5 4 3 2 1

Contents

PREFACE   vii

1   WHY RADICAL MUSLIMS AREN'T TAKING OVER GOVERNMENTS   1
     Emmanuel Sivan

2   RADICAL ISLAM IN EGYPT
     A Comparison of Two Groups   11
     David Zeidan

3   THE DEVELOPMENT OF PALESTINIAN ISLAMIC GROUPS   23
     Reuven Paz

4   RADICAL ISLAMIST MOVEMENTS IN TURKEY   41
     Ely Karmon

5   ISLAMISM AND THE STATE IN NORTH AFRICA   69
     Bruce Maddy-Weitzman and Meir Litvak

6   HIZBALLAH
     Between Armed Struggle and Domestic Politics   91
     Eyal Zisser

7   BALANCING STATE AND SOCIETY
     The Islamic Movement in Kuwait   105
     Shafeeq N. Ghabra

8   THE RISE OF THE ISLAMIST MOVEMENT IN TURKEY   125
     Nilufer Narli

9   FETHULLAH GULEN AND HIS LIBERAL 'TURKISH ISLAM'
     MOVEMENT   141
        Bulent Aras and Omer Caha

10   ISLAM AND DEMOCRACY   155
        Ali R. Abootalebi

11   MEDIATING MIDDLE EAST CONFLICTS
     An Alternative Approach   173
        George E. Irani

12   LIBERAL ISLAM
     Prospects and Challenges   191
        Charles Kurzman

13   INSIDE THE ISLAMIC REFORMATION   203
        Dale F. Eickelman

14   ISLAMIST MOVEMENTS IN THE MIDDLE EAST
     A Survey and Balance Sheet   207
        Barry Rubin

LIST OF CONTRIBUTORS   219

INDEX   221

Preface

The politics of Islam has been one of the most controversial and tumultuous issues in the Middle East. Islamist movements have established regimes in Iran and Sudan, become the principal opposition groups in every other country of the region, and created revolutionary upheavals in Algeria and Egypt. Yet unable in most cases to gain power, these movements now face a serious debate over strategy and tactics that is likely to lead either to their relative decline or dramatic transformation.

This book looks at the Islamist movements seeking power today, analyzing both groups involved in armed struggle and those trying to gain power by operating within existing systems. At the heart of this situation stands a paradox: Islamist organizations cannot muster enough support or power to gain power through revolutionary means, but are also blocked by governments from transforming their societies through elections or persuasion. Even Iran's Islamist government faces a divisive conflict over alternative visions, a mirror image of this very same debate.

Consequently, these movements face difficult choices. Certainly, they can continue failed strategies of violence or frustrated electoral efforts. Violence is always psychologically appealing to some activists and government repression may justify such a stance or even forbid any other option. Remaining an opposition party brings certain advantages ranging from power for its leaders to the freedom to maintain a network of institutions. In each case, the movement professes to transform the whole society while in practice creating a small model of that ideal goal.

An alternative, still in the process of full formulation, is a rethinking of Islamist politics to function as a pressure group to make their societies more Islamic, to reinforce the walls of semiseparate internal communities, and to reinterpret Islam in more liberal ways. This process could also require, however, a credible renunciation of any goal of fully transforming society.

To draw a rough parallel to European history, radical Islamism has been in a 'Communist party' phase, whether employing armed struggle or seeking power through elections and agitation. It could enter a 'Social Democratic' phase that could bring broader appeal, more effective lobbying for change, and perhaps eventual entrance into government. In Iran, the course proposed by President Muhammad Khatami and his supporters represents the same basic concept in reverse, paralleling recent debates in the Soviet Union and China. Rather than a 'totally Islamic' polity, the goal would be some form of Islamic-oriented society.

Again, though, it should be stressed that such a transition will not inevitably be accepted by the movements themselves, nor would it necessarily be acceptable to the incumbent rulers of these states. By examining the Islamist movements in opposition, the roots of their struggle, and their internal debates, this book tries to clarify how they approach these problems and alternative options, as well as whether such different routes are within the realm of possibility or can succeed.

The emergence of a movement around Usama bin Ladin was not a result of the radical interpretation's success in winning over the masses; rather it was a desperate reaction to its failure. Having lost in every other way, bin Ladin and his followers tried to play the anti-American card, downgrading his opposition to the Arab regimes to the point where they might tolerate him and his movement as an asset or at least not as a threat. On September 11, 2001, though, they were too successful in attacking the United States. At first, this made them very popular in the Arab street and regimes rushed, each in its own way, to profit indirectly from the event. But America was too angry for Arab states or even Iran to risk its wrath by explicitly endorsing or protecting al-Qa'ida groups. Yet, as the debate continued, and whatever his own movement's fate, bin Ladin had struck a powerful doctrinal blow for a further radicalization of Islamist thought.

Bin Ladin's great innovation was to open up a new front against Americans and to give this strategy a justification. All the basic ideas he needed, however, had already been expressed by a range of radical Islamist thinkers, from the Egyptian Sayyid Qutb in the 1950s to Khomayni in the 1970s, and a score of Islamist thinkers thereafter. Killing Americans in east Africa (the 1998 attack on U.S. embassies in Kenya and Tanzania), Yemen (the bombing of the USS Cole), and most spectacularly on America itself (September 11, 2001) was very popular in the Arab world.[1] Even those who claimed to mourn the victims cheered the gestures.

Bin Ladin had invented a new type of populist terrorism. Such activities brought Islamists not one inch closer to successfully making revolutions and seizing state power, but did make them feel and appear to be more powerful and successful. Most important of all, this type of action appealed to tens of thousands of Muslims who would never dream of becoming personally involved in violence.

The facts about Islamist politics have been clouded by Western ignorance and Islamist apologetics. It is necessary to apply the same kind of political analysis here that is used to study political movements and ideologies in other parts of the world.

Islamism has clearly become a leading factor shaping the Middle East and the main source for revolutionary, terrorist, and reformist groups alike that challenge current policies and structures. Of central importance is the fact that Islamist interpretations of Islam's political philosophy vary widely from state to state and also among different groups. The fundamentalist readings of Islam are certainly innovative and often arguably heretical in light of traditional views and practices. Thus, in this book we use the word *Islam* to indicate the religion and its theological aspect, and *Islamist* to designate political movements and philosophies that provide specific interpretations of that religion.

Among the broader questions discussed in this book are:

- How interpretations of Islam lend themselves to radical and moderate movements.
- Why radical movements have not gained more support, in part because of their unusual and unfamiliar interpretations of Islam.
- How different movements have chosen their strategy and whether they have been able to alter it in the face of changing conditions.
- Prospects for radical or reformist movements seizing power and transforming their societies.
- Strategies of governments to co-opt or repress Islamist movements.

To discuss these and other issues, the book's chapters cover the countries where Islamist movements have been most important. The book begins with case studies of revolutionary and reformist groups, followed by chapters discussing future alternatives for Islamist politics, presenting advocates and critics of a potential liberal, reformist, interest-group Islamism.

The failure of revolutionary Islamist movements to seize power is one of the most important factors in modern Middle East politics. The factors and reasons for this outcome are presented by Emmanuel Sivan. Following are four case studies of radical Islamist groups engaged in armed struggles. David Zeidan describes the doctrine, disputes, and failures of Egypt's militant Islamist organizations. A key point here is how their ideology broke with normative Islamic views. Among Palestinians, Islamist appeals have blended opposition to Israel with calls to transform society. Especially interesting is how Islamist movements have often been so appealing to those most exposed to Western thought and university training. Reuven Paz discusses the movement's origins and how it broke with the dominant nationalist movement.

In Turkey, Islamists who advocated armed struggle remained relatively marginal and dependent on Iranian sponsorship. This movement is analyzed by Ely Karmon.

Algeria and Lebanon are particularly interesting countries to examine, since they are arguably the two places where militant Islamist ideologies have won the highest proportional base of support. The Islamic Salvation Front in Algeria moved reluctantly from reformist to revolutionary tactics when the military regime there rejected its electoral victory in 1992. This situation, and its interesting contrasts to the evolution of Islamist movements in Morocco and Algeria, are described by Bruce Maddy-Weitzman and Meir Litvak.

In Lebanon, Islamism became very intermixed with ethnic-national conflicts. Thus, Hizballah was simultaneously involved in struggles to gain hegemony within the Shi'ite community, to take over Lebanon, and to lead a struggle against Israel. Following the Israeli withdrawal from southern Lebanon, Hizballah faced a difficult choice on what priority to put on these various functions. It had the opportunity to transform itself further into a political party seeking power within Lebanon, a challenge described by Eyal Zisser.

The book then presents two case studies of movements that have successfully established themselves in the context of electoral politics. In Kuwait, Islamist parties have become a regular part of the political scene, exercising influence on legislation and social life, as documented by Shafeeq N. Ghabra. Turkey is the only country where an Islamist party gained power as the result of electoral success, but the armed forces forced that government's resignation in 1997. This story is analyzed by Nilufer Narli. Turkey is also the home for one of the most coherent and advanced efforts to build a liberal, reformist Islamist philosophy, the movement of Fethullah Gulen, as described by Bulent Aras and Omer Caha.

Next, the book provides essays on three aspects of the potential development for a more liberal, reformist Islamism. Ali Abootalebi discusses the relationship between Islamist movements and democracy. George Irani suggests how traditional Islamic mediation techniques can be applied in politics. Charles Kurzman surveys the main developers and advocates of an alternative Islamist philosophy.

Finally, there are two concluding chapters that evaluate the state of Islamist movements. Dale Eickelman looks at the developmental changes that affect Islamic theory and practice, which may be underpinning a transition. Barry Rubin analyzes the status of Islamist politics across the Middle East, highlighting the paradox created in the failures of both revolutionary and reformist strategies. These factors will determine the direction of Islamist politics and, by extension, of the Middle East's future.

This book is a project of the *Middle East Review of International Affairs* (MERIA), which is part of the Global Research in International Affairs (GLORIA) Center of the Interdisciplinary Center. MERIA is a quarterly journal and monthly magazine on Middle East politics and research published and distributed through the Internet. Many of the chapters in this book originated as articles in MERIA Journal, and the authors were brought together through the project's activities. Additional books will be developed through MERIA in the future, bringing together the best scholarship from around the globe in the study of Middle East issues.

The article by Emmanuel Sivan is reprinted with the permission of the *Middle East Quarterly*. Thanks to Cameron Brown, Ozgul Erdemli, Elisheva Rosman-Stollman and Linda Sharaby for their help in preparing the manuscript.

NOTE

1. Cameron Brown, "The Shot Heard Round the World: The Middle East Reacts to September 11," *MERIA Journal,* Vol. 5, No. 4 (December 2001), pp. 69–89, <http://meria.idc.ac.il>; and Barry Rubin and Judy Colp Rubin, *Anti-American Terror and the Middle East* (NY: Oxford University Press, 2002).

1

Why Radical Muslims Aren't Taking Over Governments

Emmanuel Sivan

Twenty-odd years after its rise to prominence, radical Islam (or Islamism) is at bay. Its mixed record includes survival in the teeth of state repression, some impact on political decision-making, and sociocultural hegemony, but a general failure in the attempt to take power. This predicament of radical movements holds true particularly in the Arab-speaking world, those ancient countries where Islam has been ensconced for nearly fourteen centuries. Why has radical Islam reached this impasse?

Radical Islam has made tremendous inroads into the hearts and minds of Arabic-speaking Muslims. In the sociocultural realm, militant Islamic discourse maintains a hegemony in the public debate among Arabs, replacing Pan-Arabism and Marxism. Islamism has a profound impact on gender roles, fertility, and consumption habits, as well as on the marginalization of local Christians and the censorship of movies, plays, and books. Hyperrigorous religious practice has spread, leading to a growing social pressure toward conformity, the best example of which is the donning of the veil by women. Voluntary Islamic organizations proliferate; the popularity of Islamist media (notably audio- and videotapes) grows;[1] and religious activism resurges as the major avenue for venting both protest and the craving for change. The cultural success of radical Islam resides, above all, in the strength of voluntary Islamic associations.

Although the movement has always known a high turnover rate due to attrition or legal and administrative pressures, a large pool of new recruits, mostly young urban males in their teens, seems always to be available. As a

1

result, the number of voluntary Islamic associations, far from declining, is on the rise; their activity, despite legal and bureaucratic harassment and some scandals (such as the bankruptcy of "Islamic" banks in Egypt), remains as strong as ever.

These associations remain the backbone of radical Islam. They carry out the work of *da'wa*, spreading the word and establishing a countersociety to propagate the movement's ideas, create support networks for members, and show that Islamic values can be fully implemented in the contemporary world. The continued vigor of the Islamic associations is a consequence, above all, of the budgetary woes of most Middle Eastern countries following the decline in oil prices after 1985, a decline that had implications not just for oil exporters but also for the poor countries, as Arab foreign aid dried up and employment for expatriate "guest workers" dwindled. For some states, these woes were further exacerbated by the demise of the Soviet Union and resultant loss of assured East European markets.

The revenue crisis helped the Islamists in two ways. First, regimes responded to this problem by breaking the unwritten covenant agreed upon with their subjects in the 1950s and 1960s, in which the subjects relinquished their claims to basic human and civil rights in return for the state's undertaking to provide them with education and health care, employment, and subsidies for such necessities as staples, cooking gas, and transportation. The poorest and the young suffered these retrenchments the hardest.

The 'retreating state' of the 1990s thus created disgruntled citizens by the legion: university graduates no longer assured of a government job; workers barely able to eke out a living, let alone save for a dowry and establish a family; masses of recent rural migrants lacking such basics as shelter. All these groups provided a pool of possible recruits for Islamic associations.

Second, at a higher socioeconomic level, Islamic associations have sprung up among professionals (doctors, lawyers, journalists) whose growing wealth and sophistication enable them to act independently. They first try to shape decision-making within their respective professions, then reach out and take positions on public affairs in general. Islamism also has had political impact, though indirectly. It limits regimes' room to maneuver; for example, any plan to slash subsidies must take into account the menace of Islamic-instigated mass demonstrations, for mass public demonstrations protesting austerity measures have often occurred.[2] Family-planning policies falter or advance in a haphazard manner due to the vituperations of Friday sermons in "free" (meaning nongovernmental) mosques. National security and regional power are often handicapped by the need to allocate resources to counterterrorism and the maintenance of public order. Da'wa associations, always known for their idealism and probity, are now in demand more than ever.

The support networks thus created could serve as a base for an eventual rise to political power. But they have not. Only in Sudan did the radicals, in alliance with the army, manage to wrest power and hold it. Otherwise, radical Islamic movements in Arab countries have shown a persistent inability to become the major political player. In Algeria especially, a violent insurgency has led to many deaths but not to a takeover of the government, and the same holds to a lesser extent in Egypt and Tunisia. In Yemen and Jordan, they had a share in government as junior partners for brief periods, but exerted barely any influence on public policy. In all, the radicals have tried three avenues of approach to power—violence, da'wa and parliament—with various degrees of failure.

Many radical movements have taken recourse to violence. Hoping to follow the Iranian, Sudanese, and Afghan examples, they have sought to seize power from above and thus control the major instruments of 'heretical modernity' (meaning the state). But, after two decades of mostly failed efforts, fewer and fewer radicals believe they can take power by force. The main obstacle has proven to be the stiff and increasingly effective resistance of existing governments.

Counterterrorist operations have been devised with ingenuity and daring, relying on "sting" operations, intelligence, and changes in legislation (which permit preventive arrest, search without warrant, and transfer of suspects to the jurisdiction of military courts). Security services in many Middle East countries cooperate with their counterparts in other Muslim countries (including Turkey and Pakistan) as well as in the West. Several dictatorial regimes physically wiped out the movement: Hafiz al-Assad of Syria did so in the 1982 Hama massacre; Muammar Qadhafi of Libya did so everywhere except in Wadi al-Anjil; Saddam Hussein of Iraq liquidated cadres in 1980 and quelled the March 1991 revolt.

Authoritarian regimes rarely go to these extremes (with the exception of Algeria), but have shown themselves capable of defending their resource base: oil and gas (in the Persian Gulf, Libya, Algeria), the Suez Canal in Egypt, and even the vulnerable tourism industry in many countries. Nor do the regimes neglect the battle for hearts and minds. To deprive Islamist violence of its legitimacy, they use the resources of the Islamic establishment (notably its audiotaped spokesmen) as well as the entertainment industry (the Egyptian one has produced such successful movies as "The Terrorist" and "Terror and Meatballs," as well as the television miniseries "Layla and the Dervishes.")

The achievements of these counterterrorist efforts vary. In Tunisia, the iron-fisted President Zayn al-'Abidin 'Ali has managed to stem the tide of terrorism in just a few years following his takeover from Habib Bourghiba in November 1987. In the Algerian civil war, the scales have been tipped against an Islamic victory. Both the Islamic Salvation Army (AIS) and the Islamic Salvation Group (GIA) have suffered heavy losses and are shunned by the bulk of the population. No more can their members believe that "power is within the range of our Kalashnikovs." Protest, revenge, and extortion are the all-pervasive goals of the violence, which still goes on.

The Egyptian security services, in a sustained effort galvanized by the assassination attempt on Husni Mubarak in June 1995, have lowered the yearly level of violence to some 190 killed in 1996, compared to 1,100 in 1993, 700 in 1994, and 480 in 1995. While this deadly harvest is still greater than what Egypt experienced in the early years of the Mubarak presidency (30 killed per year), the improvement is evident. Further, the violence has been largely contained in Upper Egypt (particularly the Malawi region) far away from the loci of power and the large population centers.

Endemic violence, of the Shi'ite variety, can still be detected on a smaller scale in Bahrain, and on a sporadic scale in Morocco and Yemen. Perhaps as a result of the widespread antiterrorist activities, radical Islamic movements have experienced discord and disarray. It has reached the point that imprisoned leaders of the Jihad and Jama'at Islamiyya organizations in Egypt have called for an end to all acts of terror, despite the opposition of many leaders who are in hiding or abroad. A similar call was launched by most leaders of Algeria's Islamic Salvation Front (FIS) and its military arm, the AIS, only to be rejected out of hand by the Armed Islamic Group (GIA), which continues to massacre women and children in the countryside south of Algiers.

Discord is not a novelty in the history of radical Islam, which has known various splits and internecine wars, but its extent today is greater than anything the radical Islamic movement has known over the last quarter century.

If violent 're-Islamization from above' is on the decline, how about 're-Islamization from below,' the long-term infiltration into society's every nook and cranny as a way to gain eventual political control? This is, on the face of it, the Muslim Brotherhood strategy in Egypt and elsewhere. They engage in grassroots vigilantism to ban alcohol, pornography, and television satellite dishes, and to impose Islamic law, dress codes, and stricter regulation of tourists.

In Egypt, Lebanon, Jordan, and Kuwait, fundamentalists conduct court fights and press campaigns against "permissive" writers and artists. They mobilize popular protests against relations with Israel (a prominent topic in Jordan), launch strikes against the high cost of living (in Lebanon and Morocco), or demonstrate in favor of the constitution (in Bahrain).

Two key factors support this strategy. First, the Islamist message that the failure of the supposedly all-providing state is due to its moral dissoluteness and secularism is simple and effective, and it appeals to a deeply ingrained cultural tradition connecting private anxieties to public woes.

Second, the intricate yet elastic organizational structure of radical Islam is supple and decentralized, with a minimalistic hierarchy. This sort of 'enclave'[3] (as anthropologists call it) ensures equality of status among members without hampering decision-making; it does so by promoting charismatic local figures. In this way, it hampers repression and endows the members with a sense of empowerment and group solidarity.

The radicals are resourceful in finding new locales in which to operate: Afghanistan served as a recruiting ground for militants to gain experience, contacts, and skills, then return to their home countries; Bosnia served this same function until the Dayton agreement of 1995. The North African movements, persecuted at home, transferred much of their activity (including propaganda, support networks for terrorism and even some terror operations) to migrant communities in Western Europe. Hamas expanded financing and support ventures in both Europe and North America. The Egyptian Jihad organization moved some of its operations to Ethiopia (where it tried to assassinate President Mubarak) and Pakistan (where it blew up the Egyptian embassy).

Militants living in Europe have achieved something else: improved coordination between the Islamist movements of various countries. Migrant workers recruited for the cause frequently shuttle across the Mediterranean along with family gifts, used cars, and electrical equipment. They carry propaganda material produced in the West, as well as funds. This supple network fulfills radical Islam's claim to be an international movement that encompasses the whole *umma* (population of Muslims).

Thus do religious luminaries from one country sometimes act as the higher legal and moral authority in another country: Shaykh Yusuf al-Qaradawi of Egypt's Muslim Brotherhood lives in Qatar and serves as the supreme mufti for the Palestinian Hamas. Shaykh Ibn Qatada, a Palestinian-Jordanian living in London, is mufti for elements of the Algerian GIA. An Egyptian and former Afghan volunteer, Shaykh Abu Hamza, is one of the GIA's chief propagandists abroad.

The cause of radical Islam is advanced when regimes, realizing that the old nationalist and statist ideologies have lost their appeal, try to steal some of the radicals' thunder by relying on religious legitimacy. They infuse the school system with heavy doses of Islamic contents so that many children thus educated are later amenable to accepting the radicals' worldview, transmitted in what is for them a familiar discourse. Because schooling is predicated upon learning by rote (*talqin*), the young are conditioned to accept a dogmatic message with no sense of critical inquiry, just the mindset in which radicalism thrives.

All this helps explain the sociocultural and organizational survival of radical Islam, which is in itself quite a feat, but why have these factors not brought about an increase in political power?

The Islamist movement aims to stop, before it is too late, the seemingly ineluctable and rapid slippage of the Middle East toward apostasy, modernity and secularism. By nature a long-term effort, this campaign can hardly enthuse a membership made up in their crushing majority of people aged fifteen to twenty-five. Underlying the Muslim Brotherhood's message is that, thanks to the ongoing crisis of the state and their own resourcefulness, they ultimately will infiltrate the elites and create a popular base to exert pressure upon these secularized elites to change. At the end of the road, they would bring to power new Islamized elites (for example, judges who would interpret cases in the light of Islamic law, the *Shari'a*).

Experience has shown, however, that powerful, countervailing cultural forces operate: the audiovisual media emit hedonistic messages, which undermine the notion "Islam is the solution." The consumer culture's attraction, the lure of "Made in USA" sneakers and movies, bewitches many amongst the *shabab* (youth) upon whom the elderly leaders had pinned their hopes. More dismaying yet are the local knockoffs, such as the North African hybrid of Arabic and rock music, dubbed *Rai*. Increasingly, Islamist voices can be heard asking, "Perhaps all we can wage is a rearguard battle. Isn't it likely that our present achievements are doomed to death by attrition?"

The deadend of violence and da'wa leads Islamists to often give higher consideration than before to the parliamentary option. The proponents of parliamentarism point to its many virtues. It permits them to introduce legal reforms, shapes policy-making, and allocates resources to causes close to the radicals' hearts (notably, Islamic education).

Opponents of parliamentarism retort with several arguments. First, they are ideologically against it. For them, democracy is a value only for the despised "Westoxicated" elites. It cannot stop society's decline into infidelity, let alone reverse the curve. As a system predicated on the sovereignty of man, it runs counter to Islam's attachment to the sovereignty of God. It can be accepted at best as an instrument, and as that it dismally fails.

Second, in countries where "parties of a religious character" are illegal, such as Algeria, Tunisia, and Egypt, the radicals are barred from running at all or are allowed to do so only under a subterfuge as independent candidates or in a joint list with another party. They are subject to constant harassment of da'wa activities through control of voluntary associations, professional organizations, unofficial mosques, and preachers. Their activists do not enjoy freedom of expression and travel, may be subject to arbitrary search and detention, or may lose their government jobs.

In this respect, the distinction between Egypt and Jordan or between Tunisia and Morocco is simply one of degree. Many Islamists argue that Arab regimes offer, at best, a sort of *democracia pactada* of the type practiced in some Latin American countries during the transition period from military rule. These are democracies of what sociologists call 'partial inclusion,' built on shared rules of political competition including the right to vote and an electoral law designed to minimize the influence of extremist parties and favor more traditional-rural sectors (through a two-chamber system, for instance, as in Morocco and Jordan). These are top-down affairs whose creation presupposes the opposition's willingness to content itself indefinitely with second-tier cabinet portfolios.

Some religious organizations would be included in the system, as is the Algerian Muslim Brotherhood, led by Shaykh Nahnah, who ran in the 1997 elections under the banner of the Social Movement for Peace. Others, such as the Algerian FIS, would not be permitted to run, though its members would one day perhaps be allowed to participate as individuals.

Third, skeptics note that no Arab opposition party has ever won power through the ballot; electoral returns are, in fact, tampered with almost everywhere. And, in the one instance in which a party came closest to winning power, the first round of the June 1991 elections in Algeria when FIS won a plurality, the results were annulled by the military.

Fourth, they say that Islamists have precious little to show for playing the parliamentary game and conclude that participation in government is an error. Their impact on legislation and policy is paltry. Sadat had promised enactment of *taqnin al-Shari'a* (vetting existing laws for conformity with Islamic jurisprudence) but the Muslim Brotherhood of Egypt never succeeded even in pushing it through parliamentary committees. In Jordan, the large faction of the Islamic Action Front (also known as the Muslim Brotherhood) could neither block the signing of the "sacrilegious" peace treaty with Israel nor development of close ties with the Jewish state. The same holds true of Jama'a Islamiya (Sunni) and the Hizballah (Shi'ite) deputies in Lebanon and their counterparts in Kuwait, Bahrain, and Morocco. In Yemen, the Tajammu al-Islah party is still smarting from the debacle of the May 1997 elections and its subsequent ousting from the government.

Moreover, when an Islamic party does cross the apparently critical threshold and join the government, it has to make do with minor ministries where its efforts are quite often hampered. As a result, the party in question is discredited with its own electorate either as a sellout or as ineffectual, and loses votes in the elections following its ousting from government; this happened in Jordan in 1993 and in Yemen in 1997. Further supporting the skeptical view, last but not least, is the Turkish case, where the radical Necmettin Erbakan was actually permitted to become prime minister but was stymied in every initiative he took and forced out of power within a year.

Parliamentary initiatives create much discord. Within Tunisia's Nahda movement, a minority led by founder Rashid al-Ghannushi (now in exile in Great Britain) demanded a change in the movement's platform and its embrace of democracy; rebuffed, he set up a rival organization, the Tunisian Islamic Front (FIT). Young Muslim Brotherhood activists in Egypt are endeavoring to establish a new party (named Wasat, the median way) that endorses the parliamentary option despite the opposition of the Muslim Brotherhood leadership. Shaykh 'Imad al-Faluji, a founder of the Palestinian Hamas, established the dissident Islamic Salvation Party that competed in the 1996 elections, and he then joined Arafat's administration.

Yet in countries where this very option has long been pursued, it is now a controversial issue. In Jordan the Muslim Brotherhood decided by a majority vote in the leadership, and under pressure from mid- and low-level militants, to boycott the November 1997 elections. The predicament for fundamentalist Islam is not solely of the regimes' making. Even those liberal circles in the Arab ruling elites favoring a transition to democracy must take into account the antidemocratic nature of radical Islam, which being the most important opposition force in society, might be the beneficiary of such a transition, leading to an Iranian- (or Sudanese-) style regime. This scenario, feared by the modern middle class, recalls the situation in Latin America in the 1980s, when Marxist-Leninist parties were the ones likely to benefit from the replacement of military rule by democracy. Whether to accept *democracia pactada* Arab-style is not only the major question exercising the radicals, but also a major concern for many in Arab ruling elites.

Some independent-minded thinkers within the radical orbit have recently set this predicament in relief. Perhaps Munir Shafiq, a Christian convert to Islam from northern Jordan living in Lebanon, has done so with the greatest insight. Long active in the Palestinian movement Fatah, Shafiq later abjured nationalism and Marxism, converted to Islam, and became a widely read radical Islamist thinker. If radical Islam wishes to allay the fears it generates and join the political process, he writes, it must undergo a transformation, not a face-lift. It must wholeheartedly and as a matter of principle accept pluralism and toleration (in the modern sense, first elaborated by Spinoza). In this he includes the notion of alternation of power as well as basic human and civil rights for people of all hues and convictions. Shafiq calls for a rigorously honest rethinking of ideology and practice; mere window dressing, like the recourse to apologetic arguments, will not do, he warns.

Arguments maintaining that Islam equals democracy in that it holds to the principle of *shura* (consultation to elect a caliph) do not suffice. For one thing, apologetics are historically inaccurate: The shura was rarely implemented even in the Golden Age, and even then it encompassed notables only. For another, verbal juggling of this sort would never convince hard-bitten rulers, their ever-suspicious security services, or the liberal middle class—not after the experiences of Iran, Sudan, and Afghanistan, not after the long drawn-out confrontation with the violent brand of Muslim radicalism.

What is required, say Shafiq and his followers, is a serious effort of *ijtihad* (legal reinterpretation) to infuse the shura notion with modern pluralistic values. Furthermore, such values should then be injected into radical Islam's own internal mode of governance, which is at present autocratic, if not worse. It's a tall order. Some rethinking along these lines has been sketched out, but more remains to be done, as Shafiq would be the first to acknowledge.[4]

Moreover, voices like Shafiq's are, for the moment, solitary. Most radical groups who choose the parliamentary option are content to mouth the cliches about shura equaling democracy.[5] They dodge issues such as the status of religious minorities or whether freedom of expression encompasses agnostics, atheists, or holders of iconoclastic ("heretical") Muslim doctrines. They have come up with no constitutional-political guarantees to ensure alternation.

No wonder that all this is not enough to convince regimes or liberal public opinion, whose deep distrust of Islamists harks back to the days of Muslim Brotherhood violence in the 1950s. That Hasan al-Turabi, the most prolific writer on shura in the 1980s, has become a blood-stained leader of the present Sudanese regime certainly does not add to the credibility of the allegedly pro-democratic spokesmen in Islamist ranks.

When the exiled Tunisian leader Rashid al-Ghannushi announced a few years ago his conversion to democracy, then split the Nahda (Renaissance) movement he had founded over this issue, his past involvement in violence against the Neo-Destour Party was still a fresh memory. Doubts about his sincerity came not just from the autocratic Tunisian president and his henchmen but also from the Tunisian League of Human Rights, a bold opposition force. The Egyptian government denied a legal permit to the Wasat Party (the matter is still under appeal) and liberal opinion split over whether to believe the party's declared commitment to democracy.

Poor as the Arabic-speaking radicals' prospects for seizing power may be, it would be wrong to view them as doomed to political failure. Even in their present anti-democratic mindset, their top-down options may get a new lease on life due to changes in the economic and political environment. Power could yet be within their reach, through bullets or ballots, resulting from a military defeat, a succession crisis of the regime, or a drastic worsening of the economic situation.

NOTES

1. Emmanuel Sivan, "Eavesdropping on Radical Islam," *Middle East Quarterly*, March 1995, pp. 13–24.

2. In Algeria (1988); Egypt (1977, 1981, 1984, 1987); Jordan (1989, 1996); Kuwait (1989, 1990); Morocco (1984, 1988, 1996); South Yemen (1986, 1990); Sudan (1984, 1985, 1988).

3. Emmanuel Sivan, "The Enclave Culture," M. E. Marty and R. S. Appleby (eds.), *Fundamentalism Comprehended* (Chicago: University of Chicago Press, 1995), pp. 11–63.

4. Munir Shafiq, *Al-Nizam al-Duwali al-Jadid wa-Khiyar al-Muwajaha* (Beirut: Dar al-Nashir, 1994); Munir Shafiq, *Hawla Nazariyyat al-Taghyir* (Beirut: Dar al-Nashir, 1995). See also, Majmu'at min al-'Ulama' [a pseudonym, possibly shaykhs Jamal Hammami and Jamil Salim], *Al-Islam wal-Musharaka fil-Hukm* (Nablus: n.p., 1996).

5. Rashid Ghannushi, *Al-Hurriyat al-'Amma fil-Islam* (Beirut: Markaz Dirasat al-Wihda al-'Arabiya, 1993); 'Ali Benhajj (Algerian), *Risala ila Wazir al-Ittisal* (n.p., 1995), pp. 53–58; Abu-l-Ala' Madi (founder of the Egyptian al-Wasat party) interview, *Al-Hayat* Dec. 25, 1996; Mohammad al-'Awwa (Egyptian Muslim Brotherhood), "Al-Ta'addudiya min Manzur Islami," *Minbar al-Hiwar* (Winter 1991), pp. 129.

2

Radical Islam in Egypt

A Comparison of Two Groups

David Zeidan

History reveals cyclical patterns of Islamic revival in times of crisis. Charismatic leaders arise attempting to renew the fervor and identity of Muslims, purify the faith from accretions and corrupt religious practices, and reinstate the pristine Islam of the Prophet Muhammad's day. Leaders of revivals tend to appear either as renewers of the faith promised at the start of each century (*mujaddid*), or as the deliverers sent by God in the end of times to establish the final kingdom of justice and peace (*mahdi*).[1]

In modern times, a new wave of revival was initiated by the Muslim Brotherhood in Egypt, the main grassroots movement that emerged in response to the modern crisis in the Arab world. At a time when Egypt faced the challenges of colonialism, economic and cultural dependence, rapid industrialization and urbanization, and a massive population explosion,[2] the Muslim Brotherhood called for a return to the original fundamentals of Islam as the basis of Muslim social and political renewal. Suppressed by Nasser in the mid-1950s—after Egypt's revolution evoked nationalism rather than Islam as Egypt's main identity marker—the Muslim Brotherhood reemerged during the Sadat era (1970–1981) as a movement committed to nonviolent participation in the political process.[3]

Radical Islamic societies (*jama'at*) sprang from the Muslim Brotherhood drawing on the thought of its main ideologue, Sayyid Qutb (1906–1966), who endorsed a violent takeover of power.[4] While he himself belonged to the mainline Brotherhood, Qutb's radical reinterpretation of several key Islamic concepts inspired some to split off from the Brotherhood and use his writings to legitimize violence against the regime. For example, he argued that the existing society and government were not Muslim but rather dominated by "pagan ignorance" (*jahiliyya*). The duty of righteous Muslims was to bring about God's sovereignty (*hakimmiyya*) over society, denounce the unbelief (*takfir*) of the current national leaders, and carry out a holy struggle (jihad) against them.[5]

Two of the radical groups that emerged in Egypt in the 1970s were the Society of Muslims (*Takfir wal-Hijra*) and the Society of Struggle (*Jama'at al-Jihad*). These two organizations espoused drastically different ideologies and strategies for gaining power. The Society of Muslims (al-Takfir) had a passive, separatist and messianic ideology, delaying active confrontation with the state to an indefinite point in the future when it could reach a certain degree of strength. In comparison, the Society of Struggle (al-Jihad) followed an activist, militant ideology committed to immediate and violent action against the regime. This chapter compares these two Islamic groups and analyzes their differences in doctrine and strategy in the context of a broader examination of the history of militant Islamic groups in Egypt. The two societies furnish examples of basic types of radical Islamic movements. In addition, al-Jihad remains important in contemporary Egyptian politics and in that country's internal struggle.

A number of factors led to the proliferation of radical groups during the 1970s in Egypt and across the Muslim world. These included, as had been true of the earlier Brotherhood, a response to the impact of modernity, Western encroachment, misrule by the national elite, and a whole series of massive economic and social dislocations. The result was a crisis of identity and a search for authenticity. Heavy-handed repression by military-backed regimes armed with their own powerful Arab nationalist ideologies left no avenues for protest except through the religious idiom.[6]

Equally, the oil boom enhanced the power of Islamic Saudi Arabia and channeled much financial aid to militant groups, encouraging their growth. The 1973 war against Israel and accompanying oil embargo against the West—which seemed to demonstrate Arab-Islamic power—as well as the 1979 Iranian revolution further fueled radical zeal.

Ironically, the state apparatus in Egypt also contributed to this trend. President Anwar Sadat encouraged the development of Islamist societies (*jama'at Islamiyya*) as a counterweight to the Nasserist-dominated professional associations and student unions. These societies extended their influence through a network of educational and social services at a time when government services had collapsed in the face of economic crisis and rapid increases in the number of students and the overall population. The Islamic societies, offering identity and community as well as social welfare, became a recruiting field for the revolutionary radicals.[7]

Another phenomenon that emerged during the 1970s was a dramatic rise in the number of independent private (*ahli*) mosques, not controlled by the government, that provided a safe meeting point for militants and recruits.[8]

One of the new radical Islamic groups that appeared in the 1970s was generally called *Takfir wal-Hijra* (hereafter *Takfir*) by the media and government security agencies. *Takfir* is the legal ascription of unbelief (excommunication) to an individual or group, while *hijra* signifies Muhammad's original flight from Mecca to Medina, serving as the group's model for contemporary disentanglement from Egypt's corrupt society and regime.

Takfir was led by Shukri Mustafa, a member of the Muslim Brotherhood in Asyut, who was imprisoned in 1965 and joined the radical disciples of Qutb while in prison. Released in 1971, he soon started building up Takfir but, following the kidnapping and murder of an ex-government minister in 1978, Mustafa was arrested and executed by the authorities.

Mustafa was an autocratic leader who expected total obedience from his followers. His control was strengthened by the belief that he was the predicted savior (mahdi).[9] Given this prestige, he was able to run Takfir as a highly disciplined organization, divided into action cells, recruiting groups, and logistic units. Labeling contemporary society "infidel," Takfir aimed to set up an alternative community that would work, study, and pray together. There were gradations of membership: Full members devoted themselves totally to the community, leaving their jobs and families. Errant members were excommunicated and punished.[10]

The *Jama'at al-Jihad* (henceforth *al-Jihad*) was founded in 1979 by Muhammad Abd al-Salam Faraj, a former Muslim Brotherhood member who was disillusioned by its passivity.[11] To explain his views, Faraj wrote a short book titled "The Neglected Obligation" (*al-farida al-gha'ibah*). But al-Jihad did not restrict itself to theory alone. It quickly became involved in sectarian conflicts and disturbances in Upper Egypt and Cairo. In October 1981, the group assassinated Sadat at a military parade. Faced with an all-out campaign to shut it down, al-Jihad supporters fought a three-day revolt in Asyut seeking to spark a revolution before being defeated.

In contrast to Takfir, al-Jihad was led not by one charismatic leader but by a collective leadership apparatus[12] in charge of overall strategy, and a ten-member consultation committee (*majlis al-shura*) headed by Shaykh Umar 'Abd al-Rahman. Everyday operations were run by a three-department supervisory apparatus.[13] Members were organized in small semiautonomous groups and cells.[14] There were two distinct branches, one in Cairo and the other in Upper Egypt. The Cairo group was composed of five or six cells headed by emirs who met weekly to plan their strategy.[15]

In recruiting, both Takfir and al-Jihad relied heavily on kinship and friendship ties. Both attracted predominantly students from rural areas and lower and middle class backgrounds who had recently migrated to big cities and were alienated and disoriented in their new environment. Most members were well-educated, particularly in technology and the sciences.[16]

Takfir recruited mainly in Upper Egypt and was the only society to actively recruit women. Faraj recruited for al-Jihad in private mosques in poor neighborhoods where he delivered Friday sermons.[17] Al-Jihad succeeded in recruiting members from the presidential guard, civil bureaucracy, military intelligence, media, and academia.

Especially interesting are the differences between these two radical groups, which represent many streams of contemporary radical Islamic thought, as well as something of the traditional, still far more widely accepted Muslim theology and world view.

Both groups agreed that authentic Islam had existed only in the "Golden Age" of the Prophet's original state in Medina and under the "rightly guided" first four caliphs (622–661). Muslims must rediscover their religion's original principles, free them from innovations, and actively implement them in present society. This was in line with revivalist (*salafi*)[18] views, and contradicted the traditionalist view of Islam as the total of the sacred source texts of Quran and the Prophet's example and traditions (*Sunna*), plus all scholarly interpretation and consensus over the ages. It also differed from the reformist view in stressing active political, rather than mere educational, activity.

The ultimate goal for both groups was the establishment of a renewed universal Islamic nation (*umma*) under a true caliph,[19] fully implementing Islamic sacred law (Shari'a) as God's ideal form of Islamic government.[20] Until the establishment of this Caliphate (*khilafa*), the Islamic societies would form the embryo and vanguard of the true Islamic nation in its struggle against internal and external enemies. The takeover of power in individual Muslim states would be a necessary first step.

Takfir's ambitions did not extend to the Middle East or the Islamic world alone. It claimed that the Prophet's mandate was to fight all people in the world until they all would convert, pray, and pay the Islamic charitable tax (*zakat*). The fact that this had never before been achieved did not change the fact that it was Islam's true goal.

The group also emphasized the importance of a charismatic leader—its own—for Islam's triumph. After establishing its rule over one state, Takfir would call on all humanity to join Islam and submit to its Shari'a. The Islamic state would become the third superpower and extend its dominion over the whole world.[21] The views of al-Jihad were roughly parallel, though the group placed less emphasis on a single leader. Nonetheless, it agreed that true Muslims must wage war against the infidel rulers of all states, including Muslim states.[22]

In contrast to traditional religious scholars, who proclaimed the necessity of submission to any ruler claiming to be a Muslim, they insisted that acceptance of a government is possible only when the Islamic legal system is fully implemented.[23] Implementation of Shari'a becomes the sole criterion of the legitimacy of regimes.[24]

Traditional scholars viewed the concept of the 'age of ignorance' or paganism (jahiliyya) as an historic condition in pre-Islamic Arabia. In contrast, for both groups, 'ignorance' is a present condition of a society which is not properly Islamic because it does not implement the full Shari'a and hence is rebelling against God's sovereignty. All the regimes currently in power in Muslim countries are thus not acceptably Islamic and it is both right and necessary to rebel against them.[25]

On some points, Takfir and al-Jihad differed in a way that made clear why al-Jihad was the more successful organization. Takfir claimed that both the regime and all of society were pagan and that true Muslims must separate from them. Takfir included in this condemnation all four traditional schools of Islam (*madhabs*) and all traditional commentators. It labeled these schools "puppets" of rulers, who had monopolized Quranic interpretation to their own advantage. Takfir accused the founders of the four schools of having closed the door of creative interpretation (*ijtihad*) and set themselves up as idols (*tawaghit*), serving as mediators between God and believers. Takfir thus actually repudiated both *fiqh* and *hadith*, accepting only the Quran from traditional Islam.[26]

Al-Jihad, in contrast, selected certain commentators it favored, including the famous Hanbali medieval scholar, Ibn Taymiyya. His writings were interpreted as showing that societies are partly Muslim even when the rulers are all pagans who legislate according to their own whims.[27] Al-Jihad accepted the four traditional schools of Islam, much of scholarly consensus, and some later commentators. Consequently, it would be much easier for a Muslim to join al-Jihad or find some truth in its teachings.

While traditional scholars and the Muslim Brotherhood would not denounce a Muslim as an infidel—accepting his claim to be Muslim at face value and leaving the judgment of his intention to God—both radical groups were ready to denounce Muslims as infidels, which could imply a willingness to attack or kill them. Since Egypt's failure to implement the Shari'a made it an infidel pagan state placed under excommunication (takfir), all true Muslims were duty-bound to wage holy struggle (jihad) against the regime, an idea alien to traditional Islam.

Both Takfir and al-Jihad also agreed that the prime emphasis should be put on a national revolution first. Only when the infidel regimes of Muslim countries were overthrown and replaced by true Islamic states could the Caliphate be restored, occupied Muslim territories liberated, and Shari'a rule established throughout the world.

But in determining the targets and enemies of its revolution, Takfir declared that not only the regime but the society itself was infidel and under excommunication. This entailed two strategic decisions that ensured that Takfir would remain more of a cult than a revolutionary organization. First, it meant a personal withdrawal from society, which required a choice few people would make and a burden beyond what its infrastructure could sustain. Second, it called for a delay in action, which indefinitely postponed active militancy.[28]

While rejecting the state, Takfir also provoked it. Denouncing all symbols of the regime's legitimacy—the religious establishment, the army, and all government services—members ignored its laws, including conscription into the army and the legal or educational system. The group also forbade members from working as state employees, a real economic sacrifice given the Egyptian system.[29]

Traditional scholars view Muhammad's migration (hijra) from Mecca to Medina as an historical event that has spiritual, but not programmatic, relevance for Muslims today. Takfir, however, interpreted hijra as meaning that all true Muslims in every generation must reenact and emulate Muhammad's model of flight as a physical separation from infidel society. By departing to a safe place, they could establish a new society and prepare for the stage of return and victory. Total separation (*mufassala kamila*) is a must in the temporary stage of weakness, ending only when the alternative community becomes strong enough to challenge the regime.[30]

This plan was aborted, however, by Takfir itself. Its use of violence against "apostate" members brought police intervention, which in turn led to a confrontation that destroyed the organization. Given its program, Takfir posed no immediate danger to the government since in practice the strategy it pursued was one of passivity for an extended period.

In contrast, al-Jihad was a self-proclaimed revolutionary group employing armed struggle. Al-Jihad rejected Mustafa's insistence on total separation from society, nor would it postpone jihad until the phase of strength was achieved. While Takfir wanted to boycott state institutions, al-Jihad worked to infiltrate the military, security services, and other government institutions so as to successfully wage immediate jihad.[31]

Al-Jihad was just as determined in rejecting the regime, but much more flexible in dealing with Egyptian society. Certainly, it declared armed jihad a fundamental requirement (a sixth pillar, in its own words) of Islam. Many traditional scholars, the group asserted, had suppressed this fact. Indeed, jihad against unbelievers—including "Muslims" who did not observe the religion's requirements properly—must be the top priority of all true Muslims.[32]

The regime and its employees were infidels, al-Jihad claimed. As historical justification, it cited Ibn Taymiyya's criticism of the Mongol rulers of his day, who mixed Shari'a with customary law. In contrast to Takfir, al-Jihad advocated immediate revolt as both legitimate and imperative.[33] Such a revolution would be able to seize power and establish an Islamic state.[34] In tactical terms, Faraj argued that the assassination of Egypt's president (whom it called the "evil prince" and "the Pharaoh") would be an effective first step.[35]

While Takfir rejected traditional mainstream Islam as it had been practiced and defined, al-Jihad claimed that its principles and goals were the proper embodiment of that faith. Faraj insisted that most historically respected scholars agreed with al-Jihad's positions of waging jihad and establishing an Islamic state.[36]

Like many historic European revolutionary groups (but unlike Marxist doctrine), al-Jihad viewed political assassination and violence as acts that would mobilize the masses. A necessary assumption for this strategy to work was that people were already on al-Jihad's side and were just waiting to be shown the proper example and leadership. Indeed, this was al-Jihad's claim. Since God would grant success and the infidel regime's fall would miraculously cure all social ills, there was no need to prepare and establish one's strength beforehand.[37]

Yet such a strategy was not so easy to implement. For example, traditional Islamic doctrine was critical of killing fellow Muslims and, as noted above, viewed a government professing Islam as legitimate. Al-Jihad had to argue, using specific incidents and some commentators from Islamic history, that killing Muslims and overthrowing a Muslim-led government was the correct interpretation of Islam.[38]

While al-Jihad enthusiastically endorsed this position, its leaders knew that theirs was a distinctly minority view. Faraj criticized other groups, most importantly the Muslim Brotherhood, for their gradualist strategy and involvement in the political system. Such behavior, he insisted, only strengthened the regime. He also rejected widely accepted arguments that jihad should be postponed (as Takfir claimed) or that it required only defensive or nonviolent struggle (a widely held Muslim position).

In response, Faraj insisted they were all wrong and that active, immediate jihad would be the only strategy for achieving an Islamic state.[39] Al-Jihad immediately implemented its goals in the late 1970s by involvement in sectarian conflicts, riots, and acts of terrorism, culminating in the Sadat assassination.

Another characteristic of these two groups somewhat at odds with the traditionalist Muslim view was their strong antagonism to Christians and Jews, though even here Takfir and al-Jihad had contrasting views. Instead of seeing Jews and Christians as protected communities (dhimmis) and 'People of the Book,' the two groups viewed them as infidels both because they had deliberately rejected the truth and because of their connections to colonialism and Zionism.[40] They were accused of serving as a 'fifth column' for external enemies,[41] a Trojan Horse of the West within Muslim societies.[42]

Takfir stressed an international Jewish conspiracy and the need to fight it, while Zuhdi's group in al-Jihad viewed Christians as the first enemy to confront and was heavily involved in anti-Coptic activities. Shaykh 'Abd al-Rahman issued a religious legal edict (fatwa) legitimizing the killing and robbing of Christians who were said to be anti-Muslim.

Both groups accepted the prevalent conspiracy theories that saw the Christian West, Jewish Zionism, and atheist Communism as planning to corrupt, divide, and destroy Islam. Rulers in Muslim states were puppets of these forces, leading their countries into dependence and secularization. This battle had started right at the inception of Islam, and the Jews and Christians of the seventh century were identical with the Jews and Christians of today.[43]

Takfir accused the Jews of seducing humanity to idol-worship and of spreading corruption and immorality all over the world, while al-Jihad accused Muslim rulers of obeying Jews and Christians and opening up Muslim countries to exploitation.[44]

Finally, both groups saw themselves as messianic (*mahdist*, in Islamic terminology). Takfir was radically mahdist, believing that the world was nearing its end and Mustafa, Takfir's leader, was the *Mahdi*. Proof that the world was coming to an end was to be found in the prevalent state of disbelief, oppression, immorality, famine, wars, earthquakes, and typhoons.[45] Mustafa would be the caliph who would found a new Muslim community, conquer the world, and usher in God's final reign on Earth.

Al-Jihad accepted the tradition of the *Mahdi* who will reveal himself at the end of time to establish justice in the whole world. However, in the meantime the West was in decline, and true Muslims had to actively engage in the struggle for the implementation of true Islam.[46] Lack of messianic leadership was no excuse for postponing the struggle, and leadership should be given to the best Muslims in the community, presumably al-Jihad's leadership.

After its suppression by the government and the execution of its leader, Takfir seemed to disintegrate and its members joined other underground groups such as al-Jihad. However, there are persistent rumors that a nucleus remains active underground and that its ideas have affected many other radical groups.[47] Radical Islamic groups with the same name have surfaced in other Arab states, though it is not clear if they subscribe to the same ideology. For instance, in Algeria a group by the same name is reported to be actively linked to the GIA (Armed Islamic Group) and is blamed for urban terrorism and for some of the killings of civilians and attacks on the security forces. In Lebanon, on December 31, 1999, a group called takfir wal-Hijra ambushed a Lebanese army patrol near Assun, killing four soldiers. The army responded by launching a crackdown on militants in the hills around Tripoli, killing some 25 radicals.[48]

Al-Jihad, in contrast, survived repression. Despite the imprisonment and execution of al-Jihad's leaders following Sadat's assassination, offshoots managed to regroup, declaring jihad against Mubarak's regime. Al-Jihad has continued to be linked to terrorist incidents and outbreaks of communal violence ever since.[49] It seems to have a narrow base of support mainly in the urban centers of northern Egypt, and many of its leaders live in exile in Western countries. One wing seems to be loyal to 'Abbud al-Zammur, one of the original founders now imprisoned in Egypt. Another wing is called Vanguards of the Conquest or The New Jihad Group, and appears to be led by Afghan war veteran Dr. Ayman al-Zawahiri.[50]

In July 1986, following riots started by mutinous Central Security Forces, 75 members of an offshoot were arrested.[51] In September 1989, members of Salvation from Hell, another offshoot, were sentenced for the attempted assas-

sination of two ex-cabinet ministers and a journalist. Al-Jihad seemed to special-
ize in attacking high-level government officials and high-profile secularists; in
1990, five members of al-Jihad were arrested for the killing of the speaker of the
National Assembly.[52]

In 1993, al-Jihad members attempted unsuccessfully to assassinate Interior
Minister Hassan al-Alfi and Prime Minister 'Atef Sidky. Al-Jihad maintains links
with other international radical Islamic groups and figures such as Osama bin-
Laden, the mastermind of the 1998 U.S. embassy bombings in Kenya and
Tanzania, and of the September 11 attacks in the United States.[53]

Shaykh 'Abd al-Rahman was exiled to the United States in 1985, where he
was later implicated in the first bombing of New York's World Trade Center, put
on trial, and sentenced to imprisonment. He had kept his influence over al-Jihad
as well as the other radical movement, al-Jama'at al-Islamiyya, operating both in
Egypt and abroad.

In the 1980s members of both societies, like other radical groups in the
Arab world, fought alongside the *mujahidin* in Afghanistan against the Soviets,
gaining valuable experience in warfare and often specialist training from U.S.
agents. After the Soviet withdrawal, many returned to their home countries,
reinvigorating the violent struggle against the regimes in power.[54]

Studying these two groups reveals the impact of the new politicization of
Islam in recent decades. Yet it should be clear that these groups' theologies are no
simple revivalist returns to sacred origins but reinterpretations of historically dominant views and sectarian-type modifications on the model of the early *kharijis*.[55]
Even when they can claim historic precedents, such as Ibn Taymiyya, they use
innovative approaches lying outside the framework of mainstream Islam.

Even though these groups have a large circle of sympathizers who agree with
their goals and accept their methods, they remain a minority within Egypt.
Examining their ideologies gives important clues as to why their support has
remained limited.

First, as noted above, many of their views either revise or contradict traditionally accepted interpretations of Islam. Thus, joining or supporting the group
requires a change in one's original belief system.

Second, these groups are naive in their strategic conceptions. One could
argue that, on a strategic level, both Takfir and al-Jihad were unconsciously
pursuing a suicidal approach. Takfir's isolation and al-Jihad's launching of a
revolution without preparation and wide support could only lead to defeat.
Dependence on divine intervention is not a blueprint for success.

Third, many Egyptians will not accept their claim that a coup that establishes
the Shari'a will miraculously solve all the country's problems. The Iranian model
shows that the capture of government does not automatically yield rapid progress
or a just society. Even popular support can be difficult to maintain, while Islamist
leaders may well disagree on goals, ideology, and methods. Their utopian presentation of the projected golden age of the reinstituted Caliphate fully implementing

Shari'a inevitably raises high expectations that can never be fulfilled. Should they take power, it would mean dealing with the frustrations of unfulfilled expectations by totalitarian means. As in most revolutions, large numbers of people would have to be sacrificed on the altar of ideology. And even then, the original ideology itself might have to be sacrificed to pragmatic considerations.

NOTES

1. Hrair R. Dekmejian, *Islam In Revolution: Fundamentalism in the Arab World* (New York: Syracuse University Press, 1985), pp. 9–12,19–20. See also John L. Esposito, *Islam: The Straight Path*, (New York: Oxford University Press, 1988), pp. 117–118.

2. Dekmejian, *Islam In Revolution*, pp. 3–7, 9–12.

3. During the pre-revolution days, the Muslim Brotherhood had been equivocal on the issue of violence: while advocating participation in the parliamentary process, it had also founded a secret armed wing which was involved in some violent activities.

4. Dekmejian, *Islam In Revolution*, pp. 912, 19–20.

5. John L. Esposito, *The Islamic Threat: Myth or Reality?* (New York: Oxford University Press, 1992), pp. 133–135.

6. Dekmejian, *Islam In Revolution*, pp. 8, 31. See also John O. Voll, "The Revivalist Heritage" in Yvonne Yazbeck Haddad et al. (eds.), *The Contemporary Islamic Revival: A Critical Survey and Bibliography* (New York: Greenwood Press, 1991), p. 23; Esposito, *Islam: The Straight Path*, pp. 162–164.

7. Esposito, *The Islamic Threat*, pp. 138–139.

8. Hamid Ansari, "The Islamic Militants In Egyptian Politics," *IJMES*, Vol. 16, No. 3, (1984), p. 129.

9. Dekmejian, *Islam In Revolution*, p. 95. Mustafa's title was "prince of the princes" (*amir al-umara*), rather than the more common *amir* used by most leaders of Islamic societies.

10. Esposito, *Islam: The Straight Path*, pp. 136–137. See also Farzana Shaikh, (ed.), *Islam & Islamic Groups: A Worldwide Reference Guide*, (Harlow: Longman, 1992), p. 70.

11. Nabeel Jabbour, *The Rumbling Volcano*, (Pasadena: William Carey Library, 1993), pp. 194–212.

12. Dekmejian, *Islam In Revolution*, p. 97.

13. Ibid., pp. 97–98. Shaykh 'Abd al-Rahman became spiritual guide for both al-Jihad and the other extremist groups known as "Islamic societies" (*al-jama'at al-Islamiyya*) well into the 1990s issuing the religious legal decisions (*fatwas*) needed to legitimate their various activities. He is now serving a prison term in the United States for his involvement in the First World Trade Center bombing in New York.

14. Ibid.

15. Gilles Kepel, *Muslim Extremism in Egypt: The Prophet and the Pharaoh*, (London: Al-Saqi Books, 1985), p. 206.

16. Dekmejian, *Islam In Revolution*, pp. 95–96.

17. Afaf Lutfi al-Sayyid Marsot, "Religion Or Opposition: Urban Protest Movements in Egypt," *IJMES*, Vol. 16, (1984), pp. 549. See also Kepel, *Muslim Extremism in Egypt*, p. 206.

18. The Salafiyya movement was launched by Rashid Rida (1865–1935), disciple of the great Egyptian Muslim reformer Muhammad Abduh (1849–1905). Its goal was the revival of Islam not so much by harmonizing it with modern times as advocated by the reformers, but by a return to the pristine Islam of the pious forbears (*salaf*). Salafiyya was to some extent an amalgamation of reformist with fundamentalist Wahhabi trends.

19. Ever since Ataturk dissolved the Ottoman Caliphate in 1924 in his drive for secularization, Islamists have viewed the revival of the Caliphate—the divinely appointed succession to the Prophet and the ideal form of state leadership—as essential to the revival and political resurgence of Islam.

20. Ansari, "The Islamic Militants In Egyptian Politics," pp 136. See also Walid Mahmoud Abdelnasser, *The Islamic Movement in Egypt: Perceptions of International Relations, 1967–81*, (London: Kegan Paul, 1994) p. 111; Muhammad Abd al-Salam Faraj, "The Neglected Duty," in Johannes J. G. Jansen, *The Neglected Duty: The Creed of Sadat's Assassins and Islamic Resurgence in the Middle East*, (New York: Macmillan, 1986), pp. 162–165.

21. Abdelnasser, *The Islamic Movement in Egypt*, pp. 234–235.

22. Ibid, p. 235.

23. Ansari, "The Islamic Militants in Egyptian Politics," pp. 136–137.

24. Abdelnasser, *The Islamic Movement in Egypt*, pp. 258–259. See also Faraj, "The Neglected Duty," p. 166.

25. Abdelnasser, *The Islamic Movement in Egypt*, p. 197.

26. Ibid. See also Esposito (ed.), *The Oxford Encyclopedia of the Modern Islamic World*, (New York: Oxford University Press, 1995), Vol. 4, pp. 179–181.

27. Ibid. See also Faraj, "The Neglected Duty," pp. 166–167,170,173–175.

28. Abdelnasser, *The Islamic Movement in Egypt*, pp. 204–205.

29. Jabbour, *The Rumbling Volcano*, p. 150. See also Kepel, *Muslim Extremism In Egypt*, p. 150; Abdelnasser, pp. 205–206.

30. Jabbour, *The Rumbling Volcano*, pp 143–157. See also Kepel, *Muslim Extremism In Egypt*, pp. 95–96; Dekmejian, *Islam In Revolution*, pp. 92–96, 101; Faraj, "The Neglected Duty," pp. 200–201.

31. Abdelnasser, *The Islamic Movement in Egypt*, p. 111.

32. Ansari, "The Islamic Militants In Egyptian Politics," pp 137. See also Dekmejian, *Islam In Revolution*, p. 101.

33. Ansari, "The Islamic Militants in Egyptian Politics," pp. 123–144. See also Kepel, *Muslim Extremism in Egypt*, pp. 191–122; Faraj, "The Neglected Duty," pp. 170, 173–175.

34. Ibid.

35. Esposito, *Islam: the Straight Path*, pp. 134–135. See also Kepel, *Muslim Extremism in Egypt*, pp. 195; Ansari, "The Islamic Militants in Egyptian Politics," pp. 136–7; Abdelnasser, *The Islamic Movement in Egypt*, pp. 205–207.

36. Johannes J. G. Jansen, "Tafsir, Ijma' and Modern Muslim Extremism," *ORIENT*, Vol. 27, No. 4, (1986), p. 648. See also see Faraj, "The Neglected Duty," p. 172.

37. Jansen, "Tafsir, Ijma' and Modern Muslim Extremism," p. 648. See also Faraj, "The Neglected Duty," pp. 202–203.

38. Faraj, "The Neglected Duty," pp. 207–208, 210–213.

39. Ibid., pp. 186–189.

40. Esposito, *Islam: The Straight Path*, p. 171.

41. Abdelnasser, *The Islamic Movement in Egypt*, pp. 242–243.

42. Ibid, p. 239.

43. Ibid, pp. 226, 240–241, 244, 254.

44. Ibid, p. 226.

45. Abdelnasser, *The Islamic Movement in Egypt*, p. 216. See also Derek Hopwood, *Egypt: Politics and Society 1945–1990*, (London: Harper Collins Academic, 1991), p. 118.

46. Abdelnasser, *The Islamic Movement in Egypt*, pp. 234–235. See also Faraj, "The Neglected Duty," pp. 163–164.

47. Dekmejian, *Islam In Revolution*, pp. 96–97.

48. "Massacres in Algeria: A Domestic Tragedy and the Show-Off Positions," *'Ayn al-Yaqeen*, Internet, <http://www.ain-al-yaqeen.com/issues/19980121/feat3en.htm>. "Syria Roots Out Militants," 7 January 2000, Global Intelligence Update, *Stratfor*, Internet, <http://216.30.41.7/SERVICES/giu2000/01700.ASP>.

49. Shaikh, p. 69.

50. *Terrorist Group Profiles*, Dudley Knox Libraries, Naval Postgraduate School, published on the Internet: <http://web.nps.navy.mil/~library/tgp/jihad.htm>.

51. R. Springborg, *Mubarak's Egypt*, (Boulder: Westview, 1989), pp. 217.

52. Esposito, *Islam: The Straight Path*, pp. 134–135.

53. Hopwood, *Egypt: Politics and Society*, p. 188.

54. Adel Darwish, "On the Threshold of the 7th Millennium," *The Middle East*, June 1999.

55. The *khariji* movement was a legalistic puritan group that arose in the early years of Islam during the rule of Muhammad's son-in-law 'Ali (d.661) as fourth caliph. It was the first Muslim sect. The *kharijis* rejected all Muslims who did not accept their interpretation of Islam as infidels worthy of death. They developed an ideology of continuous jihad and rebelled against all rulers until finally suppressed after some 200 years of bloodshed. Remnants of the original *khariji* movement survive today in the *ibadis* of Oman and in the *mzabis* of Algeria.

3

The Development of Palestinian Islamic Groups

Reuven Paz

The story of how Palestinian Islamic groups evolved is one of the most interesting case studies in modern Islamist politics. By looking at the roots of these organizations and their recruitment techniques, one gets a far better appreciation of the nature, appeal, and strategy of these groups.

A key element in their development has been the struggle between Islamist and nationalist alternatives for the allegiance of individual Palestinians. Factionalism has also been an important dimension, given the multiplicity of groups deriving from the Muslim Brotherhood and Islamic Jihad tendencies. Also interesting is the relationship between Islamist organizations and educational institutions, which have served as important centers for finding, socializing, and mobilizing supporters.

Until 1967, organized Islamic groups in the West Bank and Gaza Strip (henceforth called "the Territories") were situated in socioreligious centers and mosques run by the Waqf establishment, as well as several charity funds in Jerusalem and the West Bank. These groups drew most of their support from middle class traders who were beginning to develop in urban areas of the West Bank.

In the Gaza Strip, the Muslim Brotherhood, active under the Egyptian civil regime despite Nasser's hostility to the Brotherhood's Egyptian branch, were influential in several mosques run by their supporters. In fact, until 1967, Islamic groups maintained a strong hold on the population of the Gaza Strip with almost exclusive control of all social organizations. The only Islamic group not affiliated with the Muslim Brotherhood consisted of supporters of several shaykhs who had adopted a strict Salafi or Wahhabi line during their studies in Saudi Arabia. (Saudi Arabia supported the Egyptian Muslim Brotherhood during the course of its rivalry with Nasser's regime during the 1960s.)[1]

The Muslim Brotherhood was also dominant in the Jordanian-ruled West Bank. The Brotherhood controlled the Waqf establishment, operated legally, and even participated in the Jordanian government in the 1960s, though Jordanian security services did supervise the group tightly. The Jordanians restricted its movements, arrested its followers, and barred it from certain actions.[2] The group's only Islamic competitor was the Islamic Liberation Party (*Hizb al-Tahrir al-Islami*), which was banned and persecuted by the government. Thus, the Brotherhood, which enjoyed some backing from the Saudi regime, was able to play an 'open game' by mildly criticizing the government on internal affairs.

Until 1967, the Muslim Brotherhood faced no real competition from secular nationalist groups in the Territories, such as the banned Jordanian Communist Party or the Syrian and Iraqi Ba'ath party. These groups attracted a very narrow stratum of intellectuals and university graduates. In Gaza, leftist organizations were often forced to collaborate with the Muslim Brotherhood as a result of joint imprisonment.

Israel's entry into the Territories in 1967 brought considerable change in the nature of Islamic activities there. Islamic groups now enjoyed more freedom than in the past. This newfound freedom, coupled with changes that took place during the 1970s in the organizational pattern of Palestinian society in the Territories as a whole, were central factors in the Palestinian Islamic resurrection of the 1980s.

One of the central factors influencing Palestinians in the Territories since 1967 had been socioeconomic development, to which the Israelis were indifferent. The armed struggle waged by the Palestinian nationalist secular organizations from the onset of the occupation until the 1993–1994 period diverted Israeli attention from Palestinian social processes. By the 1980s, these processes had brought about several important results, including:

• A vast increase in the Palestinian population due to a high natural birthrate and immigration beginning in the late 1970s, as the number of Palestinians employed in the Persian Gulf sharply declined.[3]
• A major drop in the average age in the Territories.[4]
• A significant rise in the level of education and the number of educational institutes in the Territories concomitant with an awakening national awareness of the importance of education to political, economic, and social development.
• An increase in the standard of living among Palestinians, especially during the first half of the 1980s. The loss of income from Palestinian employment in Gulf countries was more than made up for by an increase in the number of

laborers working in Israel and heavy funding since the late 1970s from Palestine Liberation Organization (PLO) affiliates.[5]

- The (conscious or unconscious) adoption of Israeli behavior and ways of thinking, modernization, and the forming of a middle class influenced by Israel as well as communication with the rest of the Arab world.

The combination of these factors, together with an effort by the PLO and pro-Palestinian foreign organizations, gave rise to a Palestinian sociopolitical organizational foundation. Israel offered 'covert help' in the sense that it did not interfere so long as it did not perceive an immediate military threat. This new foundation shifted the political national organizational weight from municipalities, which could easily be controlled by the Israelis, to a wide variety of new and growing institutions in the early 1980s.

The West Bank, and later also the Gaza Strip, saw the emergence of research institutes, newspapers, information offices, workers unions, professionals unions, student committees, liberal organizations, youth movements, women's organizations, social organizations, and charity funds—all somehow connected to PLO factions. Also notable is the fact that this sociopolitical base was centered in East Jerusalem, which was regaining its importance in relation to West Bank Arab municipalities.

One of the main factors enhancing the development of this national foundation was the growth of higher education institutions in the Territories at the end of the 1970s. These bodies soon became central to Palestinian political and social development in the Territories. They offered social mobility to groups that previously did not have access to the higher education system. In the West Bank, for example, and even more so in Gaza's Islamic University, a large percentage of students came from refugee camps, small villages, and lower-income families.[6]

These colleges and universities not only enhanced Palestinian national political awareness but also introduced the PLO's structure to the Territories as a supraorganization comprised of several active groups such as ideological movements and even political parties.[7] Until this point, the PLO manifested itself only in the military-terrorist field and in the prisons where convicted terrorists were sent.

The political organization that developed across university campuses in the Territories and its social impact led to two processes that quickly influenced the entire population and its organizational structure. The first process was the almost total filling of the political void in the Territories. Gradually the entire younger generation—now the vast majority of the population—identified politically with either the PLO, an Islamic faction, the Communist Party, or Jordanian supporters. Even Israel, in the early 1980s, attempted (and failed) to start an organization of village associations that would lead a faction accepting the Israeli presence in the Territories.

The second process was the politicization of almost every aspect of Palestinian life. Relatively democratic election patterns and organizations were formed under Palestinian national political influence, perhaps also due to unconscious impression of Israeli democracy. Partylike structures developed in the Territories which allowed the PLO to exercise social, political, and economic control both from inside and from outside the Territories.

These processes—beginning in the early 1980s—were actually part of a larger transformation of Palestinian society toward creating a basis for a forthcoming state. The core of Palestinian nationalism was transferred inward, from the refugee camps in Lebanon to the Territories, and from external Arab patronage to direct struggle with Israel.

Along with these sociopolitical processes, another process was also taking place— an indigenous Islamic resurrection that aimed to mold the character of the Palestinian state-to-be, which could follow in an Islamic or national secular direction.

Because of the importance of universities in the Territories in shaping the ideologies of secular nationalist activists, Islamic factions decided to pour a heavy effort into their campus presence, especially since many students came from villages and refugee camps where Islam already had a relatively strong presence. It should be noted that for the Islamic groups, education, starting at a very young age, was a primary part of their sociopolitical activity.

The Muslim Brotherhood in particular focused on education. It had consistently abstained, from the beginning of the Israeli occupation until the Palestinian uprising—intifada—twenty years later, from any "armed struggle" against Israel, a main activity of all PLO-affiliated organizations. Just as the Muslim Brotherhood hoped to offer an alternative sociopolitical character to the future Palestinian state, it was also an alternative to violent protest until the uprising.

When, in the 1990s, the Palestinian national leadership chose to compromise with Israel and abandon terrorism, the Muslim Brotherhood remained an alternative and undertook terrorism in the guise of Hamas and Islamic Jihad. The twenty years preceding the forming of Hamas were for the Brotherhood a period of building and reinforcing its social foundation through its influence in the educational arena and in the almost total control it had obtained in the mosques.

For the Muslim Brotherhood, the development of sociopolitical organizations and their student activities gave the Islamic cause a significant push, which was crucial to the revolutionary faction of Islamic Jihad. The Islamic groups in the universities began forming as soon as the national secular groups did and an overt ideological rivalry soon developed.

While Islamic groups kept pace with their national secular counterparts in universities, they lagged behind in other fields. For example, no Islamic factions were formed in organizations such as workers unions, professionals unions, or economic and social societies. No bodies, such as unions or Islamic information centers, were created, apart from student bulletins and charity funds. Until 1988, several centers for the preservation of Islamic heritage were founded, but far fewer than similar centers founded by nationalist groups. For example, in January 1983, one such center was founded in Jerusalem by the Waqf administration, which mainly documented Arab and Turkish manuscripts. In 1986, a research center which doubled as an Islamic library from the estate of the al-Husayni family, was founded on behalf of the "Arab Child's House."[8] However, until the founding of Hamas at the beginning of the intifada, universities remained the main public arena where Islamic organizations concentrated their presence.

Several reasons explain why Islamic organizations failed to engage in a full range of sociopolitical activities, like their nationalist rivals. First, outside funding from the PLO, which was crucial to building up the nationalist base, did not reach Islamic groups. Similarly, these groups—which did not turn violent until late 1986—did not enjoy the large funds that supported terrorism or compensated the families of prisoners and dead activists.

Second, the Muslim Brotherhood senior leadership, which in the West Bank was relatively older than its nationalist equivalent, worked in the traditional ways of the 1950s and 1960s. To attain public influence, it invested in social communal activities, charity funds, and religious centers such as the Waqf and mosques. For some of them, activities such as charity, selling Islamic literature, preaching, and distributing cassettes were considered much more efficient than publishing newspapers and pamphlets or building a foundation of institutes taken from Western culture. The organized propaganda used by Hamas since its inception was engineered by younger activists who had learned from their nationalist colleagues in universities in the Territories or abroad.

Third, while the revolutionary faction of Islamic Jihad mimicked the activities of the Egyptian Islamic groups, where the student arena was also very central, other factions, especially the Salafi-based ones, were composed of people with little education who emphasized secret, armed activities and not building a large public base.

Fourth, the rivalry between Islamic groups and nationalist secular parties in colleges and universities very rarely reached the public sphere, and if so, it was almost exclusively in the Gaza Strip. Thus, there was no widespread competition for public support.

Fifth, the purpose of building an organizational infrastructure was to expand national awareness of the PLO as an exclusive Palestinian leadership ahead of future statehood. It was therefore built according to the accepted Arab national model. Islamic groups, on the other hand, envisioned the founding of an Islamic state at first narrowed to the entire land of Palestine and then enlarged to include the entire Islamic Arab world. Thus, their organizational emphasis was different.

Still, the Brotherhood's limited focus is surprising given that the Egyptian Muslim Brotherhood—which served as a model for branches in other countries—had developed front organizations until the early 1950s similar to those of secular groups. The Muslim Brotherhood in Egypt, Jordan, and the Gulf states had published Islamic newspapers and periodicals, as did other Islamic groups in Europe and the United States.

While secular groups established financial institutes and became heavily involved in professionals or workers unions, Islamic groups centered their activities in mosques which served as a communal factor no less than a religious one. Through the mosques, Islamic groups promoted awareness *(wa'i)*, religious education, preaching and ideological, political, and social indoctrination, financial activity through charity funds, sports activities, and more.

After 1967, due to the relative freedom Israel granted them and constant connections with the Jordanian regime and its supporters, the national secular network did not pose a significant threat to the Islamic groups' stable position. In addition, the national base in the West Bank, where most of the population was rural and even traditional, did not have a political manifestation contradicting the Muslim Brotherhood's ideology. In the Gaza Strip, where the Muslim Brotherhood was always popular, secular nationalist groups developed slowly, and sped up only in the middle of the 1980s. In fact, in Gaza's Islamic University—which became a leading political and social center—the Muslim Brotherhood had almost full control over the administration and the male and female student councils.

To a certain extent, however, the Muslim Brotherhood underestimated the institutional strength of the PLO factions. This was proven at the onset of the intifada, when the nationalist leadership in the Territories succeeded in controlling the population and the uprising's course, even before the outside directive from the PLO. More so, the uprising itself was a manifestation of the mood fostered mainly by the nationalist factions and using their foundation built in the 1980s.

Colleges and universities, however, were an exception. Hence, they were very important to the organizational growth of the Islamic Jihad factions, especially its revolutionary one, though the Muslim Brotherhood's groups conducted the main Islamic activity.

What is special about these groups' publications is that they were locally produced, not imported like most of the Islamic literature being circulated. The percentage of local articles—as opposed to photocopied ones published in Islamic bulletins abroad—rose greatly in the 1980s. Previously, very few thinkers originated from Palestinian Islamic groups and until the establishment of Hamas, the groups imported all of their ideals.

The Islamic groups were independently organized in every one of the higher-education institutes closed down after the uprising began. Once a year the groups convened a quasigeneral assembly of their representatives, usually during al-Israa' wal-Mi'raj events in Al-Aqsa mosque. The last assembly prior to the uprising took place in April 1987[9] and dealt with current issues in the Islamic Arab world. The groups attacked Arab regimes—including that of the Palestinians—that supported a compromise with Israel. This hardline stance can perhaps be explained by the fact that the assembly took place at the same time as the

National Palestinian Council meeting in Algiers, which brought the beginning of a turn toward a political solution.

The Islamic groups' main activities were focused on events and ceremonies for Islamic holidays or ancient Islamic history. They also organized exhibits of Islamic books and fairs and circulated bulletins, books, and sundry Islamic publications, mainly published from 1982. This year marked a new stage in the organizational pattern of the Islamic groups in institutions of higher learning.

More than one factor influenced the change in Islamic groups' orientation, including Israel's invasion of Lebanon and Sadat's murder, as well as the trials of Egyptian Jihad organization members. It appears that the 'Lebanese effect' had to do not only with the Israeli control over southern Lebanon, but also with the infiltration of Iranian forces and the fallout from Iran's Islamic revolution that spurred the growth of the revolutionary faction of the Islamic Jihad.

The first publications in the spirit of the revolutionary Islamic Jihad, which probably posed a certain threat to the Muslim Brotherhood and also hastened its own publications, came from the Muslim Youth Association in Jerusalem. It was a series of three booklets which were once published under different names:[10] *Al-Nur*, *Al-Nur Al-Rabbani*, and *Al-Nur Al-Ilahi*.[11] The first was published in May–June 1982, before Israel's invasion of Lebanon, and its content reveals the influence of the Egyptian monthly *Al-Mukhtar al-Islami* of the radical Islamic groups in Egypt. The main issues featured in this publication and in subsequent ones were copied from the Egyptian publication and written by Dr. 'Iz al-Din Ibrahim, then one of the literary pseudonyms of Dr. Fathi al-Shqaqi, the founder of the revolutionary Islamic Jihad in Gaza.[12]

The first publications of the Muslim Brotherhood groups were a combination of photocopied material from abroad and handwritten articles and news items, mostly discussing the situation of Palestinian higher education. For example, a publication named *Al-Risalah* was published in November 1982 by the Hebron University student council, then led by the Muslim Brotherhood.[13] It featured an interview with a student named Muhammad Harb, an active communist who repented and became a supporter of the Islamic Group (another name for the Muslim Brotherhood).[14] The interview, propaganda against the communists, also accused nationalist groups of creating disturbances in the university aimed at causing the Israeli army to arrest Muslim students. This claim occasionally reappeared to justify why Islamic groups did not participate in demonstrations against the Israeli army, since these were viewed as provocations with no "pure" intent.

The publication also contained a list of student council activities during 1982 that indicates the Islamic groups' mode of operation. Consider the following examples:

• Opening two mosques, one for male students and one for female students.
• Distributing free robes to needy female students.

- The sale of discounted books.
- Performing a ceremony for the birth *(mawlid)* of the Prophet. Among those registered as present were leaders of the Muslim Brotherhood such as Shaykh Ahmad Yassin from Gaza and Muhammad Fuad Abu Zaid from Qabatya/Jenin.
- A medical services card.
- Performing wide scale fundraising in 'Palestine' raising 15,000 dinars.
- The noting of historic dates such as the Balfour declaration and the partition decision.
- Holding a Hebrew learning course.
- Collecting 1,600 dinars to pay for fines given to imprisoned students.
- Blood donations for several residents.[15]

One of the main issues preoccupying Islamic students was 'immoral behavior' in colleges and universities. Many students attended daily meetings between Muslims and Christians, some of whom were more liberal regarding cross-gender relations. Some Christians also belonged to the Marxist organizations that advocated relative equality between the sexes. As a rule, the move from a strict, closed village society into an open one with daily cross-gender interactions led to behavior strongly condemned by the Islamic groups.

In an *al-Muntalaq* issue published in al-Najah University's bulletin, the immoral behavior of the student council—"corruption and debauchery"—is cited as a direct reason for the founding of the Islamic group in 1987.[16]

One of the issues at the top of the Islamic groups' agenda was friction with the administrations of other universities, especially the two considered more secular and nationalist—Bir Zeit University and al-Najah University in the West Bank. In both, there was a connection (and sometimes common interest) between the administration and nationalist student parties. Apart from disagreements on mundane issues such as tuition and dorms, the Islamic groups confronted the administration while attempting to conduct separate events, usually with Islamic content, that were usually points of tension between the rival parties, interfered with studies, and led to conflicts that extended beyond university walls.

In both these institutions, and surely in Freres College (which became Bethlehem University), there was also Christian influence which added to the tension. In one *al-Muntalaq* issue, the university administration is called "the hostile crusade management."[17] Reference to Christian students in the Islamic publications was rare.

The February 1984 *al-Muntalaq* bulletin surveyed the achievements of al-Najah University's Islamic group six years after its establishment. It is interesting to see how the Islamic group's followers classified the achievements in order of importance. The first was developing an Islamic personality and saving young men and women from moral and ideological deterioration; the second was

building two separate mosques for men and women; the third was giving scholarships and loans to needy students; and the fourth was supplying Islamic books.
Only in thirteenth place one can find activities which may be viewed as
sociopolitical, copied from the nationalist groups and first introduced to the
Territories by the Communist Party: one day of volunteer work in Gaza and two
in the university itself.[18]

The volunteer framework was developed by leftist groups in the Territories
as early as the second half of the 1970s and was adopted by Fatah supporters the
following decade. It was turned into one of the main elements of the younger
generation's organization in all aspects of political and social life in the Territories
in the framework of what was called "the youth committees for social work"
(lijan al-shabibah lil-'amal al-ijtima'i), popularly known as "Shabibah." Much of
the volunteering consisted of charity work.

Volunteer days could be found only in the colleges and universities and
were part of the Islamic groups' influence there. The Islamic groups did not,
however, form voluntary front organizations, as did the nationalist groups, with
the exception of the Islamic group at Gaza's Islamic University, which operated
a voluntary labor committee. The dominant influence of the Muslim Brotherhood at Islamic University perhaps accounts for the rise of such a committee
there. Indeed, an Islamic workers union also formed at the university, which
doubled as an organizational center for the Muslim Brotherhood.[19]

Islamic groups were also concerned with the recurrent closings of educational institutions by the Israelis, whether due to violent clashes among students
or to clashes with the army and riots. The Islamic groups placed the utmost
importance on maintaining regular studies in the Territories, as demonstrated by
an *Al-Muntalaq* editorial from December 1984:

> Owing to the reopening of the university after a forced closure of four whole
> months, we cannot but congratulate the new and senior brothers and sis-
> ters. . . . We appeal to the senior students to be sensible and serve the public
> interest and abandon the activities that bring the university to give our en-
> emies a golden opportunity. . . . We call upon our new brothers to see things
> clearly and understand that regular studies and the opening of the university
> are the peak of constructive positive activity, and this is what our people and
> nation want.[20]

This position also demonstrated the Muslim Brotherhood's passivity regarding
resistance to the Israeli regime. Until the uprising, this policy advocated carrying
on with life as usual in order to enable the movement to establish itself.

The Islamic University in Gaza was different from other institutions in that
it was established initially as an Islamic institute, although it also offered secular
studies. The centerpiece of the Muslim Brotherhood's power, it became the

largest university in the Territories and the one with the most political and social weight in the Gaza Strip.

The Muslim Brotherhood controlled the student council at the university and also became the most organized of the Islamic groups in the Territories. Several active committees were established in the 1980s, including a cultural and educational committee, an art committee, a volunteer work committee, a mosque committee, and a sports committee. These became the movement's main propaganda tools in the Gaza Strip. The group distributed publications such as *al-Shihab* (on behalf of the mosque committee) and *al-Nidaa'* (on behalf of the student council) and also irregular ideological publications such as "From The Young Generation's Desk" (Bi-aqlam al-Shabab).[21] In 1986 and 1987, the student council's Islamic preaching and guidance committee published a series headed *Voice of Truth, Power and Freedom* (Sawt al-Haqq Wal-Quwwah Wal-Hurriyyah), a well-known slogan of the Muslim Brotherhood's in Egypt.[22]

The student council's culture committee was prolific, publishing some material that was openly circulated under the name of the Muslim Brotherhood.[23] The student council publications in Gaza were also more ideologically consolidated than those in the West Bank. *Al-Nidaa's* bulletins included ideologically richer material from local writers, knowledgeable in the Muslim Brotherhood's philosophy. As a rule, their bulletin and other publications were similar to those of Islamic groups abroad.

It should be noted, however, that the Islamic group's publications in Nablus' al-Najah University were better funded than those in Islamic University, probably due to the indirect Jordanian funding of the Muslim Brotherhood in Nablus and Samarea. The Jordanian Muslim Brotherhood was part of the Jordanian government even after 1967.

A prominent subject in all of the Islamic groups' publications was the rivalry with secular nationalist groups. In the West Bank, where the Muslim Brotherhood did not have as much control over popular centers as they did in parts of the Gaza Strip, the higher-education institutes became the main arena for competition between the two camps. The rivalry was most fierce in al-Najah University, which saw student clashes beyond the administration's control from the beginning of the 1980s until it was closed during the intifada.

The Islamic groups circulated pamphlets[24] which, at their core, represented the cultural and social rivalry between the two sides—a rivalry most manifested at the universities. The West Bank institutions, which employed not only secular Arab instructors but also Americans and Europeans, became the center of secular revolution for many young people who came from villages and refugee camps. Since most members of the Islamic group came from similar homes and social status, they fought hard to preserve a traditional lifestyle in the face of Western influence in the universities.

The issue of Palestine was also a prominent point of contention. The Islamic groups were mostly concerned with Islam in the Palestinian arena, though there was some mention of the jihad in Afghanistan and the trials of Muslim groups in Egypt and Syria. Mainly, the groups in the Territories addressed the PLO's political line and accused Arab governments of neglecting the Palestinian cause. They concentrated on Palestinian political problems or local problems arising from the Islamic-secular rivalry.

The Palestine focus is to be expected given that Islamic Palestinian groups grew within a conflict that was nationalist in essence. Islamic supporters were well-integrated into general Palestinian society. What is interesting, though, is that the Islamic groups were controlled by the Muslim Brotherhood, which, at least in the West Bank, was part of the Jordanian movement. But the Muslim Brotherhood's transformation into a mainly Palestinian group that viewed the problems of the Arab Islamic world and of creating a large, new Arab state as secondary was a direct result of the activities of Islamic groups in colleges and universities. Students during the 1980s had grown up fighting the Israeli occupation. Indeed, resisting the Israelis became the center of Palestinian political work in the Territories, which led Islamic activists to address a question that became significant in Palestinian society: establishing the character and nature of the future independent state.

Higher-education institutions in the Territories became one of the centers of fighting the Israeli regime, and Islamic resistance was prominent. In violent riots initiated by leftist students at Bir Zeit in December 1986, Islamic group members played an active role for the first time. Both of the students killed in these clashes belonged to the Islamic group and were residents of the Gaza Strip.[25] Their residency is noteworthy because it represents an increase in the number of Gaza Strip residents who studied in West Bank institutions and their influence on the Islamic activity in this area. This increase accelerated the militancy of Islamic groups in the West Bank.

In summary, it appears that the flourishing of sociopolitical life in colleges and universities as central to the national Palestinian foundation in the Territories accelerated the organizational development of Islamic groups. The political implications of these changes were mainly felt during the intifada when the Muslim Brotherhood, in the form of the Gaza-born Hamas, openly opposed the Israeli regime.

At the same time, though, a new Islamic opponent surfaced—the Islamic Jihad—which was more threatening ideologically than organizationally. The Muslim Brotherhood had difficulty coping with Islamic Jihad's rise in popularity in 1986 and 1987 after it committed itself to violence against Israel, something the Muslim Brotherhood had consistently refrained from doing until that point.

The strengthening of the organizational infrastructure of Islamic groups in colleges and universities gave impetus to the growth of the revolutionary faction of Islamic Jihad in the Territories. In contrast to the Muslim Brotherhood's leadership, which consisted of older, religious establishment figures, Islamic Jihad's leadership came from students and academics who had spent time in Egyptian universities in the 1970s and absorbed the revolutionary militancy of groups there.

The elitist concept of a revolutionary group whose role was to lead the masses found an attentive audience among university activists. Unlike the Muslim Brotherhood, the Palestinian Islamic Jihad was enthused by the success of Iran's Islamic revolution. From its mid-1982 founding at Islamic University in Gaza, the group publicized its disagreement with the Muslim Brotherhood over Iran's revolution. Its first publication[26] contained the movement's main ideas: Khomeini's call to the Muslims of the world; an article about the Islamic revolution of the oppressed led by 'Iz al-Din al-Qassam; a call for permanent and organized dialogue among the Islamic groups; the battle against the tyranny of the Arab regimes based on the philosophy of Sayyid Qutb; and raising jihad to the top of the Islamic struggle's agenda.

Next, the group ran in the 1982 student council elections under the name "The Independent Islamists" (Al-Islamiyyun al-Mustaqillun). In 1984, the group attempted to form a faction called "The Islamic Student Movement" (Al-Harakah al-Islamiyyah al-Tulabiyyah) and published and distributed handwritten promotional material at the end of 1983 at the Islamic University. This flyer attacked the old Muslim Brotherhood's student council for kindling the fire of disagreement instead of striving to unite the Islamic groups. It cited the council's ban on the circulation of the new group's publications and compared the Muslim Brotherhood to a repressive government.[27]

It is interesting that Islamic Jihad's first flyer in the Territories was published not in Gaza but rather in al-Najah University in Nablus in May 1983.[28] The flyer severely attacked the university's secular student council for publishing a long declaration against the Islamic movement on different issues, including the support of the Islamic revolution in Iran. One of the subjects raised in the Islamic movement's counterflyer was the Arab secular nationalists' neglect of the Palestinian cause.

The year 1985 marked a new organizational feat for Islamic Jihad. It succeeded in forming as a proper party in several universities in the Territories under the name "The Islamic Group" (al-Jama'ah al-Islamiyyah)—a name borrowed from Egyptian student groups. This name, signaling Islamic violence, was used until the university was closed during the intifada. The group became the student faction of the Jihad movement.

Islamic Jihad differed from the Muslim Brotherhood and the nationalist groups on three basic points. The first was their support of the Iranian revolution. The second concerned the Palestine issue. Islamic Jihad favored military action against Israel, which served as a common denominator with the nationalist groups, especially Fatah. Inherent in its publications was harsh criticism of the Muslim Brotherhood's passive stance. The third difference concerned the unity of Islamic groups, not only in the Territories but throughout the Arab world. Islamic Jihad was influenced here by Shi'ite Iran, which wanted to end discord with Sunni Muslims and rebuild the Caliphate state. Anyone who disagreed with Islamic Jihad's strategy was declared an enemy. (In contrast, the Muslim Brotherhood emphasized Islamic pluralism.)

The revolutionary faction within Islamic Jihad was the only one to act as an official party at the Islamic University and in the universities in the West Bank. It refrained from using the name "Islamic Jihad" until June 1987, when it distributed a flyer bearing the name "Islamic Jihad Organization" at Islamic University. By October and November of 1987, it was the only name used and became the permanent name of the group led by Shaykh As'ad al-Tamimi during the intifada. The group affiliated with Fatah in the Gaza Strip began calling itself "The Islamic Jihad Squadrons" (Saraya al-Jihad al-Islami) and in the West Bank it added the words "Jerusalem/the temple" (Bait al-Maqdes).

The Islamic Jihad's bulletins were dull in comparison to those of the Islamic groups of the Muslim Brotherhood and contained few details regarding their groups' activities in different institutes, revealing Jihad's inferior position in the higher-education institutions in numbers, organization, and finances.

Until the outbreak of the intifada, the revolutionary Islamic Jihad group was successful only in Gaza, where it originated. In Islamic University's male and female student union elections in 1984 through 1986, it obtained six to seven percent of the male students' votes and a lower percentage among the female students. In the 1987 elections, held immediately after the outbreak of the uprising, it polled 15 percent of the votes. One may assume that this relatively high percentage is mainly due to the military actions of the other Jihad factions.

It seems that the main importance of the revolutionary faction in colleges and universities in the Territories lay more in its challenge to other Islamic groups than in any of its own achievements. It did supply the ideological basis that encouraged the forming of armed Islamic Jihad groups in 1986 and 1987, which implemented the revolutionary group's callings. The group also contributed to accelerating militant processes that developed among the young generation within the Muslim Brothers. Its activity and mode of organization were based on the student arena, most strongly at Islamic University.

CONCLUSION

The higher-education institutions in the Territories had a crucial effect on the development of most Islamic groups, particularly the Muslim Brotherhood and the revolutionary faction of the Islamic Jihad. It molded a new, young, and educated generation that filled important leadership positions in these groups. This generation, which grew up in the midst of the general Palestinian national struggle in the Territories, introduced Palestinian patriotism to the Islamic arena

in lieu of the 'Islamic cosmopolitanism' that characterized the Muslim Brotherhood until the 1980s. It also emphasized the political and cultural struggle
between Islamic groups and popular nationalist secular groups. Actually, until
the December 1987 intifada, colleges and universities were the main arena for
Palestinian-Israeli conflict, a prelude of what was to engulf the whole Palestinian
community during the uprising. In time, the young veterans of the secular-
religious conflict would form the indigenous leadership of the intifada against
the Israelis.

This secular-religious conflict also had a cultural dimension. The universities and colleges in the Territories, especially those in the West Bank, accelerated
the absorption of Western secular culture, particularly among the lower class,
traditional folk who comprised the majority of the student population. Daily
exposure to Israeli society also contributed a Western influence. Bir Zeit University and Bethlehem University became the centers of the cultural struggle, with
a notable number of Christian professors, local and foreign, and even Israeli
Arab citizens. Al-Najah University in Nablus, despite having a Muslim character
and very few Christian students and professors, developed a relatively strong
Marxist element side by side with labor and professional unions.

Attempts were also made in the universities to create Palestinian cultural roots
by exhibiting clothing, food, agricultural tools, and buildings from the pre-1948
era. Similar attempts at emphasizing the Canaanite heritage of the Palestinians,
especially in Samarea, increased to a large extent immediately after the establishment of the Palestinian Authority in the 1990s. As in other Arab and Islamic
countries (Egypt with its Pharaonic culture, Lebanon with the Phoenic, Turkey
with the Pan-Turan, and Iran with its pre-Islamic Persian culture), these attempts
led to religious tension and were sometimes seen as part of an anti-Islam campaign. In general, Palestinian culture in the Territories (and outside them after
1967) developed along secular lines, largely influenced by left-wing artists.

During the second half of the 1980s—right before the uprising—the Muslim
Brotherhood was a strong rival of the secular nationalists among PLO supporters
in the Territories. Its popularity was based partly on its passivity in the struggle
against Israel. The tension between the Muslim Brotherhood and the secularists
is well illustrated by the booklets circulated by both sides during the 1987
student council elections at Islamic University.

In the Muslim Brotherhoods' *al-Haqiqah al-Gha'ibah* (The Absent Truth),[29]
the group quite apologetically presents its contribution to the Palestinian struggle
since the 1930s through the participation of the Egyptian Muslim Brotherhoods
in the wars against Israel from 1948 until 1967. The booklet's main weak spot,
exposed by the Muslim Brotherhood's opponents, was the fact that this contribution ceased in the same years in which "the Islamic holy places, foremost the
al-Aqsa mosque, fell into the hands of the Jews." The movement could not claim
any achievements for the liberation of Palestine between 1967 and 1987.

The combination of cultural and political battles was characteristic of the Palestinian students' activities in all the higher-education institutions from 1980 until the uprising. The uprising spread the battle to the entire Palestinian population. The establishment of the Palestinian Authority worsened the internal conflict. The centricity of the higher-education institutes to the development of both the Islamic and nationalist groups strongly points out two issues related to Israel that until now have not been given proper attention.

Israel completely ignored the growth of Islamic sociocultural and national-secular foundations in these institutions, as they were not violent. In certain respects, Israel's behavior was a historical repetition of British behavior toward Jewish universities during the mandate period, chiefly Hebrew University in Jerusalem and the Technion in Haifa. But unlike the British, who were foreigners and did not consider themselves responsible for the future of the country, Israel is sure to be closely involved in the development of Palestinian society even after a permanent agreement is reached.

Israel's apathy regarding Palestinian social developments in the Territories contributed to its inability to read the 'Palestinian map' correctly. It misjudged the intensity of hatred toward the Israeli occupation, the causes of the national uprising headed by the lower classes in refugee camps, and the growth of Islamic groups and their deep hold on society. This hold was achieved mainly by community sociocultural-educational activity centered in higher-education institutions.

A second point concerning Israel is its conscious and unconscious influence on Palestinian society in the Territories. Palestinian colleges and universities and social foundations, both on the Islamic side and on the nationalist-secular side, continuously nurtured the study of Israeli society—an ability to read the 'Israeli map' and analyze the events in Israel. The large-scale employment of Palestinians in Israel, which grew in the 1980s, naturally contributed to this understanding, but it was also common among the lower classes both in the Gaza Strip and in the West Bank.

When members of these classes became a main force in Palestinian higher education in the Territories, they used their familiarity with Israeli society as a means of personal and national advancement. Palestinian colleges and universities manifested the two most important elements of Israeli society: education as the key to personal and collective advancement, and democratic pluralism.

NOTES

1. Abu 'Amru, Ziad, *Usul al-Harakat al-Siyasiyyah fi Quta' Ghazah 1948–1967* (Acre: Dar Al-Aswar, 1987), pp. 70–74.

2. Regarding the Muslim Brotherhood see, Amnon Cohen, *Parties in the West Bank during the Jordanian Reign* (Jerusalem: Magnes Publishers, The Hebrew University, 1980), pp. 128–193.

3. Regarding the demographic developments in the Territories and in the entire Palestinian arena, see Gad Gilbar, *Trends in the Palestinian Demographic Development, 1870–1987* (Tel Aviv: Moshe Dayan Center, Tel Aviv University, No. 108, September 1989).

4. The age group of 0–24 formed 69.5 percent of the population in the West Bank (including East Jerusalem) and Gaza Strip in 1986. Of these, 60.5 percent were in the age group of 0–19. This is one of the world's youngest populations, and this affected the development of political awareness. The age group of 20–34, the potential age of students in higher-education institutes in the Territories, then formed 21.5 percent, more than one fifth of the population.

According to a study made by the Higher Education Council in East Jerusalem, the number of those studying in higher-education institutes in the school year 1982–83 was 10,295, which formed 0.84 percent of the population in the Territories (including East Jerusalem). See Majlis al-Ta'lim al-'Aali, *Hawl al-Ta'lim al-'Aali fi al-Dafah al-Gharbiyyah wa-Quta' Ghazah* (Arabic) (Jerusalem, 1983), p. 170.

5. Naturally, there is no data, not even in general, regarding the extent of funding from the PLO to the Territories, although this funding was not kept secret by the organization. The best-known fund for helping the national foundation in the Territories was established during the convention of the Arab League at Baghdad in 1978. The funds were to come from all the Arab states. According to Arab publications, what happened was that in the 1980s only Saudi Arabia and the Gulf States participated in the funding. In the 1980s, the Joint Jordanian-Palestinian Committee, which was to determine the distribution of the funds, operated on and off next to the Baghdad Fund. This committee's activity varied according to changes in Jordan's relations with the PLO. In July 1986 there was a long break in its activity after the expulsion of Khalil al-Wazir "Abu Jihad" from Jordan and the closing of most of the organization's offices in Aman. After that it seldom assembled, according to the state of the political relations between Jordan and the organization. For some details regarding the funding of the national institutes in the Territories see: Khalil Nakhleh, *Mu'asasatuna al-Jamahiriyyah fi Filastin: Nahwa Tatwir Ijtima'i Hadif (Our Public Institutions in Palestine: Towards Comprehensive Social Development)* (Geneva, January 1990. A PLO inner publication. Private copy with author). Dr. Nakhleh is a sociologist, an Arab Israeli citizen who left Israel in the 1970s and among other things was involved with the activities of Palestinian funds in Europe.

6. Several studies regarding the social influence of the universities and the education of the Palestinian population in the Territories were published, some in the Territories themselves. See Samir N. 'Anabtawi, *Palestinian Higher Education in the West Bank and Gaza: A Critical Assessment* (New York: Keagan Paul International, 1987); Nabil A. Badran, "The means of survival: education and the Palestinian Community 1948–1967," *Journal of Palestine Studies*, Vol. 9, No. 4 (Summer 1980), pp. 44–74; Gabi Baramki, "Aspects of Palestinian life under military occupation, with a special focus on education and development," *British Journal of Middle Eastern Studies*, Vol. 19 No. 2 (1992), pp. 125–132; Gabi Baramki, "Building Palestine Universities under occupation," *Journal of Palestine Studies*, Vol. 17, No. 1 (Autumn 1987), pp. 12–20; Munir Fasheh, "Education under occupation," in Nasser H. Aruri (ed.), *Occupation: Israel over Palestine* (Belmont: Arab American University Graduates (AAUG), 1989), pp. 511–535; Sarah Graham-Brown, "Impact on the social structure of Palestinian society," in Nasser H. Aruri (ed.), *Occupation: Israel over Palestine* (Belmont: AAUG, 1989), pp. 230–256; Muhammad Hallaj,

"Mission of Palestinian higher education," in Emile A. Nakhleh (ed.), *A Palestinian Agenda for the West Bank and Gaza* (Washington: American Enterprise Institute, 1980), pp. 58–63; Khalil Mahshi, "The Palestinian uprising and education for the future," *Harvard Education Review*, Vol. 59, No. 4 (1989), pp. 470–483; Muhsin D. Yusuf, "The potential impact of Palestinian education on a Palestinian state," *Journal of Palestine Studies*, Vol. 8, No. 4 (Summer 1979); Ahmad 'Awad Munir, *Al-Ta'lim al-'Aali fi al-Dafah al-Gharbiyyah wa-Quta' Ghazah: Tatawwuruhu wa-Ususuhu* (Nablus: Jami'at al-Najah al-Wataniya, Markaz al-Dirasat al-Rifiyyah, 1983). See also R. Shadid Muhammed, "The Muslim Brotherhood movement in the West Bank and Gaza," *Third World Quarterly*, Vol. 10, No. 2 (April 1988), pp. 658–682.

7. For a good, concise view of the nationalist groups in the higher education institutes and their political division, see Emile Sahliyeh, *In Search of Leadership: West Bank Politics since 1967* (Washington D.C.: The Brookings Institution, 1988), pp. 115–136.

8. Hamuda Samih, "Marakiz al-Turath al-Islami fi Filastin" (The Centers for Islamic Heritage in Palestine), *Al-Hilal Al-Dawli* No. 15 (May 1–15 1988), p. 10.

9. A flyer of the fourth student Islamic convention, Sha'ban 1407—April 1987.

10. Changing the names of bulletins was a known method of circumventing the need to receive a permit from the Israeli military rule for publishing a newspaper. A one-time bulletin did not need a permit in the Territories nor in East Jerusalem under Israeli law. The method was to choose a word identifying the paper to the public, and add another word or words to every issue creating a different phrase, as if it were a one-time publication.

11. *Al-Nur al-Rabbani (The Celestial Light)*, one-time publication of the culture department of The Young Muslims Association in Jerusalem. Undated, 41 pages. According to its content, it was published during the first months of 1982. *Al-Nur (The Light)*, one-time publication of the Young Muslims Association, July 26 1982, 77 pages. *Al-Nur al-Ilahi (The Divine Light)*, one-time publication of the Young Muslims Association, October 19, 1983, 73 pages.

12. This fact was related to the author from Dr. Fathi Shqaqi himself, during a discussion with him in February 1986 in the Gaza prison.

13. *Al-Risalah*, one-time publication of the student council of Hebron University, undated. According to its content, it was published on November 1.

14. Ibid., pp. 6–9.

15. Ibid., pp. 34–37.

16. *Al-Muntalaq*, the mosque committee of Al-Najah University's bulletin, No. 8 (February 1984) pp. 16–17.

17. *Al-Muntalaq*, No. 9 (April 1984), p. 49.

18. *Al-Muntalaq*, No. 8, pp. 18–19.

19. See, for example, the results of the union elections held on June 27, 1983, in which the Muslim Brotherhood won in all the faculties. *Al-Nidaa'*, a publication of the student council in the Gaza university, undated (according to its content, it was published in the summer of 1983), p. 22.

20. *Al-Muntalaq*, No. 11 (December 1984), p. 3.

21. At least four such undated publications were known to have been distributed by the culture committee in the student council. According to their content, they were published during the years 1983–1985. They included more ideological content than the group's bulletins and were probably meant to enhance the Islamic awareness.

22. See, for example: *Al-Haqiqah al-Gha'ibah (The Absent Truth)*, November 1987, 55 pages. This was the second booklet in the series.

23. See, for example, the booklet titled "The Islamic Awakening and the Muslim Brotherhood," No. 1, a one-time cultural publication of the culture committee of the student council of the Islamic University in Gaza, undated.

24. A flyer signed by the Islamic group in Al-Najah University in Nablus, September 11, 1987. It is noteworthy in that the tension at the Islamic University in Gaza in regard to the elections there continued in the first days after the outbreak of the Palestinian uprising. After the elections, Fatah supporters blamed the Islamic group for rigging the elections. See: *Al-Fajr*, December 7 and 9, 1987.

25. "The Islamic group in Bir Zeit University Mourns its Dead," an undated flyer circulated in December 1986.

26. *Voice of The Oppressed (Sawt Al-Mustad'afin)*, a publication on the occasion of culture week at the Islamic University in Gaza, June 1986, 56 pages. The Koranic term *Mustad'afin* was occasionally used by the Muslim Brotherhood, but was much more widely used in the terminology of the Islamic revolution in Iran, almost synonymous with *revolutionists*.

27. In July–August 1983, many members of the Islamic group that then called itself "The Islamic Forerunner" *(Al-Tali'ah al-Islamiyyah)*, named after the bulletin they circulated by that name in the Territories, were arrested. The arrests were for distributing illegal and inciting material, and most were sentenced to short prison terms of up to one year. Among the imprisoned was their leader, Dr. Fathi Shqaqi. During their detention and trial several members of the group blamed the Muslim Brotherhood and the Islamic group in the University of Gaza for assisting the authorities in uncovering them. Their trial revealed that they were engaged then not in any violent activity against Israel, but only in subversive activities.

28. "The War against Islam Continues," a manifest of the Islamic student movement in al-Najah University, May 23, 1983.

29. *Al-Haqiqah al-Gha'ibah* (Gaza, November 1987). This booklet was the second publication in a series named *Sawt al-Haqq wal-Quwwah wal-Huriyyah (Voice of Truth, Power, and Freedom)*, a known slogan with the Muslim Brotherhood. It may very well be that the name of the booklet was chosen to deliberately resemble the name of the book by the engineer Muhamad 'Abd al-Salam Faraj, the ideologist for the Egyptian Jihad group whose members murdered the late president Sadat: *Al-Faridah al-Gha'ibah* (The Neglected Obligation—in this case, Jihad).

4

Radical Islamist Movements in Turkey

Ely Karmon

It has been argued that the marginality of violent Islamist groups in Turkey, in contrast to the vigorous armed opposition in Egypt or Algeria, is due to the Turkish political system's pluralism and the Islamist Welfare Party's (RP) full integration into this system.[1] But the leaders and sponsors of these extremist organizations think that by using violence against the secular symbols of the Turkish state, leading secular intellectuals and journalists, and representatives of "Imperialism and Zionism," they will help install an Islamic state. The limited reaction by the authorities up to 1996 and the RP's electoral victories seemed to provide reasons for this hope.

The military coup of 1980 was intended to end a long period of widespread terrorism and extremist violence throughout the country and also to hold back the threat of radical Islam embodied in the National Salvation Party led by Necmettin Erbakan.[2] But while the 1980–1983 military government did break up the extreme left and right, the Islamic movement survived and even grew in importance during the 1980s.[3]

In marked contrast to Turkey's first two military coups, military authorities in the 1980s proclaimed the importance of religion in the nation's political life[4] and forwarded a new ideological concept called "The Turkish-Islamic Synthesis," which represented an attempt to integrate Islamists and nationalists.[5] The Islamist influence in the system was to contribute to Turkey's territorial integrity and counter revolutionary sentiments, especially among the Kurdish youth. The Islamists offered an attractive alternative even for ex-communists after the collapse of communism in the Soviet bloc.[6]

On the foreign front, the Turkish-Islamic synthesis was supposed to help contain southward Soviet expansion and combat Iran's radical Islam by constructing a coalition of U.S.-backed moderate Islamic states. Closer relations with Saudi Arabia were favored in order to gain big loans for the weak Turkish economy.[7] The geopolitical tumult of the early 1990s created a new international environment, which put Turkey in a key position, sometimes in direct competition with Iran for regional influence and economic assets.[8] Nevertheless, that strategy let the Islamic genie out of Ataturk's bottle, as one researcher put it.[9]

Islamic subversive and terrorist activity in Turkey began in the 1960s. As early as 1967 and 1973, the leaders of *Hizb al-Tahrir* (Islamic Liberation Party) were imprisoned for attempting "to bring the Islamic State Constitution to Turkey."[10] Islamic Jihad appeared as a real terrorist threat in the 1980s, after a series of assassinations of Jordanian, Saudi, and Iraqi diplomats. In October 1991, Islamic Jihad took responsibility for killing an American sergeant and wounding an Egyptian diplomat to protest the Middle East peace conference in Madrid.[11] For many years it was assumed that this group was a Lebanese Shi'ite terrorist organization until it was discovered that a Turkish branch existed, engaging in assassinations of secular intellectuals.

As Anat Lapidot correctly notes, defining the Islamic movement is a complex task. Citing Sabri Sayari, she distinguishes between traditionalists and radicals, the latter a minority inspired by the Iranian revolution.[12] Ismet Imset points to the confusion about these different groups among the general public, researchers, and government officials in Turkey. A report by the Turkish National Intelligence Organization (MIT) and the Security General Directorate of the Police in October 1991 mentioned no fewer than ten Islamic organizations active in Turkey: the Turkish Islamic Liberation Army (IKO), the Turkish Islamic Liberation Front (TIK-C), Fighters of the Islamic Revolution (IDAM), the Turkish Islamic Liberation Union (TIKB), the World Shari'a Liberation Army (DSKO), the Universal Brotherhood Front-Shari'a Revenge Squad (EKC-SIM), the Islamic Liberation Party Front (IKP-C), Turkish Fighters of the Universal Islamic War of Liberation (EIK-TM), the Turkish Islamic Fighters Army (IMO), and the Turkish Shari'a Revenge Commandos (TSIK).[13]

This chapter uses the term *Islamic movement* to describe all currents in Turkish Islam, while *Islamic Movement* refers to one of the main radical groups.

Imset distinguishes between western and southeast Turkey. In the west, the Islamic Movement (*Islami Hareket*), also called "Islamic Resistance" (*Islami Direnis*), represents the ideological influence of the original (Iranian) Hizballah.[14] Both *Movement* and *Resistance* were only temporary code names, at least until 1990. In southeast Turkey, the movement spread first under the name of Hizballah, and was then referred to as the Hizbal-contra to address its anti-PKK activity. According to Imset, Hizballah and Islamic Movement are in fact one, representing an umbrella organization of groups acting on behalf of what he calls "The International Islamic Movement."[15]

At the end of the 1970s, under the influence of the coalition between left-wing organizations and Khomeini's followers in Iran, an alliance of the left, especially Maoists, with radical Islamic elements was established in Turkey that attacked the nationalist right. The conflict peaked in February 1979 when a young Muslim leader was killed by nationalists (known as "Idealists") in the yard of the Fatih mosque in Istanbul.

The Turkish Islamic Movement, like all other radical organizations, received a serious blow during the September 1980 military coup. But, as the regime encouraged the general Islamic trend as a solution to political polarization, and as both Marxists and nationalists lost their influence, Islamic activists were afforded ample space to strengthen their position. The "Hizballah Muslims" appeared for the first time publicly in 1984 and, like the original Hizballah, proclaimed support for the Iranian revolution and the defense not of nations or sects, but of "Allah's way."

According to Imset, Kalim Siddiqui, a Pakistani active at the Muslim Institute in London, had a key role in unifying Turkey's radical Islamic Movement. Thus, the first Hizballahi appeared in Turkey as the "followers of Siddiki" (sic).[16] A pro-Hizballah magazine published in November 1987 "The guidelines of the Islamic Movement," which included acceptance of the Islamic state as the center of religious belief, the leadership of Muslim scholars, the spread of the mentality of martyrdom and the leadership of the Islamic revolution (in Iran).[17]

A significant development occurred in the middle of the 1980s with the conversion of some members of the right-wing Nationalist Movement (MHP) to Islam. The death of one of their leaders in prison in 1984 and the tortures suffered by many others convinced a group of extreme nationalist activists "to turn to Allah" and condemn the "darkness of nationalism."[18] These militants were already professionals in the field of terrorism and street fighting and represented significant operational support for the Islamic Movement.

In southeast Turkey, Islamic radicalism emerged in poor towns and villages with large Kurdish populations (Dyarbakir, Silvan, Cizre, Kiziltepe and others), especially among the young and unemployed. They followed the teachings of local Muslim scholars or shaykhs and often organized themselves around extremist Islamic publications such as *Tevhid*, *Yeryuzu* and *Objektif*. Their activity became more visible at the beginning of the 1990s, influenced more and more by Khomeini's teachings, and they were identified by the local public as Hizballah, although they considered themselves part of the Islamic Movement.

There are few sources on the Turkish Islamic organizations, although the groups' publications and manifestos are distributed quite freely even when they threaten future terrorist attacks. All the material is in Turkish and has neither been collected nor translated. The only other source consists of interviews given by anonymous leaders and activists to Turkish journalists.

In one such interview, published in February 1993, a militant declared, "We are fighters of the Islamic Liberation Movement, the sword against Satan, blasphemy, Zionism and Imperialism. We have begun taking action only recently in Turkey and our move is based on pain, suffering and patience. We do not pursue a tribal case; our objective is to establish a state for the Muslims." Asked whether he belonged to Hizballah, the militant replied that the press had given that name to the organization and that they would adopt it only when the movement was worthy of it. Meanwhile it had not reached "that level of perfection."[19]

In speaking about the special relationship of the Movement with Iran, the same militant seemed careful not to confirm "the lies of the Turkish state" about such links. Iran is seen as an example and a guide but the instructions are "from the Quran" and not from Iran, "the land of Dar al-Islam where blasphemy has been crushed." The Movement needs no instructions from any country because the Quran is the program and shows the strategies and the tactics to be adopted.[20]

It seems that the Sunni origin of the radical Turkish Islamic groups did not prevent their close cooperation with the Iranian Shi'ite regime. The material published so far in the Turkish sources does not permit an evaluation of the exact nature of these groups' ideology: declarations such as those cited above are general and not binding. Yet, it is known that various Sunni extremist organizations have viewed the Iranian revolution and its leader Khomeini as a catalyst and a model for their own revolutionary endeavor. This is the case of the Palestinian Islamic Jihad (PIJ) and its leader Fathi al-Shqaqi[21] or the Algerian *Groupe Islamique Arme* (GIA),[22] which also received direct Iranian logistic and financial support, leading the Algerian government to break diplomatic relations with Iran.

For its part, the Iranian regime, in spite of its increasing nationalism since its war with Iraq, has been keen to convince Sunni movements that it has continued to stick to Khomeini's Islamic universalistic ideology. Ayatollah Ali Khamene'i, Iran's spiritual leader, declared that his country wanted the unity of all Muslim brothers, Sunni and Shi'ite.[23]

A 1997 report prepared by the Turkish security authorities for the National Security Council (NSC) outlined the objectives of the radical religious movements and stressed that their strategy consists of three stages.[24] The first stage is the message (*teblig*), and calls for an effort by the radicals to persuade the people to adopt the Islamic religion, establish an Islamic state and administration, live in accordance with Islamic rules, and struggle to safeguard the Islamic way of life. The second stage is the community (*cemaat*) and calls for the restructuring of communities in accordance with the requirements of Islam. The third stage is the struggle (jihad) and calls for the armed struggle to safeguard the Islamic way of life.

Special mention should be made of a puzzling organization called "The Great Eastern Islamic Fighters Front" (IBDA-C), active since the middle of the 1970s but more extremist and aggressive since the beginning of the 1990s. Although it is an Islamic movement struggling for the constitution of an Islamic state, it uses leftist slogans in its publications and accepts ex-Marxists in its ranks. It is also extremely anti-Semitic and anti-Christian in its propaganda and terrorist activity. It is interesting to note that IBDA-C's publications do not show any particular pro-Iranian tendency.

A chronological analysis of Islamic terrorist activity shows that 1990 was probably the starting point for the offensive against the Turkish secular establishment: a professor, journalist, political scientist, and writer were assassinated by Islamic Jihad and the Islamic Operation (or Action), the first time this name was used.[25] Muammar Aksoy, a liberal political scientist, was also killed in 1990, marking the first time the name *Islamic Movement* appeared.[26]

In 1991, Islamic radicals entered a period of reassessment that ended after the opening of the Madrid peace talks between Arab countries and Israel. In October, an American soldier was killed and an Egyptian diplomat was wounded by Islamic Jihad.[27] The following year represented the turning point in radical Islamic terrorist activity, as the targets of attacks included exiled Iranian opposition members as well as Jews and Israelis.[28]

But the terrorist threat attracted acute national attention when Ugur Mumcu, one of Turkey's top investigative reporters, was killed on January 24, 1993 by a car bomb similar to one used in the assassinations of an American computer specialist in October 1991 and an Israeli diplomat in March 1992. Both the Islamic Liberation Organization and IBDA-C took responsibility for the murder.[29]

Several days later an attempt was made on the life of a well-known Turkish businessman and community leader of Jewish origin, Jak Kamhi, by a group of four terrorists who used automatic weapons and even a rocket launcher. He escaped uninjured. The same month, the tortured body of exiled Iranian dissident Abbas Gholizadeh, a former officer and the Shah's bodyguard, kidnapped several weeks before, was discovered by the police.

This series of terrorist events provoked a sharp reaction among the Turkish public: huge street demonstrations in favor of the secular regime, a strong press campaign, and swift action by security authorities against the perpetrators and their sponsors followed. For the first time, the Islamic Movement and Iran were directly implicated in acts of terror against the state. The arrests and interrogations of many Turkish members of these organizations unveiled the story behind the killings of Turkish secular intellectuals and anti-Khomeini Iranian exiles in the years 1990 to 1992.[30]

But the arrest and trial of dozens of Islamic terrorists did not dissuade more extremists from continuing to attack secular Turkish intellectuals. In July 1993, they set fire to a hotel hosting a cultural festival, killing thirty-seven people.[31]

The authorities' fight against the radicals continued in 1994, when 659 members of Hizballah were caught, some of them responsible for murders of exiled Iranian opposition activists. The same year, IBDA-C was responsible for ninety terrorist incidents, including five bombings in various cities.[32] A prominent cinema critic and writer, Onat Kutlar, was killed in December by a bomb attack carried out by IBDA-C aimed "at spoiling the colonialist Noel [Christmas] celebrations."[33]

One of the most controversial terrorist activities of Hizballah in southeast Turkey has been the liquidation of dozens of pro-PKK activists, journalists, intellectuals, and politicians beginning in the fall of 1991 and lasting through 1993. It has been widely assumed that this was the work of the splinter group "Hizbal-contra," because of the immunity it enjoyed from security authorities owing to its anti-PKK nature.[34]

It must be stressed that its members were mostly of Kurdish origin. The Hizballah regards the PKK as Islam's enemy and has accused it of "trying to create an atheist community, supporting the communist system, trying to divide the people through chauvinist activities and directing pressure on the Muslim people."[35] A Hizballah militant in the southeast described the goal of his organization as the establishment of an "Islamic Kurdish state in Turkey."[36]

In March 1993, the PKK signed a "cooperation protocol" with the Hizballah Kurdish Revolutionary Party aimed at ending the conflict and finding "methods for a joint struggle against the Turkish state." The agreement was signed after Hizballah recognized that it was exploited by "the colonialists" and that the clashes in no way benefited the cause of Islam.[37]

A turning point in the Turkish authorities' attitude toward the Islamic terrorist threat occurred in March 1996, with the arrest of one of the leaders of Islamic Action, Irfan Cagarici, and his confessions about the role his organization had played since the early 1990s in the assassinations of secular politicians and intellectuals, with the direct support and supervision of Iranian intelligence.[38] Relations between Turkey and Iran reached a new low as a result. But then, in June 1996, after 73 years of secular Kemalist regimes, the RP formed an Islamic government with Erbakan as prime minister.[39]

Turgut Ozal became in 1983 the first prime minister of a civilian government after the 1980 coup. His "Turkish-Islamist Synthesis," a means of countering revolutionary sentiment, included a relaxation of Kemalist and secularist policies and a public embrace of Islam as an essential component of Turkish identity. During the long period of his rule as prime minister and then president of Turkey, Muslim associations, foundations, publications, and television and radio stations flourished. Islamists also built strongholds in the Ministry of Education.[40]

The important role played by Islamic radical publications in recruiting militants and designating targets cannot be underestimated. Two Istanbul-based publications, *Akademi* and *Objektif*, and the monthlies *Yeryuzu* and *Tehvid* have been accused of backing Hizballah.[41] IBDA-C sent death threats to the head of the Jewish community in Ankara before a bomb was placed in his car, and published a list of Jewish targets in the extreme religious periodical *Akinci Yolu*.[42] IBDA-C's weekly, *Taraf*, took responsibility for the bomb attack on film critic Onat Kutlar in December 1994 and sent "a warning not to play with fire" to TV journalist Ali Kirca, whom it accused of being "anti-Islam."[43]

In this atmosphere, pro-Islamic politicians received important appointments in the sensitive field of security, such as the Ministry of Interior. Under Interior

Minister Abdulkadir Aksu, who served at the end of the 1980s, Turkey's security apparatus—especially the intelligence and personnel departments—was penetrated by pro-Islamic elements and, according to Ismet Imset, the ministry during this period was generally inclined toward "Saudi and even Iranian Islamism." Aksu was replaced at the end of 1991 and the police were purged of fundamentalist officers.[44] According to one source, 700 of the 1,600 key ministry executives, provincial governors, and other functionaries at the time were believed to be RP supporters. Yet, even in April 1994, Interior Ministry officials permitted the staging of unauthorized mass Islamist demonstrations in Ankara and Istanbul.[45] Ironically, these fundamentalist officers and functionaries were reassigned to posts in the southeast, where they supported or ignored the attacks of Hizballah against the PKK.

The RP leadership's attitude regarding violence and terror on the Islamic movement's radical fringes is at the least ambiguous, if not clearly supportive. Erbakan condemned the March 1993 assassination of the journalist Mumcu and declared it incompatible with the values of true Islam, but at the same time, important members of his party accused Israel of killing him.[46] In November 1993, Erbakan said at his party's parliamentary meeting that only "Islamic fraternity" could combat the PKK, but he did not mention the terrorism practiced by some Islamic groups.[47] Some researchers even considered Hizballah the RP's armed protector.[48]

Despite all the evidence, as late as the end of 1995, leading Islamic circles denied the existence of fundamentalist terrorist organizations. Deputy RP leader Abdullah Gul declared that no terror movement is compatible with Islam and that the accusation is "being circulated intentionally" in order to influence national elections. According to another leader, most of the crimes in Turkey blamed on the Islamic movement were in fact "international operations" and "plots of the West."[49]

Erbakan's real policy toward Islamic terrorist groups can be judged by the fact that he hosted, as prime minister, representatives of the Palestinian Hamas, Egypt's Muslim Brotherhood, and Algeria's FIS. Erbakan was not even impressed by Egyptian President Husni Mubarak's protest against including the Muslim Brotherhood, sparking a diplomatic incident with Egypt. Over the years, Erbakan maintained a strange silence about the complicity of neighboring Muslim countries in anti-Turkish terrorism.[50]

Iran's support for and incitement of Islamic terrorism in Turkey in the early 1990s can be understood as part of its drive to export the Islamic revolution to a key Muslim country, a symbol of secularism and a strategic adversary. Tehran's aggressive policy was probably encouraged by Islam's growing influence in Turkish society. Iran especially encouraged Ozal's policy in the 1980s of embracing Islam and expanding Turkey's relations with its Muslim neighbors.[51]

Good relations did not, however, prevent deep Iranian involvement in Islamic terrorism inside Turkey's borders, which at times was proven in court or leaked by security authorities to the media. Iran was involved in the 1990 murder of three intellectuals, and the murders of Mumcu, an Iranian dissident, and a Jewish businessman, all in 1993. Turkish Islamic terrorists, who were recruited through numerous Iranian cultural centers in Turkey, received military training in Iran in "pursuit, counter-pursuit, weapons and bombs."[52]

As noted previously, an abrupt change occurred in the Turkish authorities' attitude after Mumcu's killing when rampant terrorism and growing international criticism of Iran prodded Ankara to finally acknowledge that the Turkish Hizballah existed.[53] For the first time, a Turkish minister declared that members of radical Islamic organizations trained in Iranian security installations, traveled with Iranian real and forged documents, and attacked Turkish citizens and Iranian opposition militants with Iranian-supplied arms.[54] Turkey's approach toward Iran, however, was very cautious.[55] The minister absolved the Iranian state of these actions, but concluded that "the perpetrators had connections in Iran."[56]

Iran's foreign minister issued a subtle denial excluding the possibility that any anti-Turkish activity conducted on Iran's territory could escape the state's control. While denying that Iran was behind anti-Turkey movements, he accused Turkey of supporting terrorist groups opposed to the Tehran regime and suggested discussing any "mutual allegations" through a common security committee.[57]

Iran has never presented evidence of any Turkish sponsorship of terrorist organizations in Iran, though Turkey has sheltered more than a million Iranians, many of them political refugees from Khomeini's regime. The main conflict in subsequent years surrounded not Iran's support for Islamists but rather, its support of the PKK. Iran offered a safe haven to PKK fighters, who in 1994 intensified their terrorist campaign both inside and outside Turkey's borders.[58]

Iranian support for radical Islamic terrorism in Turkey was likely dampened by the vigilant campaign waged by Turkey's security forces against the Islamic groups and the consequent decline in their operations in 1994 and 1995. Radical Islamist organizations staged 86 acts of violence in 1995, compared with 464 attacks in 1994. Further, Ilim, one of Hizballah's two splinter groups (the other was Menzil), ceased most of its armed activity and many Islamic Movement militants were arrested.[59]

Turkey's fundamentalist Islamic movement has developed in a political and social environment very different from that of similar groups in other Middle Eastern countries. As Sami Zubaida notes, Turkey's Islamist ideology is also nationalist and challenges Kemalism's European leanings. At the same time, the Islamic movement's leading political force—the RP and its various predecessors and successors—is fully integrated into the Turkish pluralist system, which may account for the marginality of the violent Islamic groups.[60]

The RP's ambiguous and tortuous policy over the issue of Islamic terrorism in Turkey and Iranian involvement in it during the 1990–1996 period casts doubt about its genuine acceptance of Turkey's democratic values and secular regime. What probably most influenced the RP's moderate and cautious policies over the years has been the army's staunch secular orientation and the country's secular nationalist core. These factors also influenced the strategy of the more violent Islamic terrorist groups. They never, for example, attacked military or security personnel, although many of their members were killed during the security forces' anti-terrorist campaigns. In contrast with Egypt or Algeria, the Turkish groups have also refrained from attacking top secular politicians, though some low-level Kurdish politicians have been targeted.[61] Moreover, Turkish Islamic groups have not attacked Western targets or acted abroad, like other Islamic groups or the PKK, though they have some infrastructure in Europe.[62]

Instead, the groups limited their operations to secular intellectuals and media professionals who were important in shaping public opinion against the Islamic movement. Indeed, until Mumcu's murder, operations against these targets did not seem to provoke a strong reaction against terrorist groups and their political mentors. Islamic groups attacked Jewish personalities, the Jewish community, and also Israeli diplomats, but in this they were not different from RP, which expressed anti-Semitic and anti-Israel views.[63] Indeed, because they shared a similar ideology, if not method, it can be hypothesized that RP leaders tried to cover up the radicals' violent practices.

The tolerance shown by some in the security establishment—especially those in the Ministry of Interior and the police who came to senior positions due to their Islamic views or connections—helped terrorist groups in their formative period. Top military leaders were clearly worried by this trend and it seems that an attempt by one police agency to spy on the National Security Council fostered its decision to bring down the Erbakan government.[64] The lack of any major act of Islamic terrorism during Erbakan's premiership and until the decision of the Constitutional Court to outlaw his party, raises some questions about the strategy of these groups and the real goals of their leaders and sponsors.

Turkey's growing military and strategic cooperation with Israel, which became public in 1996 and 1997, did not generate any particularly violent activity against the government or Israeli targets, despite the RP's clear opposition and Iran's anxiety. However, the Turkish military gave no respite to the new Islamic prime minister. On August 3, 1996, the Supreme Military Council (SMC) declared that "reactionism"—that is, Islamic fundamentalism—was becoming an important threat to Turkey.[65] This meeting could be seen as the watershed leading to the Turkish army's decision to unequivocally end the Turkish-Islamic Synthesis era and eradicate both political and violent Islamist forces.

Following this first direct warning, President Suleyman Demirel sent several warning letters to the government, without result. And twice in early 1997, the NSC demanded that the government stop "illegal activities" and defend the secular regime.

The army's twenty urgent demands included "enforcement of neglected constitutional requirements on dress codes and on banning of Sufi brotherhoods; reversal of worrisome social and political trends, such as the growth of religious schools and infiltration of Islamists into the bureaucracy; special restrictions implicitly aimed at Refah, such as limits on cash transactions by Islamist groups and acceptance of party responsibility for the 'unconstitutional,' i.e., antisecular, behavior of its members; and careful monitoring of Iranian efforts to 'destabilize' Turkey."[66]

Erbakan avoided implementing the NSC's decisions and persisted in anticipating the possibility of "defense industrial cooperation" with Iran. After the February 1997 Jerusalem Day incident in Ankara's Sincan district, when inflammatory remarks by Iran's ambassador to Turkey and the city's RP mayor triggered a show of force by the Turkish military resulting in the ambassador's recall, Erbakan was finished. On June 18, 1997, under army pressure, Erbakan resigned; on January 16, 1998 the Constitutional Court outlawed the Refah Party and barred Erbakan from political activity for five years. The following month, a new party, the Virtue Party (FP), replaced the RP, gathering in its ranks some 130 parliamentarians from the old movement.

The Turkish army's views on the threat of Islamic extremism were unequivocal. Consider the following remarks given by the General Staff's chief of intelligence in June 1997:

> Following the transition to a multiparty system and as a result of concessions made to the detriment of Ataturkist principles and reforms, the reactionary sector stepped up its work to organize nationally under the umbrella of democracy . . . [resulting in a] situation [that] has turned individual fundamentalist activities into a mass movement [and] has created a climate that encourages and rewards those who raise a green banner instead of the sacred flag of the Turkish Republic.

Even the appearance of separatist movements (that is, the Kurdish problem) was attributed to "the authority vacuum," and to "[t]hose who do not wish to recognize the Turkish national identity and . . . have undertaken activities behind the guise of the more international religious identity . . . as a first step toward their ultimate goal of destroying the unity and harmony of the Turkish Republic."[67]

The speech detailed how, particularly since the Erbakan government, Islamic groups were able to build a huge political,[68] social,[69] economic,[70] and propaganda[71] infrastructure. It equated the threat from the "reactionary sector" with that of the Kurdistan Workers' Party (PKK) in Turkey's east and southeast, drew a link between the two anti-regime movements, and accused Iran of systematically providing every type of material and moral support to violent Turkish Islamic groups such as Hizballah, Selam, and the Islamic Movement.

In late July 1997, violence erupted in the first major Islamic demonstration since Erbakan's forced resignation a month earlier. At least thirteen people were wounded and scores arrested in clashes in Ankara between police and thousands of Islamists protesting a government plan to severely curtail religious education in secondary schools.[72]

The impact of the secular military and civil establishment's firm policy could be felt after the April 1999 parliamentary elections. The Virtue Party took only 15 percent of the vote, suffering a bitter defeat, although its candidates were re-elected as mayors of the country's two largest cities, Istanbul and Ankara. The real winners of these elections were Prime Minister Bulent Ecevit and his Democratic Left Party (DLP) and the Nationalist Action Party (MHP), which took about 18 percent of the vote, astonishing even its own leaders.[73] "Virtue's decline will pull Turkey away from the appearance of a country where radical Islam is on the rise," commented Ertugrul Ozkok, editor of the *Hurriyet* newspaper.[74] The Constitutional Court opened a closure case against the Virtue Party after the April 18, 1999 elections on charges that the party was carrying out anti-secular activities and was the successor of the RP.[75]

It is difficult to draw an accurate picture of the terrorist activity of Islamist groups in Turkey since 1997. Most of the data published by the Turkish press relates to IBDA-C terrorism in big cities such as Istanbul and Ankara. Hizballah is active mainly in eastern and southeastern Anatolia and the national press rarely reports its attacks.[76] The group's actions surface when members of Hizballah are detained in police operations and generally are not detailed. There is also a difference between the targets attacked by the two main organizations: while IBDA-C targeted secular journalists and intellectuals, symbolic sites of the secular regime, Christian (Greek) shrines, and even brothels, Hizballah focused on killing people in the southeastern provinces (including militants suspected of being informers), extorting money, and engaging in organizational activities in primary and high schools, universities, mosques, and shrines.[77]

After a lull in IBDA-C's activity in 1997 and 1998, the organization staged a series of attacks beginning in October 1999 that could be regarded as a campaign to emphasize its renewed strength.[78] The most important and striking attack was the assassination on October 21, 1999 of Ahmet Taner Kislali, a former minister, academic, and respected newspaper columnist. Earlier, in June 1999, the General Directorate of Security affirmed that it had received a tip-off that IBDA-C was preparing to assassinate Premier Bulent Ecevit.[79]

One of the reasons for the autumn terrorist campaign could be the April 1999 trial of Salih Izzet Erdis (alias Salih Mirzabeyoglu), considered to be the leader of IBDA-C, and three of his deputies. During the trial, dozens of IBDA-C sympathizers protested violently in front of the court and more than thirty were arrested. As a result, Turkish security authorities intensified their counterterrorist measures and arrested many active members of the organization, although they did not find the connection with Kislali's assassination. On November 15, 1999, twenty IBDA-C members were caught with weapons and bomb-making materials, planning to execute sensational acts of terrorism in Istanbul. Suspected targets included several well-known personalities such as Professor Yasar Nuri Ozturk, dean of the theology school at Istanbul University, and writer and columnist Fatih Altayli.[80] The group was also preparing to stage bomb attacks on November 6, to protest the anniversary of the founding of the Institution of Higher Education (YOK). Hasan Ozdemir, the director general of the Istanbul police, stressed that Erdis, IBDA-C's imprisoned leader, declared 1999 "The Year of Conquest."[81] According to Turkish officials, twenty separate operations were staged against IBDA-C in 1998 and 1999, netting 166 suspects and accounting for thirty-five acts of terror.

Security authorities have also waged a relentless campaign against the military and civil infrastructure of all the branches of Hizballah, considered to be the most powerful and dangerous of all the violent Islamist organizations. These extensive counterterrorist operations paralleled the well-publicized war against PKK guerrilla forces in southeastern Turkey and northern Iraq, but received no attention from the foreign media.

On April 22, 1998, Interior Minister Murat Basesgioglu announced the first wave of intensive operations against Hizballah, particularly in the eastern and southeastern Anatolian provinces. By the end of the month, 130 of the 1,000 wanted militants were captured in Diyarbakir alone. Dozens of other militants were arrested in May in Batman, Mersin, and Mus.

The second significant counterterrorist wave came in March 1999, when 400 Hizballah members were captured in the southeastern Diyarbakir, Mardin, and Batman provinces. Several dozen more Hizballah militants were captured that June.[82] Parallel to tracking IBDA-C terrorists in October and November 1999, operations against Hizballah continued with the arrests of nearly 100 militants in Diyarbakir, including a number of senior figures. In November, the government announced that Hizballah's infrastructure in eastern Turkey had been completely cracked.[83]

In January 1999, Kemal Donmez, chairman of the Struggle Against Terrorism Department, declared that a total of 3,793 people had been captured in ten years of operations against illegal fundamentalist organizations like Hizballah, IBDA-C, the Islamist Movement, and the Islamic Communities Union.[84] The arrest of many Hizballah militants helped solve 800 crimes, 400 of which were murders.

Despite the successes of the Turkish security forces, at least 20,000 supporters of violent Islamic groups strived to establish a "Kurdish-Islam" state in the southeastern Anatolian region. Operations in 1999 revealed that the organizational skills and overall strength of Hizballah were much greater than previously assumed.

In March 1999, allegations against Erbakan for the first time accused the former Islamist prime minister of being directly connected to terrorist organizations.

State Prosecutor Nuh Mete Yuksel accused Erbakan of participating in December 25, 1993 meetings in Tehran with the Greek 17 November organization, Fatah, the Lebanese Hizballah, the Japanese Red Army, the Abu-Nidal Group, Turkish Hizballah, and RP members under the chairmanship of Iran's spiritual leader, Ali Khamene'i. The accusation was based on the testimony of Altan Karamanoglu, Turkey's former ambassador to Baku. Participants in that meeting decided to establish a joint command, provisionally headquartered in Iran but slated to move to Turkey when a theocratic regime would be set up there.[85]

According to an indictment prepared by Yuksel, the RP's former Deputy Chairman Ahmet Tekdal and former Deputies Sevki Yilmaz, Hasan Huseyin Ceylan, and Ibrahim Halil Celik face death sentences on charges that they tried to undermine the current constitutional state system and replace it with a state based on religious principles. The 75-page indictment states that the National View, the Islamists' main ideological body, aimed to replace the current democratic system with an Islam-based one.[86]

The Virtue Party and the RP were also accused of having links to radical Islamic organizations abroad, such as the Islamic Salvation Front (FIS) of Algeria and the Muslim Brotherhood of Syria. The indictment also charged the National View with having contacts with IBDA-C. Most importantly, representatives of the National View were reportedly connected to the PKK. The indictment accused Erbakan of promising to legitimize the "status of bandits" during his tenure as prime minister.

The same prosecutor launched a probe into remarks against secularism broadcast on a private television channel by the well-known and respected Islamic preacher Fethullah Gulen. Gulen had warned a group of his followers that, "If they come out early, the world will squash their heads. They would make Muslims once again relive incidents such as those that occurred in Algeria, Syria and Egypt." In the recording, Gulen also underlined the importance of expanding his group within the civil and justice administrations. "In these entities will be our guarantee for the future," he said. Prosecutors apparently believe that Gulen was warning his followers that if they rose up before they were fully prepared, they would face defeat. They therefore sought capital punishment for Gulen on suspicion of plotting religious unrest in Turkey.[87]

Finally, in July 1999, Uzbek dissidents convicted of playing a role in a February 1999 assassination attempt against Uzbek President Islam Karimov claimed that Erbakan had helped them financially.[88]

One of the possible consequences of the PKK's decline as a fighting organization after the new peace strategy devised by its imprisoned leader Abdullah Ocalan could be a strengthening of radical Islamist groups, mainly Hizballah.

Relations between the PKK and some of the Islamic radical groups at the beginning of the 1990s were marked by ideological conflict and rivalry over the same Kurdish constituency in southeastern Turkey. At times this conflict permitted

Turkish authorities to use the more extremist elements of the Islamic Kurdish Hizballah in their fight against the nationalist PKK. In 1993, however, the two sides, acknowledging the danger of the internecine strife, agreed to a modus-vivendi and common struggle against the Kemalist regime. Since then, the PKK and most of the Islamist radicals have cooperated in the local operational arena.[89]

Hasan Yalcin, acting leader of the Labor Party, has claimed that a cooperation agreement, including the perpetrating of some attacks, was signed between the People's Liberation Army of Kurdistan, the PKK's military wing, and the fundamentalist Rahmet Group. He affirmed that a PKK-IBDA-C protocol about common terrorist training existed. Within this framework, the PKK trained some IBDA-C militants in Greece in acts of sabotage. According to Yalcin, the agreement between the PKK and Hizballah was also still in force.

According to the Istanbul *Hurriyet*, Hizballah has avoided armed clashes with the PKK since 1995 and rarely taken punitive measures against it because it considers PKK militants as a "ready military force." The Hizballah views PKK property as "free of charge," inheritable if Ocalan is executed and his organization dismembered.[90]

Emin Gurses of Sakarya University thinks that the PKK is in a process of disintegration and that the new threat will be Hizbul-PKK. Umit Ozdag of Gazi University believes that it will be very difficult for the PKK to survive without Ocalan's leadership, which was critical to raising money in Europe. Hizballah, according to Ozdag, is building up seriously, although it does not yet have the practical experience of the PKK.[91]

While Iran welcomed Erbakan's pro-Islamic policy, the warming in relations did not interfere with the overall strategy of furthering the Islamization of Turkey, as the 1997 Sincan incident revealed. In an interview with the Istanbul *Turkiye*, the Iranian ambassador said that at Sincan he spoke only about facts concerning Israel and that beyond that he did not even hint about Turkey: "I did not mention Hizballah or anything like that. I simply produced historic examples to show that Israel is a fundamentalist state. I did not even mention Yasir Arafat." He added, candidly, that the year before he had presented a far tougher speech at Jerusalem Day, but then the press did not even devote a line to it. "Had the RP not been in government this year, the press would again not have mentioned it. It is inconceivable to use a neighboring country to get rid of the RP, and that without justification," complained the ambassador.[92]

The expanding military cooperation between Turkey and Israel, which Erbakan could not erase, caused great concern in Iranian governmental circles and was considered a new American-Zionist plot to isolate and encircle Iran.[93] Tehran considers its conflict with Turkey not merely as a strategic and political competition between two regional rivals, but mostly as an ideological battle between its radical Islamic worldview and Turkey's "adamant [will] to translate into practice the western concept of secularism."[94]

After the PKK's expulsion from Syria in October 1998 and Ocalan's February 1999 capture in Kenya, Iran was accused of actively supporting the Kurdish organization's attacks against Turkey. Turkish intelligence established that Osman Ocalan, Abdullah's brother, who aspired to be the new leader of the PKK, was under government protection in Iran and occasionally met Iranian officials for talks. It was reported that Iran was preparing Osman Ocalan and his men for bloody terrorist attacks against Turkey and providing them with logistic and technical aid in pursuit of the same anti-Turkey policy that Syria employed.[95]

According to the Turkish press, Tehran wanted to control not only the PKK but also Turkish Hizballah, which was organized in the same region. During his interrogation, PKK's leader Abdullah Ocalan admitted that Iran mediated between the PKK and Hizballah.[96]

In July 1999, Turkish authorities reported again that Abdulaziz Tunc, the first Hizballah 'confessor' and an assistant to its escaped leader, Huseyin Velioglu, affirmed that Iran was a supporter. Tunc and other Hizballah members were trained in Iran in 1988 on how to use hand grenades, automatic weapons, and rockets.[97]

Also in July 1999, Tehran complained that Turkey had bombed an Iranian town at the mountainous junction of the Iranian, Iraqi, and Turkish borders—an area used by PKK guerrillas—killing five people and wounding ten. Iran retaliated by capturing two Turkish soldiers accused of straying into Iranian territory while pursuing the PKK; rather than return the soldiers immediately, Iran initially announced that they would be put on trial. These incidents fueled the tension between the two countries.[98]

The military incidents were accompanied by harsh criticism of the Iranian regime by Turkish prime minister Bulent Ecevit, who labeled student protests in Iran's cities a "natural" reaction against an "outdated regime of oppression." Ecevit also accused Iran of replacing Syria as the biggest base for PKK rebels.

The tension dissipated after the return of the two soldier-prisoners and a series of Turkish-Iranian security meetings focusing on Tehran's alleged growing support of anti-Turkish organizations. Korkmaz Haktanir, undersecretary of the Turkish Foreign Ministry, visited Iran on October 17 and 18 and asked Iranian leaders to act vigilantly against terrorists using their country for transit purposes. Positive security mechanisms between Turkey and Iran were also set up.[99]

The Turkish daily *Milliyet* analyzed Iran's policy in this context: "Democratic and modern Turkey that nonetheless respects and is committed to its religion constitutes a model for the Iranians, and the Tehran regime is uneasy about that." Tehran was also aware of its military weakness. Iran's frail economy and the most recent student protests had demonstrated that many dissatisfied people opposed the regime. Moreover, Iran was worried by the possible attitude of its important Azeri Turk minority. All these factors indicated that Iran was unlikely to risk a hot war with Turkey. But, the Turkish newspaper speculated that even after the end of the prisoners' crisis, Iran would not pursue friendship with Turkey so long as it did not have a democratic and strong regime, and that the stormy relationship between the two countries would continue.[100]

The Iranian view, according to the Tehran daily *Resalat*, was not optimistic either. The Turkish bombing of Iranian territory "has put the Iranian nation in psychological conditions of war and rancor toward the government and the military ruling over Turkey." The newspaper accused Ecevit of directing Turkish anger against Iran, because it regarded Islam in Turkey as an extension of Iran's Islamism. Moreover, the Turkish military aggression against Iran had to be seen not only "in terms of that country's national interests and objectives . . . but also as the direct result of Turkey's membership of NATO . . . and its special ties with America and the Zionist regime." It stressed the fact that the recent incidents coincided with President Demirel's visit "to the occupied Palestine." Turkey was presented therefore as a linking platform between military activity against Iran and "the centers controlling those activities in the West and the Zionist regime." Thus, even if the crisis were to end, "enmity and hatred would still continue to remain in the minds of the Iranian nation."[101]

According to Alan Makovsky, part of Turkey's post-Gulf War self-confidence and activism is its new relationship with Israel. Turkey and Israel are both Western-oriented and pro-United States, and deeply concerned about terrorism and Islamic fundamentalism. The only democracies in the Middle East, Turkey and Israel are also the two most economically dynamic and militarily powerful states in the region.[102] Therefore, it is quite natural for them to have finally announced in 1996 a strategic agreement including common military training, defense-industrial co-operation, collaboration in gathering intelligence on Syria, Iran, and Iraq, and free trade. Indeed, bilateral trade, virtually nonexistent in 1990 and roughly $450 million in 1998, was expected to reach more than $1 billion in 2000.[103]

Ironically, the relationship came to light during Erbakan's premiership. Although the RP and Erbakan were staunch opponents of the Turkish-Israeli alliance, they were forced by the military "to swallow the frog" and accept it against their will. Erbakan's signing of the agreement himself signaled to his followers, and opponents, the weakness of the Islamist movement and the limits of its political weight.

This event indicated the final step of the secular Turkish establishment, under the pressure of the unanimous military command, to resolutely leave behind the failed Turkish-Islamic Synthesis strategy, subdue the growing Islamist movement, and neutralize its political, social, and violent strongholds. The alliance also allowed for the military defeat of the PKK, seen more and more as an objective ally of the Islamists, by forcing Syria to expel its leader and other militants and stop any support for the Kurdish separatist movement.

On October 26, 1999, Cevik Bir, former deputy chief of the Turkish General Staff, remarked in an address at The Washington Institute for Near East Policy that "Turkey became a 'front country' in the region when new threats emerged after the Cold War . . . The initiation of Turkish-Israeli relations should be seen in this light. Contrary to the beliefs of some, neither the United States nor any other third party initiated Turkish-Israeli cooperation or the 1996 military training and cooperation agreement. These were the initiatives of the Turkish leadership."[104] General Bir affirmed that this military agreement paved the way for a resolution of the Autumn 1998 Turkish-Syrian crisis and, in his opinion, Syria's more responsive attitude toward Turkey since then proves that the Turkish-Israeli agreement works.[105]

The Islamic fundamentalist movement in Turkey shares many common features with movements in many Muslim countries but it understands the dangers of a direct clash with the nationalist Kemalist ideology and a military sworn to defend it. The politicization of Islam by the new intellectual and economic elite and military—who believed they could transform it into a pillar of the regime—has been skillfully exploited by the Islamic movement in its bid to achieve power and install an Islamic regime.

This is also true regarding the more radical, violent Islamic offshoots. Their expansion and relative freedom of action was tolerated until they became a real threat to internal political stability. The RP's parallel growth, its electoral success, and its leadership's indulgence of the Islamists' terror no doubt encouraged further violence.

It is noteworthy that following the RP's biggest electoral success in December 1995 and until the resignation of Erbakan's government in June 1997, Islamic groups perpetrated no serious terrorist acts, with the exception of low-level attacks by the IBDA-C, the most independent of the groups. Erbakan's policy of boosting relations with Iran and Libya possibly gave the radical groups the impression—or hope—that the RP government would indeed follow a more extremist Islamic policy.

Erbakan's resignation under army pressure, the succeeding government's steps to curtail the Islamic influence on the education system, the outlawing of the RP, and the recent move to ban its successor, the FP, have changed the rules of the game. The secular establishment, feeling the double pressure of the powerful military and of anxious Turkish civilians who favor the Kemalist ideology and regime, has definitely shown that the Turkish-Islamic Synthesis does not present a solution to Turkey's intricate problems.

Turkey has been able to resolutely challenge and foil growing domestic Islamic radicals due to a number of developments: its new self-confidence and strategic status that emerged as a result of the Gulf War; the fall of the Soviet empire; the liberation of the Turkic peoples of Central Asia; the weakening of Iran's regime; and the strategic agreement with Israel.

Until 1996, Iran paid a very low price for its support of Islamic terrorist activity in Turkey. The countries' bilateral relations were especially smooth during Erbakan's term of office. But Iran is entangled in internal strife between moderates, led by President Muhammad Khatami, and the old revolutionary strategy sustained by the spiritual leader, Khamene'i, whose supporters remain in key political and security posts.[106] The radicals seem to have the upper hand regarding relations with Turkey and have continued the strategy of subversion through the enfeebled PKK and the remnants of the violent Islamist movement.

According to Alan Makovsky, Turkey's relations with Iran are similar to its relations with Syria before Ocalan's expulsion. Turkey does not want a confrontation with Iran. "Given Turkey's more assertive regional policies of recent times, Ankara likely will continue to press Tehran—over time perhaps with threats or even limited use of force—if the Iranians do not alter their behavior and rein in the PKK," according to Makovsky.[107] However, Turkey might not hesitate to threaten Iran if its national security interests are compromised. In 1998, for example, Turkey threatened to use force unless Syria dismantled PKK bases on its territory and expelled Ocalan. Syria bowed to Turkish pressure. Asked whether the row with Iran could reach the same intensity, president Suleyman Demirel said, "No, no, I don't think so; at least not for the time being."[108]

RADICAL ISLAMIC ORGANIZATIONS IN TURKEY

National Security Council (NSC) report on radical groupings

In a twenty-page report on "reactionism" the NSC lists the radical Islamic groups as follows:

The organizations with religious motives: Hizbullah, IBDA-C [Islamic Great Eastern Raiders Front], Islami Hareket [Islamic Movement], and Vasat [al-Wasat].

The radical religious groups such as Yeryuzu, Tevhid, and Yildiz have their roots outside the country and gather around a bookshop, publication, or individual.

Indicating that the organizations with religious motives and the radical religious groups do not enjoy broad support, the report says these groups regard the Turkish Republic as the antithesis of Islam and consider it against their religious beliefs to form any legal organization sanctioned by the existing political system.

The radical religious groups in Turkey differ among themselves. These groups were further divided as being centered in Iran, Egypt, Pakistan, Saudi Arabia, and Sudan and in various countries simultaneously.

The report lists the prominent groups of the "reactionary" movement thus: Malatyalilar (or Safak), Hizbullahi Vahdet, Hizbullahi Davet, Yildiz, Vahdet, Tevhid (or Selam), Tefkir (or Cumasizlar), Akabe, Yeryuzu, Tevhid-i Cekirdek (or Kimliksizler), Yonelis (or Hak Soz), Ekin, Buruc (or Tohum), Mucadele, Fecr, Vehhabi, Ceysullah, Mazlum-Der.[109]

Prime Minister's Monitoring Council [PMMC] Report

According to a report by the PMMC, there are in Turkey 4,500 "reactionary" foundations whose activities are inconsistent with the purpose declared at the time of their establishment. The report says that only 15 percent of these foundations are audited and that most of them are controlled by the Nurist (Divine Light) religious order. The other leading operators of foundations are the National Youth Foundation, the Nakshibendis, the Kadiris, and Hizballah.[110]

The Istanbul Police Report on Illegal Organizations

The Directorate of Police in Istanbul has drawn up a report on the activities of the radical and reactionary organizations in the city.

The report states that the radical right-wing and reactionary groups have thirteen organizations under different names in Istanbul. Hizballah and the IBDA-C (Great Eastern Islamic Fighters Front) are the leading groups among the armed organizations. The report also says that the supporters of Hizballah operate as five different groups and notes that the Islamic Youth Organization organizes their unarmed popular activities.[111]

Organizations and Areas of Activity

IBDA-C: The organization is an extension of the THKP-C (Turkish People's Liberation Party Front) of the Islamic community. Its members work during the day and meet to carry out their activities at night. They return to their homes and families afterward. Consequently, officials find it difficult to control them. The organization does not seem to have any particular hierarchy. It is organized in Istanbul's Umraniye and Gaziosmanpasa districts and has nearly 300 militants and sympathizers. Its *vakif* (foundation) is the Islamic Studies and Arts Research Foundation (Islami Ilimler ve Sanatlar Arastirma Vakfi) in Sirinevler. Its founders are Yasar Sadoglu, Mehmet Salih Sadoglu, Sitki Dogan, Fikri Ozer, and Selma Sadoglu.

ICCB (Union of Islamic Associations and Societies): The organization is trying to get organized on the Western and Anatolian sides of the city. It uses one of its small mosques as a meeting center. It attracts new members with its propaganda activities run through publications and videotapes mailed from Germany. It has nearly sixty sympathizers in the city.

Ceysullah [God's Army]: The organization was established in 1987 by members of a group in the Umraniye and Uskudar Districts calling themselves Selefis. It has nearly 100 sympathizers. Some fifteen members of the group from various provinces, mainly Istanbul, Sakarya, and Izmir, have been sent to train at a camp in Pakistan. Its vakif is the Scientific Research Foundation (Ilim Arastirma Vakfi). Its founders are Ali Isik, Muharrem Iler, Sabri Salman, Mehmet Nur Gulluoglu, Mehmet Uyanikoglu, Mehmet Sukru Bakir.

Islamic Movement: The organization was established in Batman in 1986. High-ranking militants in the group agreed to arm their organization. Its militants were trained by the secret service in Iran, the SAVAMA. Significant blows were dealt to the organization in 1995 and 1996. Its members are trying to reorganize.

Hizbullah Tevhid Selam Gurubu [Unity and Salutation Group]: Some of the high-ranking members of the organization are from the former grassroots of left-wing factions. It has established close links with religious groups in Istanbul. Its members have rallied around the daily *Selam*, known for its articles from Iran. Its vakif is the Peace, Science and Service Foundation (Selam, Ilim ve Hizmet Vakfi) in Fatih. Its founders are A. Kemal Tuna, Mustafa Celik, Kenan Yabanigil, M. Burhan Genc, Isa Uzun, Ahmet Yurdakul, Suleyman Akboga, and M. Baki Seyda.

Hizballah Vasat [Moderate or Center] Group: The organization was established with the help of Sahabe, a periodical in Gaziantep. It later carried out activities in Pendik and Kaynarca and in Istanbul's Umraniye, Sultanbeyli, Bagcilar, and Gaziosmanpasa districts. Its members train at temporary camps in Kocaeli and Yalova. The organization has mosques in Kaynarca and Umraniye and a legal radio network known as Ozel (Special) FM. Its vakif is the Islamic Unification Foundation (Tevhid Vakfi) in Uskudar. Its founder is Mehmet Cakar.

Hizbullah Menzil (Course or House) Group: The organization is trying to legalize its activities. It is known to have nearly fifty militants and sympathizers. Its vakif is the Perseverance Social and Cultural Service Foundation (Sebat Sosyal ve Kulturel Hizmet Vakfi) in Fatih. Its founders are Mehmet Haydari, Ismail Oruc, and Mustafa Celik.

Hizbullah Vahdet (Unity) Group: The organization is trying to recruit new members through the Vahdet Foundation and its branches in Istanbul and the Abdulkadir Geylani Foundation in Diyarbakir. It has 150 members in Istanbul. Its vakif is the Invitation Educational, Cultural, and Fraternity Foundation (Davet Egitim, Kultur ve Kardeslik Vakfi) in Fatih. Its founders are Faris Karak, Ahmet varol, Adem Kiziltepe, Bulent Kaya, and Recep Celik.

Musluman Genclik (Yildiz) (Islamic Youth-Yildiz): The organization was created by a group headed by Tahir Gul at the Yildiz Technical University in Istanbul to struggle against the decision to ban students with head scarves from attending the university. Its vakif is the Human Education, Cultural and Solidarity Foundation (Insan Egitim, Kultur ve Yardimlasma Vakfi) in Fatih. Its founders are Husnu Turan, Yunus Torpil, Serif Enis, Cemal Tellioglu, and Kadir Tingiroglu.

Sirinevler Ulu Cami Egitim ve Hizmet Vakfi (Sirinevler Ulu Cami Education and Service Foundation) in Fatih. Its founders are Ibrahim Firat, Ozcan Kocaman, Binali Pala, Vehdettin Tasdemir, Mehmet Acikgoz, Idris Mutlu, and Elbeyli Celik. Its leader is Serif Eris.

Musluman Genclik (Maltyalilar) (Islamic Youth-Malatya): The organization was established by a group from eastern Turkey. Its high-ranking militants are from Malatya. It supports the Islamic Republic of Iran and has 100 supporters in Istanbul. Its vakif is the Islamic Thought and Solidarity Foundation [Islami Dusunce ve Dayanisma Vakfi]. Its founders are A. Riza Gokce, Taner Bayraktar, Abdurrahman Suayip, and Cetin Mitat.

Vahdet Egitim Yardimlasma Vakfi (Unity Education and Solidarity Foundation) in Ankara. Its founders are Recep Ozkan, Ahmet Altintepe, and Fatih Yildirim.

Asri Saadet (In the lifetime of Prophet Muhammad) Ilim, Hizmet ve Kultur Vakfi (Asri Saadet Service and Cultural Foundation) in Sultanciftligi. Its founder is Recep Aydin.

NOTES

1. See Sami Zubaida, "Turkish Islam and National Identity," *Middle East Report* (April–June 1996), p. 11.

2. See Ertugrul Kurkucu, "The Crisis of the Turkish State," *Middle East Report* (April–June 1996), pp. 2–7.

3. See Binnaz Toprak, "Religion as State Ideology in a Secular Setting: The Turkish-Islamic Synthesis" in Malcolm Wagstaff (ed.), *Aspects of Religion in Secular Turkey*, (Durham: University of Durham, Center for Middle Eastern and Islamic Studies, Occasional Paper Series No. 40, 1990), p.10.

4. Ibid.

5. Ibid.

6. See Anat Lapidot, "Islamic Activism in Turkey since the 1980 Military Takeover" in *Terrorism and Political Violence*, Vol. 3, (1997), (special issue on "Religious Radicalism in the Greater Middle East" edited by Bruce Maddy-Weitzman and Efraim Inbar), p. 64.

7. Kurkucu, "The Crisis of the Turkish State," p. 65.

8. For an evaluation of Turkey's strategic interests and policy in the region, see Kemal Kirisci's article "Post Cold-War Turkish Security and the Middle East," *Middle East Review of International Affairs (MERIA) Journal*, Vol. 1, No. 2, (June 1997).

9. See Ben Lombard, "Turkey—Return of the Reluctant Generals?" *Political Science Quarterly* 112 (Summer 1997), <http://epn.org/psq/lombardi.html>.

10. Hizb al-Tahrir, founded in Jordan in 1953, is dedicated to the creation of a Khilafah (unified Islamic state) and is banned throughout the Middle East due to its attempts to foment Islamic revolution. It began activity in Turkey in 1962. See *Cumhuriyet*, October 30, 1991. In the 1980s this organization had only limited propaganda activity in Turkey.

11. U.S. Department of State, *Patterns of Global Terrorism: 1991*, p. 14.

12. Lapidot, "Islamic Activism in Turkey," p. 65.

13. Cited by *Cumhuriyet*, October 30, 1991.

14. *Hezbollah* is the spelling used by *TDN* and other Turkish sources.

15. For this reason the names of the organizations mentioned in this article are those used by the various sources and do not always concord with the real group hiding behind the name.

16. Kalim Siddiqui was the founder of the Muslim Parliament and the Muslim Institute in London, which have close links with Iran and many of the world's violent Islamist groups. He died in 1996. See also *The Antisemitism World Report*, (London: Institute of Jewish Affairs, 1995), pp. 241–242.

17. According to the Turkish journalist Tunkay Ozkan, the Islamic Movement was established in Batman in 1987 as one of the branches of the Islamic terror organization called Hizballahiler, active in the southeast, and moved its headquarters to Istanbul in 1990. See *Cumhuriyet*, June 23, 1993.

18. It is interesting to note the similarity of this conversion to radical Islam as a consequence of harsh conditions in prison with the radicalization of Islamic militants in the prisons of Nasserist Egypt and Baathist Syria in the middle 1960s. See Emmanuel Sivan, *Radical Islam: Medieval Theology and Modern Politics* (Tel-Aviv: Am Oved Publishers, 1986, in Hebrew), p. 37.

19. See *Cumhuriyet*, February 16, 1993.

20. Ibid.

21. See Meir Hatina, "Iran and the Palestinian Islamic Movement," *Orient*, Vol. 38, No. 1 (Marz 1997), pp. 108–110.

22. See Gilles Millet, in *Liberation*, October 9, 1995, and James Philips, "The Rising Threat of Revolutionary Islam in Algeria," *Backgrounder—The Heritage Foundation*, 9 (November 1995), p. 6.

23. See Haggay Ram, "Exporting Iran's Islamic Revolution: Steering a Path between Pan-Islam and Nationalism," in *Terrorism and Political Violence,* Vol. 3 (1997), special issue on "Religious Radicalism in the Greater Middle East" edited by Bruce Maddy-Weitzman and Efraim Inbar, pp. 12–16.

24. *Milliyet*, February 27, 1997.

25. Professor Bahriye Ucok, writer Turan Dursan and journalist Cetin Emec (editor of the daily newspaper *Hurriyet*) were assassinated because they served "the idolatrous regime" and in order "to bring about the resurrection." See *Hurriyet*, October 10, 1993, and *Cumhuriyet*, February 6 and June 23, 1993.

26. See Imset, *TDN*, May 14, 1993.

27. It is interesting to note that most of the anti-American and anti-Western terrorist activity during the Gulf War was perpetrated by the extreme left-wing Turkish organization Dev-Sol and not by Islamic groups, although they were also fiercely opposed to the allied intervention (with Turkish participation) in Iraq. See also U.S. Department of State, *Patterns of Global Terrorism: 1991*, p. 14.

28. A security officer at the Israeli embassy in Ankara was killed by a bomb in his car (March 7, 1992); grenades were thrown at the Neve Shalom synagogue in Istanbul (March 1, 1992); bombs were placed in the cars of two Iranian opposition militants (June

1992); the same month a member of the Iranian Mujahedin-e Halq was kidnapped and assassinated.

29. See *Anatolia Radio* (in English), January 24, 1993.

30. See for instance *TDN*, January 29, 1993, and reports of Ankara Turkiye Radyolari Network (FBIS-WEU-93-023 4.2.1993).

31. On July 2, 1993, during the traditional Pir Sultan Abdal Culture festival in the southeast city of Sivan, fundamentalists set fire to the Madimak Hotel, where all the guests had been staying.

32. *TDN*, January 19, 1995.

33. See *Inter Press Service*, January 11, 1995.

34. See Imset, *TDN*, February 8, 1993 and May 14, 1993 and *Cumhuriyet*, February 4, 1993.

35. See *Hurriyet*, February 10, 1993.

36. See *Cumhuriyet*, February 16, 1993.

37. See *TDN*, March 12, 1993 and May 15, 1993.

38. Irfan Cagarici, the arrested leader of Islamic Action, was also behind the attack on the Jewish businessman Jak Kamhi in January 1993. See *Jane's Intelligence Review*, August 1996, p. 374.

39. See Sabri Sayari, "Turkey's Islamist Challenge," *Middle East Quarterly*, September 1996, pp. 35–37. The RP obtained 21.3 percent of the vote and 158 seats out of the 550-member National Assembly and became the largest party in Parliament.

40. See Zubaida, "Turkish Islam and National Identity," pp. 11–12. See also Feroz Ahmad, *The Making of Modern Turkey* (London: Routledge, 1993), pp. 219–222.

41. *TDN*, February 26, 1993.

42. The Project for the Study of Anti-Semitism, *Anti-Semitism Worldwide: 1995/96* (Tel-Aviv University, 1996), p. 202.

43. See *Inter Press Service*, January 11, 1995.

44. Imset, *TDN*, May 14 and 16, 1993.

45. See Zubaida, "Turkish Islam and National Identity," p. 12.

46. The vice-president of the RP declared on February 9, 1993 in the Turkish Parliament that a team of six Israeli Mossad agents assassinated Mumcu and that the West was interested in inciting public opinion to believe that Iran was responsible. This accusation was apparently based on a secret report of pro-Islamic elements in the police. See *Middle East International*, February 19, 1993.

47. See *Kanal 6 Television*, November 24, 1993.

48. See Nur Bilge Criss, "The Nature of PKK Terrorism in Turkey," *Studies in Conflict and Terrorism*, Vol. 18, (1995), p. 21.

49. The pro-Islamic daily *Turkiye*, December 3, 1995, published a series of such declarations, such as that of Muhsin Yazicioglu (leader of the Grand Unity Party-BBP) or that of Professor Mahir Kaynak, ex-intelligence officer.

50. See Alan Makovsky, "Turkey: Erbakan at Six Months," *Policywatch*, No. 230 (December 27, 1996), p. 3.

51. This interesting analysis of Iran's 'three-phase' relations with Turkey appeared in the *Tehran Salam*, December 19, 1996, on the occasion of Rafsanjani's visit to Turkey.

52. *Cumhuriyet*, June 23, 1993.

53. See Imset, *TDN*, May 14, 1993.

54. *Cumhuriyet* and other newspapers, February 5–6, 1993.

55. Unfortunately, there is no room in this chapter for a detailed evaluation of the economic, strategic and political reasons behind the cautious approach of the various Turkish governments in their relations with Iran.

56. See *TDN*, January 29, 1993.

57. See Gungor Mengi's column in reaction to Velayati's interview on February 15, 1993 in *Sabah*, February 16, 1993.

58. See U.S. Department of State, *Patterns of Global Terrorism: 1994*, pp. 11–12, 25, and U.S. Department of State, *Patterns of Global Terrorism: 1995*, pp. 12, 25. See also Criss, "The Nature of PKK Terrorism in Turkey," p. 31.

59. See *TDN*, January 8, 1996.

60. For a discussion of RP's characteristics as an Islamic movement see Zubaida, "Turkish Islam and National Identity," pp. 10–11, and Sayari, "Turkey's Islamist Challenge," p. 37.

61. See Elie Podeh, "Egypt's Struggle against the Militant Islamic Groups" in *Terrorism and Political Violence*, Vol. 3 (1997), special issue on "Religious Radicalism in the Greater Middle East," edited by Bruce Maddy-Weitzman and Efraim Inbar, p. 48.

62. IBDA-C's monthly, *Taraf*, gives some addresses of its representatives in Europe. In Germany there are several extremist Islamic Turkish organizations. The most active is "The Islamic Communities Union" led by Cemalettin Kaplan. See "Islamischer Extremismus und seine Auswirkungen auf die Bundesrepublik Deutschland," Bonn, Bundesamtfar Verfassungschutz (November 1994).

63. According to Erbakan, Western "imperialist" institutions and "Zionist Wall Street bankers" seek mainly to exploit Turkey and the Islamic countries, and Washington is the tool of "Zionist forces." RP's politicians and daily newspapers have blamed the Jews, Zionism and Israel for every domestic and foreign problem of Turkey. See Sayari, "Turkey's Islamist Challenge," p. 41, and *The Antisemitism World Report* (1995), p. 228.

64. See the interview with Admiral Guven Erkaya in *Milliyet*, August 14, 1997.

65. For a full account of the events from the point of view of the military see the extraordinary interview with Admiral Guven Erkaya by *Milliyet* columnist Yavuz Donat, *Milliyet*, August 14, 1997.

66. Cited from Alan Makovsky, *Policywatch*, No. 239, March 12, 1997, p. 1.

67. *Sabah*, June 12, 1997. [FBIS-WEU-97-114]. The speech was cited fully by the newspaper.

68. Political Islam has accumulated considerable power with its 2,500 associations, 500 foundations, more than 1,000 corporations, 1,200 student dormitories and more than 800 private schools and classrooms.

69. It has been determined that there are 1,685,000 continuing students registered in Quranic courses and that their numbers double every five years. It is forecasted that this figure will rise to 7 million by 2005. According to a study based on 1995 figures,

492,809 students attend 561 imam-preacher lyceums in Turkey, and 53,553 students graduate from these schools each year. Meanwhile, the demand for imams is only 2,288 per year. The remaining 51,345 graduates are deliberately trained in schools of law and in the political sciences and in police academies. The purpose of that is to build an Islamist state structure, within the context of political Islam, by occupying government positions over the short and medium terms.

70. The donors of financial assistance to Islamist organizations include Islamist individuals whose shares of the national income are among the highest in the country. The status of these individuals, who are publicly known as the "100 political Islamist bosses," is as follows: six are worth more than 100 trillion Turkish lira; five are worth between 20 and 50 trillion Turkish lira; fifteen are worth between 10 and 20 trillion Turkish lira; thirteen are worth between 1 and 10 trillion Turkish lira; the rest are worth less than 1 trillion Turkish lira.

71. The propaganda activities are conducted through nineteen newspapers, 110 magazines, fifty-one radio stations, and twenty television stations.

72. See James M. Dorsey, "Turkey's Military Continues Crackdown on Islam in Public Life," *Washington Report on Middle East Affairs*, October–November 1997, p. 36 <http://www.washington-report.org/backissues/1097/9710036.html>.

73. In the 1995 election it did not manage to pass the 10 percent threshold.

74. See *CNN*, Ankara, April 19, 1999.

75. For a detailed analysis of the political Islamist movement see Nilufer Narli, 'The Rise of the Islamist Movement in Turkey," *MERIA Journal*, Vol. 3, No. 3, (September 1999).

76. By the end of 1996 the term *Hizballah* came to be used instead of the previous *Hezbollah.*

77. See the statement of Cemil Serhadli, the governor of Diyarbakir, in *Ankara Anatolia*, October 20, 1999.

78. October 7—A homemade bomb exploded a Greek lyceum in Istanbul; October 17—A bomb exploded in front of a bookstore in Istanbul selling the publications of the Religious Affairs Foundation; October 21—Ahmet Taner Kislali, a former minister, academic and newspaper columnist, was killed outside his home in Ankara by a homemade pipe bomb placed on top of his car; October 29—A time bomb exploded on the campus of the University of Marmara in the Goztepe district of Istanbul, causing minor damage; November 18—Unidentified assailants damaged pictures of Kemal Ataturk and planted a pipe bomb in the Istanbul headquarters of the Ataturk Association.

79. See *Ankara Anatolia*, June 4, 1999.

80. See *Ankara Anatolia*, November 15, 1999.

81. See *Ankara Anatolia*, November 1, 1999.

82. In June 1999, thirty militants, including four policemen, of the "Vasat Group" of Hizballah were captured in an operation carried out in Malatya; ten members of Hizballah were captured in the Batman province; eight militants of Hizballah were captured in Kovancilar county of eastern Elazig province.

83. In Erzurum, a total of fourteen persons were detained on grounds that they aided the Menzil group. In operations conducted in Agri, the security forces caught

twenty-eight Hizballah militants, including the five members of the "Province Council." Security officials reported that the Hizballah members—who began organizing in the region in the early 1990s—from time to time also undertake activities in Turkey's other provinces.

84. See *Ankara Anatolia*, January 1, 1999.

85. See *Istanbul Hurriyet*, March 16, 1999.

86. See *TDN*, March 6, 1999.

87. See *TDN*, June 21, 1999.

88. See *TDN*, July 5, 1999.

89. For a detailed analysis of PKK's strategy and Turkey's policy see this author's articles: Ely Karmon, "The Showdown Between the PKK and Turkey: Syria's Setback," November 20, 1998, <http://www.ict.org.il> and "The Arrest of Abdullah Ocalan: The last stage in the Turkey-PKK showdown?" February 17, 1999, <http://www.ict.org.il/articles/articledet.cfm?articleid=72>.

90. See *Hurriyet*, March 5, 1999.

91. See *Zaman*, June 5, 1999.

92. See *Turkiye*, February 8, 1997. The relations between Turkey and Iran improved again after the mutual appointment of ambassadors in March 1998.

93. See *Tehran Times*, January 13, 1998.

94. Ibid.

95. As of spring 1999, three Iranian officers were training some 200 PKK militants in a camp set up by the PKK in the Piransehir district in Iran. In another camp named Jerme, seventy PKK terrorists were being trained. It has been found out that Iran was planning to have all these militants infiltrate Turkey to stage terrorist attacks. It has also been ascertained that the districts of Maku and Dambak in Iran served as the PKK's military depots and that personnel and materiel were sent from there to the PKK groups active in Turkey. PKK leaders Osman Ocalan, Nizamettin Tas, and Mustafa Karasu were in Iran. See *Hurriyet*, May 17, 1999.

96. See *Hurriyet*, May 29, 1999.

97. See *Milliyet*, July 5, 1999.

98. For a detailed analysis of these events, see Alan Makovsky, 'Turkish-Iranian Tension: a New Regional Flashpoint?" *Policywatch*, Number 404 (August 9, 1999).

99. See *Ankara Anatolia*, October 27, 1999.

100. See *Milliyet*, August 7, 1999.

101. *Tehran Resalat*, July 20, 1999.

102. See Alan Makovsky, "Israeli-Turkish Cooperation: Full Steam Ahead," *Policywatch*, Number 292 (January 6, 1998).

103. Ibid.

104. The French commentator Alain Gresh also asserts that "Contrary to what people think in the Arab world, in particular in Damascus, the impetus of the alliance does not come from Israel, but from the Turkish generals." See Alain Gresh, "Grandes Manoeuvres Regionales Autour De L'alliance Israelo-Turque," *Le Monde Diplomatique*, Decembre 1997.

105. See General Cevik Bir, "Reflections on Turkish-Israeli Relations and Turkish Security," *Policywatch*, Number 422 (November 5, 1999).

106. The conflict between the two camps and strategies regarding the future foreign policy of Iran has found an echo even in Iranian academic circles, which are well aware of the discrepancy between the regime's ideology and the constraints of international and internal realities. See, for instance, the publication of the revealing roundtable discussion between Dr. Ebrahim Mottaqi, assistant professor of political science at the University of Tehran, Dr. Dehshiri, member of the faculty of Allameh Tabataba'i University, and Dr. Javat Eta'at, the head of the Research Division of the Center of Islamic Revolution Documents, in *Tehran Salam* of August 11, 1997. It is interesting to note that in this professional, theoretical discussion on Iranian foreign policy, Turkey is one of the very few countries mentioned by name, and in this context Dr. Eta'at proposes a policy of confronting it and putting it in a reactive position by seeking a "reverse alliance" with one of its neighbors.

107. See Makovsky, *Policywatch*, No. 404.

108. See *Tehran Times*, July 27, 1999.

109. See Istanbul *Sabah*, 26 June 1998.

110. See Istanbul *Hurriyet*, 11 July 1998.

111. See Istanbul *Milliyet*, 12 and 13 August 1998.

5

Islamism and the State in North Africa

Bruce Maddy-Weitzman and Meir Litvak

The confrontation in Algeria between the military regime and the Islamic opposition caused a near meltdown of the Algerian state during the last decade. Algeria was the metaphorical *gharb* (West), a place were "all terrors are possible."[1] Many pundits were quick to predict an Iranian-style outcome, with corresponding effects on Algeria's neighbors. However, their rush to judgment betrayed a lack of understanding of both the Maghrib region and the highly varied realities within each Maghrib state. What is required is a proper understanding of the Islamic challenge in Algeria in relation to that which occurred in Morocco and Tunisia.

The ideological roots of modern-day Islamic fundamentalism are not solely recent: the ideas of the *salafiyya* current of Islamic reform and purification were present in preprotectorate Morocco among both the *'ulama* and various sultans,[2] and became widespread in the Maghrib in the era between the two world wars. One can argue that more than in the *Mashriq* (the Arab East), Islam was one of the core values for Algerian, Moroccan, and Tunisian nationalist movements that opposed European domination. In Algeria, the crystallization of a modern national identity between the two world wars was considerably shaped by the Islamic reformist movement led by Shaykh 'Abd al-Hamid Bin Badis. The movement promoted both the purification of Islamic practices from "polythe-

Earlier versions of this article appeared in *Religious Radicalism in the Greater Middle East*, Bruce Maddy-Weitzman and Efraim Inbar (eds.), (London: Frank Cass, 1997); *Terrorism and Political Violence*, Volume 8, No. 2 (Summer 1996) pp. 171–188; and *Middle East Review of International Affairs (MERIA), Journal*, No. 3. (Spring 1997).

ism" (maraboutic practices) and creation of an educational network that would stress that Islam and the Arabic language, and not French culture, are at the core of modern Algerian identity.[3]

Similarly, *Salafi* activity in Morocco played an important role in shaping the nationalist movement, personified in the 1920s by 'Allal al-Fasi, the religio-nationalist leader of the Istiqlal party.[4] Likewise in Tunisia, Islam "as a component of Tunisian identity and a legitimizing value . . . suffused the first generation nationalist movement [in the decades prior to World War I] and . . . persisted even into the age of Bourguibist secularism."[5]

In contrast to the general *Salafi* current, political Islam in North Africa was not a 'pan' movement. Nor, again in contrast to the Mashriq, was pan-Arabism a competing ideology. Thus, the legitimacy of the state in North Africa has never been in doubt: "The state appears more as an appropriately adjusted transfer of technology than as an alien institution."[6]

State power grew exponentially during the post-independence generation, intruding decisively into every sphere of society. However, in the words of the Tunisian scholar Abd al-Baki Hermassi, by the 1980s, policies once seen favorably as constituting the "etatization" of society increasingly began to look like the privatization of the state as small numbers of individuals accumulated great wealth from their privileged positions. This occurred at a time of austerity imposed by international financial institutions.[7] Also, the resources available for development were sharply cut by the post-oil boom economic contraction. The effect was felt across the Arab world among both petroleum-based economies, including Algeria, and "labor-exporters" such as Egypt, Jordan, and Tunisia. What resulted was the obvious inability of Arab regimes, *maghribi* and *mashriqi* alike, to deliver the social, economic, political, and psychological goods to their expanding, increasingly youthful, urbanized, and literate populations. This failure caused a profound sense of crisis (*azma*) among wide sectors of their populations and endless debate among intellectuals over what should be done (spawning a cottage industry, "azmatology," in the words of Muhammad Guessous, a Moroccan sociologist).[8]

The Maghrib's proximity to Europe rendered its youthful population (two-thirds under 30 years of age) especially vulnerable to psychological dislocation, especially since North Africa had already been widely penetrated by the gharb (primarily France) during the prior 150 years. The proliferation of satellite dishes and powerful television transmitters brought images of Europe's material glitter into people's living rooms, raising expectations and prompting demands that had no chance of being fulfilled, thus opening the way to profound disillusionment. In Mernissi's words, "[W]hat strikes me as a sociologist [when visiting a Muslim country] is the strong feeling of bitterness in the people—the intellectuals, the young, peasants. I see bitterness over blocked ambition, over frustrated desires for consumption—of clothes, commodities, and gadgets, but also of cultural products like books and quality films and performances which give meaning to life and reconcile the individual with his environment and his country. . . . In our country [Morocco] what is unbearable, especially when you listen to the young men and women of the poor class, is the awful waste of talent. '*Ana daya°* ('My life is a mess') is a leitmotif that one hears constantly."[9]

The crisis, which took root during the 1970s and gathered strength during the 1980s, spawned a new kind of dissent, articulated most forcefully by Islamist movements. They spoke not only on issues or strategies of development, but on matters concerned with justice and cultural identity.[10] Given the dual legacy of popular-maraboutic Islamic practice and the Maghrib's penetration by the modern gharb, it is not surprising that Maghribi Salafists-fundamentalists often found themselves alienated from their own societies and thus sought guidance and inspiration from outside the Maghrib: e.g., the Egyptian-based Muslim Brotherhood, Iran's Islamic Revolution, and Sudan's Hasan al-Turabi. This interaction marked a departure from premodern historical patterns.

MOROCCO

Despite the strongly similar development patterns of their Islamist movements, the specific sociopolitical and historical circumstances of the three Maghrib states varied widely. This produced a disparate state-society/regime-opposition dynamic which, in each case, produced a very different political outcome. Consider Morocco: apart from Saudi Arabia, no other Arab regime has so thoroughly draped itself in Islam's mantle. King Hassan II, who reigned and ruled from 1961 until his death in July 1999, was constitutionally the *amir al-mu'minin* ("Commander of the Faithful") deputized by virtue of his descent from the Prophet Muhammad to lead the Moroccan Islamic *umma* in all matters, temporal and spiritual.[11] His own erudition in religious matters, displayed in dialogues with religious scholars on Moroccan television, reinforced this dual role. His son and heir, King Muhammad VI, has inherited this constitutionally grounded spiritual-temporal standing.

One can argue against the oft-made claim that the monarchy is the central religious institution of Moroccan life and that Hassan's longevity rested less on blind obedience and belief in his special sacredness (*baraka*) than on his astutely wielding the levers of power at his disposal, including repression.[12] As Hassan himself told his biographer, "One doesn't maintain order by wielding croissants."[13] At the same time, it seems reasonable to conclude that the Moroccan regime has been a relatively successful "modernizing monarchy" because it situated itself firmly within Moroccan political and sociocultural traditions. This enabled it to avoid some of the harsher social, political, and psychological dislocations of revolutionary Arab regimes and Pahlavi Iran.[14]

One of these traditions is the institution of the monarchy itself: the ruling Alawite dynasty is almost 350 years old. At the same time, as I. W. Zartman argues, the monarchy under Hassan has evolved through interaction with society.[15]

Part of this involved Hassan's modification of religious traditions to reinforce his legitimacy.[16] More prosaic factors promoting relative political stability include a liberal economy and multiparty politics. Hassan described his political strategy as "homeopathic democracy," a process of controlled, well-managed change that maintains social peace while promoting economic development and the general welfare. His ultimate declared goal was a "bipolarized democracy," in which two parliamentary blocs would alternate in power, with the monarch serving as the ultimate arbiter and source of authority.

Hassan's strategy slowly but successfully bore fruit. Efforts to entice the historical opposition parties into power-sharing following the 1993 parliamentary elections foundered on their unwillingness to serve alongside the all-powerful Interior Minister Driss Basri, as well as on their own internal divisions. Four years later, the pieces fell into place, following further constitutional reform. The November parliamentary elections produced a balance of forces in the Chamber of Deputies, with a slight advantage to the Union Socialiste des Forces Populaires (USFP). In early 1998, Hassan charged its leader, the historical opposition figure Abd al-Rahmane Youssoufi, with forming the long-sought-after *alternance* government. The new government, consisting of seven parties and six nonparty officials, including Basri, took office in March, amid great expectations for change.

Inevitably, the promise of reform did not immediately live up to its advanced billing. Modernizing administrative procedures and the judicial, commercial, and educational spheres took time, and the results, if at all meaningful, would not be quickly apparent.[17] Nonetheless, the atmosphere did improve, particularly in the area of human rights. It was perhaps fortuitous that just as the last vestiges of optimism for Youssoufi's government were fading away in the summer of 1999, King Hassan died and was replaced by Muhammad. The new king surprised observers by moving quickly to put his own stamp on affairs of state, with a more open, populist style, further gestures in the human rights arena, and, most dramatically, the sacking of Interior Minister Basri. While continuing his father's legacy, Muhammad gave unmistakable signs of desiring to accelerate the pace of change.

No less significant than the evolution of Moroccan political life has been the growth in recent years of authentic 'civil society' elements, notwithstanding considerable odds.[18] Labor unions have become increasingly combative; human rights groups have bucked considerable pressure to make their voices heard; women's organizations gathered one million signatures in 1992–1993 on a petition to change the *mudawanna*, Morocco's personal status law, which discriminates against women in many areas.[19] Of related interest has been a significant lowering of the population growth rate from 3 percent per annum in the early 1970s to under 2 percent in 1998, and a corresponding halving of the average family size.[20]

The downside of Hassan's controlled-change strategy was that his reliance on existing economic and political elites carried a danger of stagnation, a lack of attention to social and economic distress, and displeasure among the educated classes. The slow pace of change undoubtedly bred cynicism among the latter and did little to make the urban poor feel empowered. Hassan's International Monetary Fund-directed policies of structural readjustment, involving debt rescheduling, subsidy cuts, liberalizing capital movements, and initial privatizing of state firms, won considerable praise from the Paris Club governments and international and commercial lending agencies. The budget deficit, which in the early 1980s reached 12 percent of the gross domestic product, was cut to less than 2 percent in a decade, foreign investment rose fourfold between 1988 and 1992, and annual growth rates were impressive. King Muhammad remained committed to his father's economic reform package. So too was Prime Minister Youssoufi, who resisted pressures from within his own party and from coalition partners to significantly increase Morocco's already crushing debt burden (one-third of the GDP) in order to expand social services.

On the microeconomic level, however, the picture was far from rosy. Gaps between rich and poor, in a society where the average per capita income is just over $1,000, further widened; urban unemployment remained high (officially 16 percent, unofficially far higher), and two years of severe drought in 1992–1993, followed by the "drought of the century" in the winter of 1994–1995, exacerbated the plight of rural areas and reinforced longstanding trends toward migration to urban areas. Subsequent winters again demonstrated Morocco's overdependence on climatic vagaries: bountiful rains produced a record 11 percent growth rate in 1996; the failure of late winter rains in 1997 produced a negative growth rate for the year.

Like many Middle East governments, Hassan initially gave budding Islamist movements some freedom of action in order to balance opposition from the radical left. The assassination of USFP leader Omar Benjelloun in 1975 by radical Islamists, apparently with the connivance of the authorities, may have been the most extreme manifestation of regime-Islamist cooperation.[21] Thereafter, while permitting nonpolitical activities, Hassan adopted a strategy of manipulation and co-optation and severely restricted the ability of Islamists to operate politically. It was only in the late 1990s, as part of the process of controlled political liberalization, that Hassan permitted, and indeed sought, Islamist activity within the formal political system. The regime's efforts to control Islamism were made easier by the fact that Moroccan Islamists are not homogeneous. One researcher counted no less than twenty-three politicized religious associations in the early 1980s. However, these are generally grouped into three trends. By summer 1996, three weekly newspapers representing the three main trends had a combined circulation of 40,000.[22]

One of these trends has been explicitly reformist but not overtly political, concentrating on matters of individual piety and righteousness, criticizing corruption, and affecting certain styles of traditional Islamic clothing, wedding celebrations, and rhetoric. As such, it has been the least restricted. The leading figure of this Sunni trend, before his death in the late 1980s, was an elderly mosque preacher in Tangier named Fqih al-Zamzami. Venerated by peddlers, laborers, and shopkeepers, cassettes of his sermons are sold in most cities. His three sons have tried to follow in his path. The Zamzami Sunni trend appears to have become intermingled with the *Tabligh*, an Islamic proselytizing movement originating in the Indian subcontinent.[23]

At the other extreme was a small group, *al-Shabiba al-Islamiyya* (Islamic Youth), drawn mostly from student and high school movements, which advocated the regime's violent overthrow. Its leader, 'Abd al-Karim al-Muti', is in exile somewhere in Europe. Some of the Shabiba, led by 'Abdallah Benkirane, broke with Muti' in 1981 and chose a nonconfrontational, reformist posture which accepted the inviolability of the monarchy and sought to work for the peaceful pursuit of an Islamic society. Benkirane operated under the banner of *Harakat al-Islah wal-Tajdid* (Movement for Reform and Renewal). By the 1990s, Benkirane was seeking to become overtly involved in the political process.[24] In 1996, his movement joined forces with another group, *Rabitat al-Mustaqbal al-Islami* (League of the Islamic Future), with the new group being called *Harakat al-Tawhid wal-Islah* (Movement for Unification and Reform). The regime's approach to Benkirane was twofold. On the one hand, it encouraged his group's activities, as a tamed, regime-legitimizing alternative to more radical groups. On the other, it was unwilling to have an explicitly Islamic party running for public office. The solution was to incorporate Benkirane's movement into an existing, albeit moribund, party, the Mouvment Populaire Democratique et Constitutionnel (MPDC), headed by the venerable 'Abd al-Karim Khatib. The MPDC put up 140 candidates in the November 1997 parliamentary elections (out of a possible 325 seats). Nine won seats, four from Casablanca alone; a tenth seat was subsequently obtained (also from a Casablanca district) when the ostensible USFP winner resigned after discovering that his victory was fraudulent. In the spring of 1999, with his party now renamed the Party de la Justice et du Development (PJD), Benkirane himself was victorious in a special election to fill a vacant parliamentary seat from Sale. Rumors were widespread that he had been assisted by the authorities.[25] What was clear was that both the government and moderate Islamists had a common interest in having an Islamist voice participate in the public discourse.

The best-known Moroccan Islamist figure is 'Abd al-Salam Yasin, a former Education Ministry school inspector and Sufi-like figure who leads the banned *al-'Adl wal-Ihsan* (Justice and Charity) movement. According to the leading analyst of Moroccan Islamism, Mohamed Tozy, the Justice and Charity movement would not exist if it weren't for Yasin, whose mystical and doctrinal authority is absolute.[26] Yasin's followers are more educated and more radical than Zamzami's. Yasin openly challenged Hassan's legitimacy—and that of any monarch in Islam—back in 1974. He later admitted to having prepared his burial shroud for the occasion.[27] Instead, King Hassan felt confident enough not to have him executed and thereafter merely kept him under various forms of detention, including a spell in a psychiatric hospital, for much of the time thereafter. During the Gulf War, 30,000 of Yasin's followers gathered under their own banner as part of a massive anti-war march, providing the only public indication of their strength. In December 1994, the government briefly eased Yasin's house arrest but swiftly reimposed it when Yasin declined to refrain from political sermons.

The authorities' effort to coax Yasin into working within the system indicates their recognition of the Islamists' potential strength and the need to defuse it by co-optation and dialogue, while not eschewing more traditional containment strategies. The Youssoufi government's tone regarding Yasin was more accommodating than its predecessor, with Human Rights Minister Mohammed Aujjar characterizing Yasin as a "grand 'alim and a nationalist."[28] Given the new king's and Youssoufi government's determination to 'turn the page' and work toward increased democratization and the rule of law, Yasin's release was only a matter of time. The declaration by one Justice and Charity official that the movement had distanced itself from politics for good, and would instead concentrate on propagating Yasin's nonviolent, purifying teachings[29] was probably an attempt to make it easier for the authorities to release Yasin. They eventually did so in May 2000, notwithstanding the stir he caused in the beginning of the year by dispatching a 19-page memorandum to King Muhammad asking him to return to the Moroccan people $40 allegedly stolen by Muhammad's late father, King Hassan.

Although the main Islamist currents in Morocco were nonviolent, an incident in the summer of 1994 provided evidence that Morocco was not entirely immune to radical, violent Islamic currents of the kind manifesting themselves in Algeria and Egypt. On August 24, two Spanish tourists were shot to death in the lobby of a hotel in Marrakesh, the first, and so far only, violent attack against foreigners. The government immediately blamed Algerian intelligence services for supporting the perpetrators, precipitating renewed Algerian-Moroccan tensions and the closing of their border. Two weeks later, four alleged perpetrators were arrested. They turned out to be a group of young French-Moroccan and French-Algerian fundamentalists, possibly connected to the remnants of Muti''s al-Shabiba al-Islamiyya, who in the late 1980s organized themselves into a group to advance the cause of Islamic revolution. Their activities included receiving weapons training in Peshawar, Pakistan, near the Afghan frontier, smuggling weapons to Algerian Islamists via Morocco, and a number of robberies in France to support themselves and the cause.[30] Their alleged head, Tariq Fellah, a Moroccan, was arrested in Germany in December 1994 (another person, 'Abd al-Ilah Ziyad, also a member of al-Shabiba, subsequently claimed he had organized the hotel attack during his trial in France). In January 1995, the group of four plus fourteen others were tried in Fez for the shooting plus other violent acts carried out during 1994. Three of the eighteen were sentenced to death (the sentences have not been carried out); the others to sentences ranging from six months to life imprisonment. Official Algerian involvement was never confirmed, and the affair pointed more to the common danger posed by Islamist radicals to both the Moroccan and Algerian regimes.

At the same time, the swift arrest and trial of the group confirmed anew that the Moroccan Islamists' ability to pose a serious challenge to the regime is extremely limited. Nonetheless, their activities, particularly on university campuses where Islamists control nearly all student unions and periodically clash violently with leftist groups, were publicly acknowledged by at least one government minister as constituting a worrisome development.[31] In November 1998, state security officers and campus guards attacked Islamist students at the Casablanca science college on the grounds of ensuring public order. Justice and Charity spokesman Fathallah Arslan declared that incorrect charges of Islamist student violence were part of an effort to frighten the public by falsely tarring Moroccan Islamists with the brush of Algerian Islamist violence. The roots of the latter, he declared, stemmed from the actions of the Algerian authorities.[32]

As Morocco entered the uncharted political and societal waters of the twenty-first century under the rule of a young new king, with the bounds of the permissible in political and social spheres being increasingly tested and contested, Islamist discourse and Islamist groups were clearly permanent features of the Moroccan landscape. In the summers of 1999 and 2000, Islamists demonstrated their mobilizing capacities by transforming public beaches into "camps" for religious, educational, cultural, and charitable activities.

Even more dramatic was a march in Casablanca in March 2001 of about 200,000 persons "in defense of the Moroccan family," protesting a government-sponsored plan to promote the integration of women into development schemes, including making far-reaching changes in the *mudawanna*, such as abolishing polygamy, equalizing the right of divorce and improving child custody rights for mothers, and raising the official minimum marriage age to eighteen. Islamist spokespersons, including Shaykh Yasin's daughter Nadia Yasin, took pains to clarify that the *mudawanna* was "not a sacred text" and that the humiliating situation of Moroccan women, including high rates of illiteracy, poverty, and prostitution, needed to be ameliorated. They framed their opposition to the plan in terms of protecting Moroccan society's "authentic identity" against the corrosive and odious anti-Islamic schemes of international organizations promoting Western-style globalization, imperialism and, for good measure, Zionism.[33]

The massive turnout for the march dwarfed that of a concurrent pro-plan demonstration in Rabat, and led the government to shelve the plan for the time being. Although Morocco's stability, controlled political evolution, and steadily increasing links with the global market seemed assured for the time being, the lines in Morocco's quickening "culture wars" seemed to be increasingly drawn.

TUNISIA

Tunisia's Islamists have enjoyed a higher international profile than their Moroccan counterparts but suffer even greater repression. As in other cases in the

Middle East, the Tunisian Islamists' protests can be seen partly as a response to socioeconomic dislocations stemming from the complex processes of modernization and development. Also contributing is Tunisia's clogged political system. However, the most important factor has been the 'psychosocial alienation' that has resulted from the predominant Western liberal model of modernity.[34]

This model has been the objective of President Habib Bourguiba since Algeria's independence in 1956.[35] Notwithstanding Bourguiba's efforts to legitimize his policies in Islamic modernist terms, his initiatives brought more secularization than in any other Arab country. An example is the Personal Status Code, which guarantees equality between men and women in matters of divorce and forbids polygamy. A second example is the relatively large number of women in managerial and executive positions. President Zayn 'Abidin Ben 'Ali, who assumed power in November 1987, softened some of Bourguiba's strident secularism and put more emphasis on Tunisia's Arab-Islamic heritage. The regime permitted Islamists to run in elections as independents in 1989. Officially, they captured about 14 percent of the vote and came close to winning a majority in several urban areas. Some have claimed that the real percentage attained by Islamist candidates was 30–32 percent.[36] The regime quickly took notice and cracked down harshly on Islamists, banning the newly formed Nahda (Renaissance) Party and taking advantage of violent acts by some Islamists to imprison thousands of activists. Stern reprimands from international human rights organizations did not deter the regime.

For now, Ben 'Ali rules Tunisia with a firm hand and, unlike in Morocco, guided political pluralism is only in its infancy: all but nineteen of the 163 seats in Tunisia's parliament, elected in 1999, are held by the ruling Rassemblement Constitutionnel Democratique. This is an improvement from the early 1990s, when the parliament contained no opposition deputies, but marks no change since the 1994 elections. Economically, the Tunisians have followed a course similar to Morocco's, instituting structural reforms and obtaining good results. Tunisia's small population, reinforced by the lowest rate of population growth in the Arab world, its educated middle class, high rate of literacy, relatively high percentage of women in the work force, and European orientation make the state a less fertile ground for Islamists than other countries in the region. Nonetheless, the groundswell of support for Islamist movements during the 1970s and 1980s indicates that Tunisia is not immune from regionwide currents.

Like their counterparts elsewhere in North Africa and the Sunni world in general, Tunisia's Islamists have been influenced by Egypt's Muslim Brotherhood and the teachings of Sayyid Qutb and Pakistan's Mawlana Mawdudi.[37] Nonetheless, there was considerable talk during the 1980s within Islamist circles of developing a specifically "Tunisian Islam."[38] Part of the rationale was the rejection of the predominant Islamist view that legitimacy is solely divine, in favor of the idea of popular will as the source of legitimacy.[39] The Islamic notion of *shura* (consultation), declared Rashid Ghannushi, the movement's leading figure, legitimizes multiparty politics, alternation in power, and the protection of human rights.[40] In November 1995, Ghannushi and a group of non-Islamist exiled opposition members, including former Prime Minister Muhammad Mzali, published a joint communiqué appealing for democracy in Tunisia via the election of a parliament representing diverse views and political parties.[41] The problem, Ghannushi stressed, was the repressive Ben 'Ali regime and most Arab governments, for that matter, which rejected all notions of civil society (al-mujtama' al-madani). Ghannushi's avowed goal to promote a modernist-Islamic synthesis in opposition to the Tunisian regime's "superficial modernity" makes him one of the more interesting and original of contemporary Islamist thinkers.[42]

To be sure, his views are not entirely congruent with Western liberal values. As he said in one interview, state-building must begin with recognition of the umma's Arab and Islamic identity. Without first agreeing on this central pillar, the "cultural context" of state-society relations, there can be no stable, legitimate authority.[43] Once the identity question is resolved, he continued, democracy can be practiced. He did not address the place in society of those without an Arab-Islamic identity. Ghannushi, in exile in London, frequently speaks of the need to open a dialogue (hiwar) with the West, rejecting the "clash of civilizations" notion put forth by both Samuel Huntington and numerous Islamists. At the same time and in contrast to other Tunisian Islamists, his rhetoric has become increasingly radical in recent years.[44] His condemnations of the allegedly perfidious Western domination of the New World Order, praise for Sudan's regime as a state founded on Islamic concepts, and efforts to promote the cause of Algeria's FIS have weakened his credibility and appeal to Western governments. In a wide-ranging conversation with the New York Times, he repeatedly placed primary blame for excesses committed by Islamic regimes on Western "rejectionist attitudes" and justified the murder of Arab and Muslim intellectuals who had embraced secularism, referring to several as "the devil's advocate[s] . . . Pharaoh's witches. The educated who put their brains and their talent in the service of an oppressive regime have made their own decisions. They must bear the responsibility for their choice."[45]

Ghannushi has also repeatedly emphasized that Western hostility to Islam is due to the activities of Zionism, which, in order to retain aid and support, is striving to convince the West that following the collapse of communism and the failure of Arab nationalism, Islam is the new evil force in the world.[46] Speaking in closed sessions at radical Islamic conferences, his rhetoric was even more fiery:

"Zionism does not only target Arabs and Muslims. It targets goodness . . . the entirety of values that have crystallized in humanity. Every evil in the world, the Zionists are behind it. This is no exaggeration. There are so many evils in the world, and behind which are the Children of Israel."[47]

Speaking in May 1995 at the Royal Institute of International Affairs, Ghannushi expressed the hope that the Algerian crisis would soon be resolved in the Islamists' favor. This would be followed by a "swift end" to the deadlock in Tunisia, "either as a result of an initiative by the regime itself, which we would prefer, or due to a massive popular pressure, which is more likely to happen. However, should Algeria continue to bleed slowly, the political situation in Tunisia will move in the same direction, but slowly too."[48] It seems that Ghannushi may have been overly optimistic. His continued denunciations of the Tunisian regime throughout the remainder of the decade seemed to have no effect. The government, Ben 'Ali claimed, had "taken the wind out of the fundamentalists' sails" through wide-ranging economic and social reforms and the country's tradition of toleration and moderation. Left unmentioned were the regime's effective modes of repression. The immediate future for the Islamists in Tunisia does not appear to be a promising one.

ALGERIA

As for Algeria, nowhere has the *azma* been more acutely felt. The socioeconomic dimension is obviously crucial in explaining Algeria's slide into chaos. A generation of misguided, mismanaged "state capitalist" policies, the worldwide slump in the hydrocarbon sector beginning in the mid-1980s, rampant corruption, rapid population growth, and high unemployment all fueled the breakdown of the ruling FLN (Front de Liberation Nationale) regime and the Islamists' rise. Taken alone, however, the socioeconomic explanation for the rise of Islamism in Algeria is insufficient. Cultural aspects must be addressed as well.

Islam has always constituted the central component of collective identity in Algeria, dating back to the pre-colonial period, when Algeria was not a unified political unit. Under French rule, Islam served as a major divide between the colonial government and its subjects. The latters' refusal to abandon Islamic personal status laws enabled the French to avoid awarding them the legal rights of French citizenship and served as a barrier to the adoption of French culture. Furthermore, since Algeria was never fully Arabized, Islam unified Arabic- and Berber-speakers against the French, providing the religio-national content to the struggle for independence and serving as the kernel of Algerian nationalism.[49]

During the post-independence period, the ruling FLN elite sought to nationalize and manipulate Islam in the regime's service. Measures taken included the enactment of a personal status code in 1984 adhering closely to Islamic precepts, banning alcohol in some cities, making Friday the day of rest, promoting religious education in schools, and implementing an Arabization program in schools and public institutions. In order to advance Arabization, the regime imported schoolteachers from Egypt, many of them sympathizers of the Muslim

Brotherhood, who used their position to disseminate Islamist ideology. At the same time, the FLN regime, under Houari Boummedienne and then Chedli Benjedid, sought to wed Islam to the governing socialist revolutionary ideology and block any independent Islamic political activity, whether urban-reformist or rural-popular. It is thus not surprising that Algeria has not produced Islamist theoreticians comparable to Khomeini, Turabi, or Ghannoushi.[50]

Notwithstanding the regime's efforts to monopolize and manipulate Islam, signs of an Islamic revival outside authorized state structures were widespread during the 1970s and 1980s. The Islamist movement developed along two parallel paths: a public one, of educational and social activities in order to disseminate the Islamic ideology and way of life; and a violent one, led by Mustafa Bouyali, an ex-FLN fighter in the war of independence who attempted to promote an armed insurrection in the countryside between 1984 and 1987. The regime responded by placing hundreds of activists in detention. Bouyali and most of his men were killed in 1987, but the survivors would play important roles in the fighting during the 1990s.[51]

The 1988 food riots and subsequent political liberalization initiated by Benjedid prompted the Islamist organizations to unite under the banner of the Front Islamique du Salut (Islamic Salvation Front), better known as FIS. Unlike previous groupings, the FIS, led by Dr. 'Abbasi Madani, sought to seize power through the electoral process. It demonstrated remarkable mobilizing capabilities, gaining major victories in the 1990 municipal elections and the first round of the 1991 parliamentary elections. It owed its success to an effective use of its network of about 8,000 mosques throughout Algeria, an appropriating of the Islamic aspect of the FLN's governing vision,[52] and an explicit claim to be the new bearers of the FLN's torch and the authentic inheritor of its legacy. The FIS-FLN connection was further strengthened by the fact that Shaykh Madani, first among equals in the FIS leadership, was an early member of the FLN, and was even imprisoned for his activities for most of the 1954–1962 period. Also like the FLN, the FIS maintained a sort of collective leadership. But what was most important was that the FIS constituted a political body that gave primacy to political action over religious activities. The two more moderate, "gradualist" Islamist parties, Hamas, led by Mahfoud Nahnah, and al-Nahdah, headed by Shaykh 'Abdallah Djaballah, were completely overwhelmed by the FIS and won only minimal support in the 1990 and 1991 elections.[53]

Its two most prominent figures prior to their imprisonment in June 1991, Madani and 'Ali Belhadj, epitomize FIS's two faces. Madani, by almost forty years the older of the two holds a doctorate from the Institute of Education at the University of London. He has been unswerving in insisting on establishing an Islamic state governed by the *Shari'a* and on the need to reinstate allegedly Islamic norms, such as the separation of men and women in the workplace. Nonetheless, his tone prior to imprisonment was relatively benign and his commitment to political pluralism, while ultimately tactical, at least left room for a dialogue with other political forces in Algeria. He told an interviewer that pluralism was absolutely necessary for a just society, promising to make "Algeria a Hyde Park, not only for free expression but also for choice and behavior."[54]

While Madani was talking about Hyde Park, Belhadj, a young preacher based in a mosque in the overcrowded Bab al-Oued quarter of Algiers, was exerting a powerful appeal on the masses of deprived, frustrated youth. His militant message was unadorned: combat the "French" (meaning the secular forces in Algeria), transform Algeria into an Islamic state immediately, by elections, if possible, and by force if the authorities reject the peaceful transfer of power, and exact retribution on all those who have committed crimes against the people.[55]

Concurrently, the crystallization of the FIS out of a wide array of small groups, which coalesced following a cataclysmic political event, foreshadowed great diversity and lack of cohesion within the movement. In addition, the FIS leadership underestimated the army's refusal to relinquish its power as the real force in Algerian politics and its determination to fight for its privileges. Nevertheless, the Islamists were able to survive a brutal crackdown by the Algerian military authorities after January 1992 and to inflict heavy punishment of their own.

Apparently, they were able to attract activists from a variety of social backgrounds ranging from academics and ex-army officers to radical militants who had already served prison terms in the 1980s and the so-called "Afghans," Algerian veterans of the Afghanistan war against the Soviet-backed regime in Kabul. In particular, they attracted a continuous stream of desperate young men from the sprawling slums of Algeria's cities who had no hope of improving their dire economic conditions.[56]

The armed struggle against the regime has been waged by two loosely organized bodies. The larger was the l'Armée Islamique du Salut (AIS), known until May 1994 as the Mouvement Islamique Armée (MIA), which functioned as the FIS's armed wing. The other, smaller coalition of armed Islamist networks was the Group Islamique Armée (GIA).

The FIS strategy aimed at forcing the regime to accept an arrangement that would relegalize its activities and enable it to resume its bid for power through political means. For that purpose, it employed armed struggle as a means of leveraging the government and sought an alliance with non-Islamist opposition forces that would isolate the regime, expose it as illegitimate, and force it to compromise. These efforts bore fruit in the January 1995 "national contract" signed by representatives of eight opposition parties, meeting in Rome. The contract, whose main outlines were proposed by Madani and Belhadj, called for the "progressive return of civil peace," based on the relegalization of the FIS and freeing of jailed FIS activists in return for a gradual end to violence and its rejection as a means to attain power, negotiations for establishing a transitional government to prepare for multiparty elections, and the formation of an independent commission to investigate abuses of human rights.[57]

The regime, however, managed to split the Rome alliance by co-opting some its signatories and launched a series of constitutional measures during the 1995–1997 period designed to endow Algeria with political institutions that provided badly needed legitimacy while keeping real power in the army's hands. The semi-free presidential elections in November 1995, in which Gen. Liamine Zeroual won with a 61 percent majority, were followed by constitutional amendments approved in a referendum in November 1996 as well as by parliamentary and municipal elections on June 5 and October 23, 1997, respectively. Each time, the government party, the Rassemblement National Democratique (RND), secured a comfortable majority, often by rigging the electoral process.[58]

The FIS was forced into a reactive mode. Its organizational structures were almost paralyzed, having been outlawed by the army, while the physical separation between the detained leaders, Madani and Belhadj, the military commanders operating in the mountains, the shaykhs (political leaders in Algiers), whose operations were partially curtailed by the army, and the Executive Committee abroad, headed by Rabah Kabir, hampered its political activity.[59]

In the military sphere, the AIS attacked only army and other security forces units. It refrained from targeting the state's hydrocarbon facilities, possibly to demonstrate its national responsibility, thereby preserving a crucial source of revenues for the regime. Initially, FIS field commanders argued that the "best organization is no organization," but in view of the growing challenge by the GIA, the FIS National *Shura* (consultative) Council appointed Madani Merzaq, an Afghanistan veteran and former prayer leader, as the AIS "national emir" (commander) in March 1995. The appointment was not accepted easily, causing some defections among field commanders, but Merzaq was eventually able to consolidate his position as a major player in determining FIS's political line as well.[60]

The GIA, by contrast, adopted the purist approach, based on the teaching of Sayyid Qutb, which regards all of society as "apostate" unless it accepts the GIA's own strict interpretation of Islam, and consequently, rejected any suggestion of dialogue with the regime. Moreover, the GIA did not fight only the army, but targeted all representatives of Western culture such as intellectuals, athletes, scientists, and musicians and particularly "immodestly" dressed or Western-educated women. It viewed all those serving or collaborating with the "apostate" regime, including those using government facilities such as schools and buses, as deserving of death. Consequently, the GIA was responsible for some of the more shocking acts of murder and terror during the civil war, including burning villagers alive, hacking people with saws and axes, disemboweling women, and setting off car bombs in crowded city streets. In addition, GIA units abducted and raped hundreds of young women under the guise of "temporary marriages" (*zawaj mut'a*). A Shi'ite custom abhorred by Sunni Islam, it was adopted by Algerian Islamists who had fought in Afghanistan. GIA terror and its impact on the country's social and cultural life prompted one foreign journalist to observe that the GIA's "war against intellectuals" had begun to resemble a "Khmer Rouge-style slaughter of the elite."[61]

The army, too, employed brutal methods, including arbitrary and secret detention, torture, area bombing of suspected Islamist strongholds, and extrajudicial executions. It also set up loyalist militias comprising up to about 200,000 fighters. Some of these militias showed the same degree of ferocity demonstrated by the GIA, while others used their weapons to settle old tribal or clan feuds over land and water rights, or for Mafia-like extortion practices.[62]

Unlike the FIS, the GIA maintained its decentralized structure, which also exposed it to greater infiltration by the regime's intelligence services and resulted in the killings of several of its leaders. Moreover, it was divided between units adhering to the *Jazá'ira* (Algerianists, those subscribing to a typical Algerian model of Islam) and *Salafi* trends of the Algerian Islamist movement, as well as by personal rivalries, which occasionally ended in fighting and the elimination of rivals. Two national GIA amirs, Jamal Zeituni and 'Antar Zoubri, were deposed in July and December 1996, respectively, with Zeituni killed by government forces shortly after his deposition. In addition, various units associated with the *Jazá'ira* trend seceded from the movement, some rejoining the AIS while others tried to establish a middle course.[63]

The initial rivalry between the FIS and GIA escalated into actual fighting. The FIS constantly condemned the massacres carried out by GIA units as contrary to Islam and tarnishing its image. It accused the army of turning a blind eye, or even of manipulating the GIA, in order to turn people away from Islam. The GIA, for its part, regarded as a form of paganism attempts by the FIS to reach political accommodation with the regime and its apparent acceptance of democracy.[64]

By late 1997 it became evident that the military had gained the upper hand strategically, even though the Islamists could continue fighting and at times inflict heavy casualties. The FIS realized its weakness in the military and political arenas. Even more so, it sensed that the GIA actions were turning the people against the Islamists as a whole. Consequently, AIS commander Merzaq, after holding secret talks with the military, accepted the army's conditions for renewing a dialogue and declared a unilateral truce starting on October 1, 1997. Several GIA units gradually joined the truce, while others kept fighting. Occasionally, the AIS cooperated with the army in fighting the latter.[65] Opponents of the truce, located mainly outside Algeria, set up the FIS Coordination Council as an organized opposition within the movement.[66]

The unilateral truce deprived the FIS of almost any leverage on the government. FIS spokesmen conceded that the resort to violence after the 1992 coup had "benefited only the government" and exacted a heavy price from their movement. The Islamist movement realized, they added, that it was "essential" to manage the political arena peacefully and have "recourse to compromise." They advocated, therefore, a "Chilean-style solution," whereby a general amnesty would be decreed, following which the army would return to its barracks, refrain from politics, and allow a genuine electoral contest to take place. While seeking to allay fears of its ideology among secularists, the FIS insisted that it advocated a "Muslim democracy," which would not be "imbued with Western values" but which would apply the principles "common to all democracies."

They acknowledged, however, that while many unjust oppressive measures against women should be removed, women could not be legally equal to men.[67]

The army's tactical victory exacerbated factional infighting culminating in the forced resignation of President Zeroual on September 11, 1998. The new president, 'Abd al-'Aziz Bouteflika, who served as foreign minister under Boumedienne, was elected on April 15, 1999 with the army's backing and the withdrawal of the six opposition candidates.[68]

Although his authority was clearly subject to the army's approval, Bouteflika launched a policy of national reconciliation. It culminated in a clemency law, approved by an overwhelming majority in a referendum on September 16, 1999. He ruled out, however, the relegalization of the FIS, even under a new name. Several hundred GIA fighters responded to the amnesty, which enabled them to lay down their arms peacefully. The FIS, which felt cheated by the regime's continued refusal to relegalize it, could do little but threaten to withdraw from the truce, but it remained unclear how much credibility these threats had.[69]

By early 2001, the Algerian ruling elites were again secure in power, thanks to their ruthless determination to fight and to crucial mistakes by the Islamists. Despite internal divisions, the elites had remained largely unified in the struggle. The continuous flow of revenues from the hydrocarbon sector enabled the regime to sustain itself. Financial and political support by European countries, particularly France, and the United States proved important as well. Even more importantly, the atrocities committed by the GIA pushed important social sectors (e.g. workers, government employees, and peasants) to cooperate with the regime, however unpopular it was, because they feared the Islamists even more. Concurrently, the FIS failed to build a broad anti-government coalition, as Khomeini had done in the Iranian revolution, because its secular partners did not trust its declared adherence to political pluralism. GIA units, for their part, remained fragmented but were still able to carry out periodic attacks against government and civilian targets. However, these did not pose a strategic threat to the regime. While the regime has won the short-term military struggle, the Islamist alternative seems unlikely to vanish as long as the country's economic crisis remains unresolved and the political system unable to incorporate broad sectors of society.

The victory of the Algerian *pouvoir* over its Islamist challengers put to rest the notion of the inevitability of an Islamist triumph in North Africa. Even during the most difficult years of the Algerian civil war, however, it was clear that the diversity within the Maghrib, and the successful coping strategies of the Moroccan and Tunisian regimes toward their own Islamist movements, meant that Algeria's neighbors were far from being mere dominos waiting to fall into line behind a triumphant Algerian-driven Islamist order. Moreover, Algeria has always been *sui generis* in the Arab world. It had the least distinct historical identity in precolonial times of any of the Maghrib's geopolitical units. It experienced the most thorough colonization, the most brutal, violent independence struggle, the application of the Soviet/Eastern European model of development and political organization, and now, the most comprehensive collapse (Lebanon excepted). Other Arab regimes never imitated Algeria's model of development nor did Algeria ever really project power beyond its borders, apart from the vacuum in the western Sahara. Thus, if historical patterns are any guide, whatever the course of events in Algeria, its influence on its neighbors can be expected to be limited.

In any case, the real challenge facing Arab regimes in the Maghrib will continue to come from within, as they seek to reconcile their political cultures and domestic exigencies with the requirements of an increasingly globalized international system. The degree of mutual aid and succor among the Islamists (more of an Islamic "global village" than an "internationale"),[70] while not negligible, does not represent an irresistible force. As the experience of the Maghrib states during the last two decades shows, modern states, singly and in alliances, possess considerable capacities of their own.

NOTES

1. The *gharb*, writes Moroccan sociologist Fatima Mernissi, is "the place of darkness and the incomprehensible, always frightening. *Gharb* is the territory of the strange, the foreign . . . the place where the sun sets and where darkness awaits. It is in the West that the night snaps up the sun and swallows it; then all terrors are possible. It is there that *gharaba* (strangeness) has taken up its abode." As she also points out, in Arab-Islamic spatial terms, the land of the setting sun, the Far West, is *al-maghrib al-aqsa*, with not dissimilar connotations. Fatima Mernissi, *Islam and Democracy: Fear of the Modern World* (Reading, Mass.: Addison-Wesley, 1992) pp. 13–14.

2. Mohamed El Mansour, "Salafis and Modernists in the Moroccan Nationalist Movement," in John Ruedy (ed.), *Islamism and Secularism in North Africa* (New York: St. Martin's Press, 1996), pp. 61–62.

3. Jamil M. Abun-Nasr, *A History of the Maghrib in the Islamic Period* (Cambridge: Cambridge University Press, 1987), pp. 334–335.

4. Ibid, pp. 38–91; Jamil M. Abun-Nasr, "The Salafiyya Movement in Morocco: the Religious Bases of the Moroccan Nationalist Movement," in Albert Hourani (ed.), *St. Antony's Papers, Middle Eastern Affairs*, No. 3. (London, 1963); Mansour, "Salafis and Modernists," pp. 59–69.

5. Michael Hudson, *Arab Politics: The Search for Legitimacy* (New Haven: Yale University Press, 1977), p. 379.

6. Remy Leveau, "Reflections on the State in the Maghreb," in George Joffe (ed.), *North Africa: Nation, State and Region* (London: Routledge, 1993), p. 247.

7. Abdelbaki Hermassi, "State and Democratization in the Maghreb," in Ellis Goldberg, Resat Kasalen, and Joel Migdal (eds.), *Rules and Rights in the Middle East* (Seattle, University of Washington Press, 1993), pp. 106–107.

8. Kevin Dwyer, *Arab Voices* (Berkeley: University of California Press, 1991), p. 15; Ali El-Kenz, *Algerian Reflections on Arab Crises* (Austin: University of Texas Press, 1991).

9. Mernissi, *Islam and Democracy*, p. 56.

10. Hermassi, "State and Democratization," pp. 111–112.

11. Remy Leveau points out the irony that the term *amir al-mu'minin* did not appear in the initial text of the 1962 constitution. Ironically, "it was the representatives of the [political] parties who reintroduced divine right among the instruments of power." ("Islam et controle politique au Maroc," cited in Francois Burgat and William Dowell, *The Islamic Movement in North Africa* (Austin: University of Texas Press, 1993), p. 167, n. 3.

12. Henry Munson, *Religion and Power in Morocco* (New Haven and London: Yale University Press, 1993), makes a cogent argument to this effect, taking issue with Clifford Geertz's classic *Islam Observed: Religious Development in Morocco and Indonesia* (New Haven: Yale University Press, 1968).

13. Hassan II (Avec Eric Laurent), *Hassan II: Le Memoire d'un Roi. Entretiens* (Paris: Plons, 1993), p. 103.

14. Along the lines laid down by John Entelis, *Culture and Counterculture in Moroccan Politics* (Boulder: Westview Press, 1989). The term "modernizing monarchy" is taken from Hudson's *Arab Politics* (note 6) pp. 25–27, 165–229.

15. I. William Zartman, "King Hassan's New Morocco," in I. W. Zartman (ed.), *The Political Economy of Morocco* (New York: Praeger, 1987), pp. 1–33.

16. Elaine Combs-Schilling, *Sacred Performances: Islam, Sexuality and Sacrifice* (New York: Columbia University Press, 1989).

17. Bruce Maddy-Weitzman, "Morocco," in: B. Maddy-Weitzman (ed.), *Middle East Contemporary Survey (MECS)*, Vol. XXII, 1998 (Boulder: Westview Press, 2001), pp. 454–463.

18. Azzedine Layachi, *State, Society and Democracy in Morocco: The Limits of Associative Life* (Washington: Center for Contemporary Arab Studies, 1998); B. Maddy-Weitzman, "God, King, Country and . . . Civil Society? The Evolution of the Moroccan Polity in the 1990s," paper delivered at the annual conference of the Middle East Studies Association, Chicago, December 1998.

19. M. Al-Ahnaf, "Maroc. Le Code du statute personnel," *Monde Arab Maghreb-Machrek*, No. 145 (July–September 1994), pp. 11–12.

20. For an analysis of these trends, see B. Maddy-Weitzman, "Population Growth and Family Planning in Morocco," *Asian and African Studies*, Vol. 26, No. 1 (March 1992), pp. 63–80.

21. Interview with Mohamed Tozy, *Jeune Afrique*, February 9–15, 1999; Emad Eldin Shahin, *Political Ascent: Contemporary Islamic Movements in North Africa* (Boulder: Westview Press, 1998), pp. 186–187.

22. Mohammed Tozy, "Champ et contre champ politico-religieux au Maroc," cited by Burgat and Dowell, *The Islamic Movement in North Africa*, p. 170; *al-Majalla*, June 23–29, 1996.

23. Munson, *Religion and Power in Morocco*, pp. 153–158; Tozy interview in *Jeune Afrique*, February 9–15, 1999; Shahin, *Political Ascent*, pp. 179–181.

24. Shahin, *Political Ascent* pp. 188–192; Shahin, "Under the Shadow of the Imam," *Middle East Insight*, Vol.11, No. 2 (January–February 1995), pp. 42–43.

25. *Marco Hebdo Internatonal*, May 7–13, 1999.

26. Tozy interview in *Jeune Afrique*, February 9–15, 1999.

27. Burgat and Dowell, *The Islamic Movement in North Africa*, pp. 166–167.

28. Interview in the Casablanca daily *al-Bayane*, quoted by *Marco Hebdo Internatonal*, December 12–18, 1998.

29. *Al-Sharq al-Awsat*, January 9, 1999.

30. For the details of their activities, see *Jeune Afrique*, January 12–18, 1995.

31. See the statement by Driss Khalil, the minister of higher education, that certain Moroccan universities were "confronting a wave of Islamic fundamentalism." *Agence France Press*, April 24, 1995.

32. *Al-Quds al-'Arabi*, April 22, 1998 (WNC-Daily Report).

33. *Al-'Alam* (Rabat), 14 March 2000.

34. Susan Waltz, "Islamist Appeal in Tunisia," *Middle East Journal*, Vol. 40, No. 4 (Autumn 1986), pp. 651–670.

35. Nikkie Keddie makes the important point that Bourguiba's policies, e.g., the adoption of the Personal Status Code in 1956, were not simply blind imitations of Western policies (unlike those of Ataturk in Turkey), but contained features from the Shari'a. Keddie, "The Islamist Movement in Tunisia," *The Maghreb Review*, Vol. 11, No. 1 (1986), p. 26.

36. Burgat and Dowell, *The Islamic Movement in North Africa*, p. 234.

37. For the essence of their thinking and activities, see Yvonne Y. Haddad, "Sayyid Qutb: Ideologue of Islamic Revival," and Charles J. Adams, "Mawdudi and the Islamic State," in John L. Esposito (ed.), *Voices of Resurgent Islam* (New York: Oxford University Press, 1983), pp. 67–98, 99–133; and Emmanuel Sivan, *Radical Islam* (New Haven: Yale University Press, 1985), pp. 21–49.

38. See statement by Ahmad Enneifer, one of the Tunisian "progressive Islamists" who separated from Ghannushi, in Burgat and Dowell, *The Islamic Movement in North Africa*, pp. 217–218.

39. Norma Salem, "Tunisia," in Shireen T. Hunter (ed.), *The Politics of Islamic Revivalism* (Bloomington: Indiana University Press), p. 164.

40. Nicolas Beau, Rached Channouchi: "Penseur et Tribun," interview, *Le Cahiers De L'Orient*, no. 27, (1992), pp. 45–52; *The Observer*, January 19, 1992, quoted in Emad Eldin Shahin, "Tunisia's Renaissance Party," *Middle East Insight*, Vol. 11, No. 2 (January–February 1995), p. 41.

41. Marie Miran, "Tunisia," in Bruce Maddy-Weitzman (ed.) *MECS*, Vol. XIX, 1995 (Boulder: Westview Press, 1997), pp. 630–631.

42. For a detailed study of Ghannushi's thinking on key issues, see Khaled Elgindy, "The Rhetoric of Rashid Ghannushi," *Arab Studies Journal*, Vol. 3, No. 1 (Spring 1995), pp. 101–119.

43. *Al-Shira'*, October 24, 1994.

44. Michael Collins Dunn, "The Al-Nahda Movement in Tunisia: From Renaissance to Revolution," in Ruedy, (ed.), *Islamism and Secularism in North Africa*, pp. 149–165.

45. *New York Times*, January 9, 1994.

46. *Al-Shira'*, October 24, 1994—MSANEWS, July 8, 1995; text of speech at the Royal Institute of International Affairs, Chatham House, London, May 9, 1995—MSANEWS, May 23, 1995.

47. MSANEWS, May 23, 1995.

48. Daniel Zisenwine, "Tunisia," in Bruce Maddy-Weitzman (ed.), *MECS*, Vol. XXI, 1997 (Boulder: Westview Press, 1999), p. 701.

49. John Entelis, *Comparative Politics of North Africa* (Syracuse: Syracuse University Press, 1980), p. 105; Severine Labat, *Les Islamistes Algeriens: entre les urnes et le maquis* (Paris: Seul, 1995), pp. 23, 59–60; Mohammed Tozy, "Les tendances de l'islamisme en Algerie," *Confluences Mediterranee*, No. 12 (Automne 1994), pp. 51–54.

50. Boutheina Cheriet, "Islamism and Feminism: Algeria's 'Rites of Passage' to Democracy," in John P. Entelis and Phillip C. Naylor (eds.), *State and Society in Algeria* (Boulder: Westview Press, 1992), pp. 171–215; Mohammed Tozy, "Islam and the State," in I. William Zartman and William Mark Habeeb (eds.), *Polity and Society in Contemporary North Africa* (Boulder: Westview Press, 1993), pp. 108–109, 199–200.

51. Rabia Bekkar, "Taking Up Space in Tlemcen: The Islamist Opposition in Urban Algeria," *Middle East Report*, Vol. 22, No. 6 (November/December 1992), pp. 11–15.

52. Hugh Roberts, "A Trial of Strength: Algerian Islamism," in James P. Piscatori (ed.), *Islamic Fundamentalisms and the Gulf Crisis* (Chicago: American Academy of Arts and Sciences, 1991), p. 144.

53. Remy Leveau, *Le sabre et le turban* (Paris: Francois Burin, 1993), pp. 194–197; Hugh Roberts, "From Radical Mission to Equivocal Ambition: The Expansion and Manipulation of Algerian Islamism, 1979–1992," in Martin E. Marty and R. Scott Appleby (eds.), *Accounting for Fundamentalisms: The Dynamic Character of Movements* (The Fundamentalism Project, Vol. 4), (Chicago: University of Chicago Press, 1994), pp. 428–489.

54. *Al-Watan*, June 22—FBIS-NES, Daily Report (DR), June 27, 1990.

55. Roberts argues forcefully that Madani's and Belhadj's voices complemented rather than contradicted each other. For the richest, and at times most provocative analysis of regime-Islamist dynamics in Algeria up until the 1992 military coup, see Roberts, "From Radical Mission to Equivocal Ambition," pp. 428–489.

56. Gideon Gera, "Algeria," in B. Maddy-Weitzman (ed.), *MECS*, Vol. XVIII, 1994 (Boulder: Westview Press, 1996), p. 237; Meir Litvak, "Algeria," in B. Maddy-Weitzman (ed.), *MECS*, Vol. XIX, 1995 (Boulder: Westview Press, 1997), pp. 225–226.

57. Litvak, *MECS*, 1995, pp. 213–215.

58. Ibid, pp. 216–217, 219–222; Litvak, "Algeria," in *MECS*, Vol. XX, 1996 (Boulder: Westview Press, 1998), pp. 232–234; and "Algeria," *MECS*, in B. Maddy-Weitzman (ed.), Vol. XXI, 1997 (Boulder: Westview Press, 1998), pp. 266–269.

59. Litvak, *MECS*, 1996, p. 238; and *MECS*, 1997, pp. 274–275.

60. Litvak, *MECS*, 1995, p. 226; and *MECS*, 1997, pp. 273–274.

61. *The Independent*, February 1, 1995; Litvak, *MECS* 1995, p. 223; Litvak, *MECS* 1997, pp. 279–280; *al-Hayat*, January 12, April 14; *al-Sharq al-Awsat*, March 6; *al-Wasat*, June 1, 1998.

62. *Mideast Mirror*, March 6, 1998; *al-Majalla*, March 15–21, 1998.

63. Litvak, *MECS*, 1996, pp. 237–238; Litvak, *MECS*, 1997, p. 283.

64. Litvak, *MECS*, 1995, pp. 227–228; Litvak, *MECS*, 1996, pp. 236–237; *al-Hayat*, January 12, 1998.

65. Litvak, *MECS*, 1997, pp. 273–274.

66. Litvak, *MECS*, 1997, p. 275; *al-Hayat*, January 9; *al-Wasat*, May 11; *Middle East International*, June 19, 1998.

67. *Le Nouvel Observateur*, January 15–21, 1998.

68. *Al-Watan*, April 17, 1999 (WNC-DR).

69. *Mideast Mirror*, June 8 and July 28, 1999, and January 7, 2000.

70. We owe this distinction to Martin Kramer.

6

Hizballah

Between Armed Struggle and Domestic Politics

Eyal Zisser

On May 24, 2000, Israeli forces completed their withdrawal from south Lebanon, ending what Israeli Prime Minister Ehud Barak called Israel's involvement in "the Lebanese tragedy."[1] The military's definition of this pullout as "an achievement and even an extraordinary success"[2] would be judged by whether the future brought peace along the border or a continued battle with Hizballah. In Lebanon, Hizballah activists led celebrations at what they considered a huge victory for the organization. After all, this struggle had been a major reason for the group's establishment in 1983 and one of the main factors making it a leading force within the Shi'ite community in Lebanon.

One cannot easily downplay this achievement by Hizballah, since throughout the 1990s it had remained almost the sole group in any Arab state committed to implementing an armed struggle against Israel. It would be argued that Hizballah achieved what no other Arab country or army had been able to do: oust Israel from Arab territory without the Arab side committing to any concession.[3]

As an Islamist movement seeking influence and power within Lebanon in order to transform Lebanese society, however, Hizballah found that its victory brought serious problems and posed serious decisions about its future. After all, it was the long, successful struggle against Israel that maintained the group, bolstered its standing within the Shi'ite community, and made it strong in Lebanon's public opinion and political system. The same factor gave it foreign support, especially from Iran and Syria. After the Israeli withdrawal, the organization lost some of its luster in the face of day-to-day challenges from Lebanese life and the harsh choices of Lebanese domestic politics.

In its favor, Hizballah was deeply rooted in the Shi'ite and Lebanese experience and had been preparing for a decade to make this transition. It strengthened its political wing, information apparatus, and widespread system of educational, health and social services. Clearly, Hizballah will survive. The question is how its new status will affect its goals and tactics, the nature of its Islamist campaign to transform the country, and the internal affairs of Lebanon itself. One critical question is to what extent Hizballah will undergo a process of "normalization," becoming more of a political party than an armed militia and a reformist rather than a revolutionary movement. If this happens, Hizballah would be cut down to its "natural size" as one more Shi'ite communal party and interest group, making deals with rivals in the Lebanese political mosaic, vying for prestige, power, and patronage.

The organization is quite aware of this danger and is trying to meet it. One potential solution would be to accept this framework and preserve a quiet south Lebanon along the border with Israel. Another would be to renew its armed struggle, precisely to revive the past days of glory. In any event, what is clear is that an important and decisive chapter in the organization's history has ended; but its story is far from over.

Hizballah stormed onto the Lebanese scene in late 1983 with a series of attacks on Western and Israeli targets in the country that brought hundreds of casualties, leading the United States and France to end their involvement in Lebanon, and Israel to complete a quick withdrawal of its direct presence.[4] The military struggle against the West, and especially against Israel, has been since the early 1980s one of the organization's main activities. This was an expression of the influence of two major events in Middle East history that set the group on its path. One was Iran's Islamic revolution, a direct source of inspiration and role model for the organization. By the early 1980s Hizballah had already bound itself to Tehran and since then has received Iran's economic and political support. The second event was the Israeli invasion of Lebanon in June 1982, which led the Shi'ite community onto the path of a violent struggle against the Israeli presence in south Lebanon. This struggle became an important focal point for the organization, one from which it drew legitimacy and support at home and abroad.

Despite all this, the organization's emergence came purely from the Lebanese context, as a result of domestic processes in Lebanon and within the Shi'ite community. The most prominent of these factors were: the Shi'ite community's increasing demographic weight in Lebanon's population (from 19 percent in 1950 to more than 40 percent at the end of the 1990s); increased migration of community members from rural regions in the Biqua'a and south to slums on the outskirts of cities; and, as a result, a stronger religious identification of

Shi'ites that turned Shi'ite clerics into the community's leaders, replacing the traditional leadership based on the notable Shi'ite families.[5]

These processes eventually turned the Shi'ite community from a weak, passive, and to some extent marginal community in the Lebanese arena into an active, powerful community struggling for a central role. This effort was first led by Musa al-Sadr, a cleric born in Iran who arrived in Lebanon in 1959 and became the community's most prominent leader. In 1975, with the outbreak of civil war, al-Sadr founded the Amal movement as a military force to strengthen the community's bargaining power. In the wake of al-Sadr's disappearance during a visit to Libya in 1978, he was replaced as Amal leader by Nabih Barri, a lawyer by training and not a cleric.[6]

Even before his disappearance, there emerged those who opposed Musa al-Sadr, believing that the Shi'ites should adopt a more radical worldview. These people refused to accept Amal's moderate line, as inspired by Musa al-Sadr, to improve the Shi'ites' status based on accepting Lebanon's existing political system. With al-Sadr gone and in the shadow of Iran's Islamic revolution and Israel's invasion of Lebanon, these people established Hizballah, whose activities began in 1983.[7]

Hizballah's platform, published in February 1985, left no room for doubt regarding its long-term objectives. These focused on the establishment of an Islamic republic in Lebanon, based on the Iranian model, as a stage in establishing a united Islamic state all over the Islamic world. At the same time, there was an obvious attempt by the organization to don a cloak of pragmatism and moderation, mainly in the Lebanese domestic context.[8] This reflected its realization that it was operating within the limitations of Lebanese realities that made it difficult for Hizballah to implement its ideological concepts. Lebanese society is a mosaic of religious and ethnic communities, none of which has the ability to impose itself on its rivals. In addition, the Shi'ite community was an insignificant minority on the eastern shores of the Mediterranean, outnumbered by a sometimes hostile Sunni majority. Finally, it seemed for a long time that it was Amal and not Hizballah that enjoyed support from the majority in the Shi'ite community.

Hizballah reached the pinnacle of its power within the Lebanese Shi'ite community in the late 1980s, when it gained both political and military control over most of West Beirut and large areas of south Lebanon. However, it was at this high point that Hizballah found itself faced with challenges threatening its continued activities and even its very existence. First and foremost among these problems was the Ta'if Agreement signed in October 1989, ending the Lebanese civil war—during which Hizballah had flourished—and marking the start of a process of rehabilitating the state institutions and disarming most of the militias. Hizballah was also forced to give up weapons, although it was permitted to continue carrying arms in south Lebanon in the struggle against Israel. Moreover, the Ta'if Agreement laid the foundation for establishing a new Maronite-Sunni order in Lebanon, with Syrian backing and support, relegating the larger

Shi'ite community to the sidelines. Another challenge facing the organization was the Middle East peace process that began in 1991 and threatened to bring an end to the organization's struggle against Israel, thus seriously weakening one of its sources of legitimacy and power.[9]

In the face of these realities, Hizballah reinvented itself as a pragmatic organization, ostensibly ready to abandon commitment to its ideological concepts or at least to postpone their implementation until far into the future. At first, the organization expressed opposition to the Ta'if Agreement and was apparently responsible for the assassination of Lebanon's President Rene Mu'awad, in November 1989, a way to prevent the agreement's implementation.[10] However, it quite quickly came to terms with the "Tai'f Republic" and began taking steps toward becoming integrated into the latter's institutions.

Hizballah participated in the 1992 parliamentary elections and its "Loyalty to the Resistance" slate won eight seats. It also participated in the parliamentary elections of 1996 and 2000, and in the 1998 municipal elections.[11] Throughout these years, Hizballah engaged in contacts designed to bring it into the government coalition. As the organization's Secretary General Na'im al-Qasim explained: "Our decision to participate in the parliamentary elections in 1992 meant that it was possible to participate in the government . . . [d]epending only on what government it is to be, and so far as we are concerned it has nothing to do with any matter of principle."[12]

In all of this, it was possible to observe a clear process of Lebanonization that the organization had undergone, as part of which it had in fact accepted the existence of the Lebanese state and had begun to work toward integration into its institutions. Already in the organization's platform for the 1992 parliamentary elections, it stated that Hizballah would work toward preserving "One Lebanon," though adding that "preserving one Lebanon and its affiliation with its Muslim and Arab environment, makes it incumbent on all of us to adhere to the resistance to the Zionist occupation and the liberation of the occupied lands."[13]

In April 1997, as part of its effort to establish dialogue and even cooperation with all parties and political forces active in Lebanon—including the Maronites—Hizballah's Secretary-General Hasan Nasrallah declared that: "Hizballah is a movement whose members are Lebanese, its leadership is Lebanese, the decision is Lebanese and it is made by a Lebanese leadership. The movement is fighting on Lebanese soil for the cause of liberating Lebanese territory and for the honor and freedom of the Lebanese people and the nation in general. . . . Hizballah is an Islamic-Lebanese movement."[14]

In addition to its moves in the political arena, the organization expanded its activity within the Shi'ite community. With Iran's generous assistance, it established a network of educational and cultural institutions, and also health and social welfare services. The latter included an Islamic health authority that operated pharmacies, clinics and even hospitals where thousands of people were treated every day. The organization also established a construction company that not only built houses, mosques and schools, but also paved roads and even supplied water to Shi'ite villages. Particularly prominent in all of this was its contribution to the reconstruction of thousands of houses damaged in the battles with Israel in south Lebanon.[15] In addition, Hizballah maintained a Martyrs' *(shuhada)* Fund, which provided assistance to thousands of families of dead, injured and imprisoned Shi'ites.[16] However, it should be borne in mind that as the rehabilitation of the state institutions in Lebanon progressed, they began pushing aside and limiting the organization's activities, and it was forced to concentrate on matters of education, health, and social welfare.

Of course, all this provided the basis for transforming Hizballah from a radical militia movement to a social-political organization which had at first tried to present itself as an alternative to the Lebanese state but gradually came to terms with the state's existence and slowly became part of the political order.

In view of the progress made in the Arab-Israeli peace process, particularly in the years 1992 to 1996, the organization's leaders began hinting that they might be ready to accept an Israeli-Lebanese peace agreement and to end the armed struggle against Israel. Hizballah apparently wanted to adopt the approach of the Islamist organizations in Egypt and Jordan regarding the peace process. They had come to the realization that they were unable to prevent a peace agreement between Israel and the Arab regimes in their countries, but also hoped and believed they could prevent the normalization of relations between the Arab world and Israel.[17]

Nevertheless, the impasse in the peace process, especially on the Syrian and Lebanese tracks during the latter half of the 1990s, allowed the organization to refrain from reaching a decision on the question of its future character and path and to continue to enjoy the best of both worlds. On the one hand, it worked toward integration into the Lebanese political system, becoming a legitimate part of the Lebanese political mosaic. On the other hand, it carried on the struggle against Israel, thus preserving its image and standing as a radical armed movement. There can be no doubt that the organization increased its circle of supporters thanks to its political activities, as well as its social welfare activities. But this was insignificant compared to the prestige and support gained within the Shi'ite community and Lebanese public opinion, as well as from Syria and Iran, because of its armed struggle against Israel. This struggle differentiated it from its rivals in the Shi'ite or Lebanese arena, made it unique, and added to its renowned glory.

In view of all this, the organization's determination to ensure Israel's continued presence in south Lebanon as much as possible is understandable. Ostensibly, one might have expected Hizballah to encourage the voices that began to be heard in Israel beginning in the mid-1990s calling for Israeli's unilateral withdrawal from south Lebanon. All it had to do was to hint that it was ready to end its armed struggle against Israel if this happened, thus pushing Israeli policy and public debate toward a quick withdrawal. However, exactly the opposite occurred. After all, Israel's continued presence in south Lebanon allowed the organization to maintain a struggle against it that ensured the organization's relative advantage over all other Lebanese forces, especially its Shi'ite rivals.

Thus the organization spoke in vague terms every time it was called upon the discuss the question of its future in the event that Israel unilaterally withdrew from south Lebanon. Although the organization's spokesmen repeatedly claimed that its activities were focused on driving Israel out of Lebanon, they also repeated their commitment to the liberation of all Palestine, thus implying the possibility of continued armed struggle against Israel even if the latter withdrew its forces to the international border with Lebanon.[18]

Thus Hizballah gained the image of defending the Shi'ites of south Lebanon.[19] In the weeks before and after the Israeli withdrawal, the organization became a symbol and object of admiration throughout the Arab and Muslim world. Even the Lebanese government, which had viewed the organization as an element undermining its sovereignty, recognized it as representing Lebanese patriotism and thus worthy of support. A clear expression of international recognition was the meeting between UN Secretary-General Kofi Annan and Hasan Nasrallah during the former's administration because of the central role the UN had played and would play in Israel's withdrawal from south Lebanon.[20]

Thus, the withdrawal from south Lebanon allowed the organization to hold victory celebrations and take up the positions Israel had evacuated. Hizballah's activists became lords over the region, while the Lebanese government was wary of deploying its forces and enforcing its sovereignty there. The organization even began organizing visits of Lebanese as well as Arab tourists to areas in south Lebanon from which Israel had withdrawn, during which the big thrill for tourists was organized stone-throwing at the Fatma Gate toward Israeli soldiers across the border. Nevertheless, the organization was careful to preserve order and calm along the border, and even prevented acts of vengeance against South Lebanese Army (SLA) soldiers who surrendered to it. These soldiers were turned over to the Lebanese authorities for trial.[21]

However, this alleged victory over Israel may be revealed as a false one and may mark the beginning of Hizballah's decline in standing and prestige. After all, having no battle with Israel may in the future cost the organization some of its dynamism, uniqueness, and foreign support. It was the struggle against Israel that had effectively prevented the organization from sinking into the Lebanese political quagmire and becoming just one of many political parties operating in Lebanon.

An example of the serious problem already facing Hizballah was provided several weeks after the withdrawal from south Lebanon by the death of two Hizballah fighters in the village of Markaba in south Lebanon during a battle against the rival group Amal for control over the area Israel had left. The leaders of both groups were quick to calm things down and to present the incident as a local affair. Yet such clashes could occur many times in the future, and the struggle for influence will remain intense.[22]

Amal is indeed emerging as a serious rival of Hizballah in the battle for control of the Shi'ite street. Amal has a certain advantage over Hizballah in that it is a more deeply entrenched organization headed by a pragmatic, moderate leadership. Amal's approach reflects recognition of the Lebanese reality, and its readiness to use that framework for promoting Shi'ite interests can make it a more effective lobbying group. Many Shi'ites do indeed prefer Amal and view Hizballah as too radical. Amal's largely secular leadership also appeals more to many individuals.

The power balance and Amal's advantages over Hizballah may be seen in the parliamentary elections of the 1990s, and in the 1998 municipal elections in which Amal's candidates gained control over many Shi'ite strongholds in south Lebanon and the Biqua'a. Among these were the city of Tyre, the largest Shi'ite concentration in the south, and Baalbek, the largest and most important town in the Lebanese Biqa'a. Until then both had been considered Hizballah strongholds.[23]

However, the struggle against Amal is only one of the series of challenges facing Hizballah. In July 1997, Shaykh Subhi al-Tufayli, former Hizballah secretary-general who left the organization when he lost a bid to lead it, announced the founding of a new organization called the "Revolution of the Hungry." Tufayli had hoped through this movement to lead a campaign of civil disobedience for the purpose of advancing the Shi'ite community, which he claimed had been neglected by the governing institutions as well as by the leaderships of both Amal and Hizballah.[24]

The new movement's founding was a kind of coming full circle for Hizballah, and also for Amal. After all, both were founded as protest movements by sectors of the Shi'ite community dissatisfied with the high-handedness and ineffectiveness of the current leaders, viewing them as part of an indifferent establishment. Hizballah's own creation expressed the criticisms of many Shi'ite clerics regarding Amal's moderate position and readiness to integrate into the existing Lebanese order. In addition, the founding of Hizballah was also an expression of frustration by many in the Shi'ite community who had not gained influence or leadership in Amal institutions. Thus, Hizballah was not just a militant group but also a fascinating coalition of forces within the Shi'ite community working toward advancing their interests under the guise of a comprehensive effort to improve the status of the Shi'ite community.[25] Yet now Hizballah had also become institutionalized and the object of criticism by those who felt left out by its composition.

As Musa al-Sadr had done before him, Muhammad Husayn Fadlallah, the spiritual leader of Hizballah, held these elements together, assisted by the anti-Israel struggle as a political and ideological glue.[26] However, it is clear that among these political and social forces that have joined together in Hizballah, there are fissures and differences of opinion on political and personal grounds which have long been pushed aside because of the priority granted to the struggle against Israel but in time might break out onto the surface.

One problem, which also affects Hizballah's relationship to Iran, is Fadlallah's pretensions to the role of Shi'ite's supreme spiritual leader (Marj'a Taqlid), a position that became vacant with the death of Ayatollah Ruhollah Khomeini in

1989. In this ambition, Fadlallah found himself in confrontation with Iran's spiritual leader Ayatollah 'Ali Khamene'i. Thus far, the organization has indeed avoided involvement in this confrontation but at the price of distancing itself somewhat from Fadlallah.[27] The question of religious leadership over the Shi'ites remains unresolved and could cast a threatening shadow over Iranian-Hizballah relations and even over the organization's internal cohesion.

However, Hizballah's main problem is rooted, as with Amal, in the fact that the group has become a part of the Lebanese political establishment. This is illustrated by its willingness, even eagerness, to join the Lebanese government. It is therefore no wonder that now Hizballah is being accused of no longer reflecting the misery and distress of the Shi'ite community in Lebanon, a claim on which Tyfayli wants to build. There is no doubt that the emergence of Tyfayli caused Hizballah considerable embarrassment. Indications of the organization's difficulty in directly facing up to Tufayli can be seen in its readiness to support the Lebanese government's moves against Tufayli and his movement.

The Lebanese government issued a warrant for Tufayli's arrest and took steps to prevent his supporters' activities. However, this was not enough to prevent Tufayli from continuing his efforts, although he maintained a low profile and for a time even went underground.[28] Moreover, in July 2000 he appeared at the graveside of the late Syrian President Hafiz al-Assad in Qurdaha on the Syrian shore for a condolence call and prayers for the soul of the departed. This showed Tufayli's aspirations to continue an active role in the Lebanese scene but also, more important, the fact that he enjoys the support and backing of Syria, which apparently wishes to use him as a card against the Lebanese regime and Hizballah.[29]

Hizballah, of course, remains a well-established, deep-rooted organization with broad support from the Shi'ite community, not to mention backing from Syria and Iran. Yet if Hizballah provides neither its constituents the passion of anti-Israel struggle nor its patrons a useful card in regional conflicts, how might this base be eroded?

Israel's withdrawal brought to the fore other issues on the Lebanese agenda. For some, especially the hard-core Maronites, the new focus is on Syrian presence in Lebanon, and voices have already been heard calling for the departure of Syrian forces from Lebanon.[30]

Others, especially members of the Shi'ite community, have an entirely different agenda and set of priorities. They are well aware that the new Lebanese order arising from the Syrian-backed Ta'if Agreement has left Lebanon a country under a Maronite-Sunni hegemony. The balance of power between these two communities, which have ruled Lebanon together since the founding of that state in 1943, has become more equal. Nevertheless, the Shi'ite community, which is now the largest community in Lebanon, has remained discriminated against in everything that has to do with apportioning of financial and regime resources.

Therefore, it may be assumed that the Shi'ites will make their voices heard demanding a fair share of the Lebanese national pie. Experience teaches that these demands could develop, sooner or later, into a violent confrontation, especially since they represent not just hunger for political power and resources, but also real economic distress in the urban slums, Biaq'a and the south. It may be assumed that in such a situation in the future, Hizballah will play a substantial, albeit not exclusive, role in the Shi'ite community's struggle. Yet with Syria opposing its ambitions, Iran reluctant to become too entangled in internal Lebanese politics, and other groups fighting Hizballah (instead of cheering it on against Israel), this would be a far more difficult period for the organization.

Of course, it cannot be assumed that the group's struggle against Israel is over, especially since such a strategy has certain attractions. Yet if Hizballah were to be responsible for renewing a cross-border war with Israel (on behalf of the unpopular Palestinians) and for bringing Israeli attacks on the south (bringing new flights of refugees and a halt to or even reversal of reconstruction), an anti-Israel battle would be far less popular than it was in the past.

The death of Hafiz al-Assad undoubtedly upset the apple cart from Syria's point of view. The Syrians had a clear interest in encouraging Hizballah to continue its struggle against Israel along the Israeli-Lebanese international border. After all, in Syria's view, shedding Israeli blood in south Lebanon gave Syria the only powerful bargaining chip it had in pressuring Israel to accept Damascus's conditions for an Israeli-Syrian peace agreement. Hafiz al-Assad had raised this kind of use of violence to gain his political objectives to a fine art. He did not eschew brinkmanship, being prepared to deal with possible escalation and flare-up.

With Assad's passing, though, and given his son and successor Bashar's clear interest in firmly establishing his status at home, Syria's interest or temptation in risking a border war that could escalate into a direct Syrian-Israel confrontation has diminished. Israeli spokesmen have on more than one occasion warned that any escalation along the border will force Israel to strike with unprecedented force again Syrian targets in Lebanon, with all that would entail.[31]

As for Iran, its distance from the Israeli-Arab arena of confrontation spurred it on to ignite fires there. After all, it was Iran's regime that reaped the fruits of Hizballah's achievements—which comprised the Islamic revolution's only foreign success—without paying any price at all for them. Thus, Iran has a basic interest in fanning the flames along the border, though this might be limited by that country's own internal struggle.

Nevertheless, the final decision was, and remains, in Hizballah's hands. The organization is aware of the great profits it could gain with the renewal of the struggle against Israel, but it also knows what harm might be done to its image and status inside Lebanon if its actions create a conflagration that could spread all over Lebanon. In such an event, it could lose a great deal of its legitimacy both inside Lebanon and in the international arena, as well as the support of the Shi'ite community, which might come to see it more as provocateur than as protector.

The organization has preferred to remain vague and to spread contradictory messages regarding its future path. For example, at funeral services for members of the organization killed in the clashes with Amal in Markaba in July 2000, Hizballah's Deputy Secretary General Na'im al-Qasim declared, "There are those who tell us how nice things are at present, is peace not sweet and is reaching an understanding with Israel not logical and desirable? On the other hand, there are those who now wish to turn into revolutionaries although they were not like that in the past, and they ask why we are not shooting at Israeli soldiers standing opposite us . . . We answer all of these people that we believe in Jihad and resistance and we will not deviate from this belief, but we will choose our own tactics and will not be dragged along by provocation. We conduct ourselves with wisdom, intelligence and Jihad, in a manner that incorporates all of this. Therefore we will not show our hand."[32] On another occasion, Na'im added: "This stage [in the struggle against Israel] has not finished, in view of the fact that the Palestinian [track of the peace negotiations] is in trouble, the Syrian track is stuck and the other elements of the Arab-Israeli conflict have also remained unchanged."[33]

The organization's Secretary-General Hasan Nasrallah explained in an interview that: "Hizballah is based on opposition to the Zionist project in our region. Hizballah adheres to this idea . . . The expulsion of Israel from the region and the liberation of Palestine and Jerusalem form the Hizballah's principal belief, and as such they are more sacred than a set goal . . . However, the question before us is our order of priorities in the next stage. There is no doubt that Hizballah enjoys a certain status in the Arab world. We want to preserve this and harness this status in favor of the awakening of the entire nation, to reinforce the condition of hostility towards our Israeli enemy to ensure that Israel was and has remained our enemy. Towards this end, we will invest efforts in formulating our opposition to normalization, and in order to perpetuate the isolation and siege of Israel, at the level of the people and after that at the cultural and economic level."[34]

However, the organization did take care to retain a pretext to continue its struggle against Israel, at the time and place it chooses. This pretext focuses on the claim that Israel's withdrawal is not complete, since it has retained some Lebanese territory. Reference is mainly to the Shab'a Farms, which Lebanon claims form part of its lands. Israel claims, however, and the UN agrees, that they are part of the Golan Heights, in other words part of Syria, and therefore Israel does not have to withdraw from them in the framework of UN Resolution 425. Hizballah can hardly count on Syria to agree that this land should be given to Lebanon.

The issue of the Lebanese prisoners, 'Abd al-Karim 'Ubayd and Mustafa Dirani, being held by Israel as leverage to obtain the release of a captured Israeli airman has remained an open issue for the organization. Moreover, Hizballah's military wing continues to operate and is deployed like any army along the border with Israel. It has established observation points and armed patrols along the border.

A major regional crisis as a result of the collapse of the Israeli-Palestinian negotiations or the lack of any progress in the Syrian-Israeli track may encourage

Iran and Syria, Hizballah's main allies, to pressure it to resume military struggle against Israel. The organization may choose as an alternative option the resumption of terror activity against Israeli and Jewish targets outside Israel, or use Palestinians living in Lebanon. Indeed, according to Israeli intelligence sources, Hizballah has been training Palestinians, mainly members of the Islamic Jihad under Ramadan Shalah, for this purpose. Some of these individuals already took part in the beginning of 2000 in some Hizballah attacks against Israeli targets in south Lebanon.[35]

Indeed, on October 7, 2000, a few days after the eruption of the Palestinian intifada, Hizballah abducted three Israeli soldiers in the Shaba'a Farms region. A few days later, Hasan Nasrallah announced that his men had kidnapped another Israeli senior reserve officer, promising to continue the struggle against Israel along the border.[36] In the months that followed, Hizballah continued its attacks in the Shaba'a region. For some time, Israel refrained from any retaliation but, on the night of April 16, 2001, the Israeli air force attacked a Syrian radar position in Mt. Lebanon, signaling the beginning of a new policy in Lebanon. The attack was a response to an attack by Hizballah on an Israeli position in the Shaba'a Farms three days earlier.[37] Although Hizballah continued its attack against Israeli targets in the Shaba'a Farms, it was clear that the new Israeli policy increased Hizballah's dilemma as to what should be its future course. The increasing criticism in Lebanon against the attacks on Israel, as endangering Lebanon's political stability and economic growth, led to an apologetic response from Hizballah, for example, a declaration by Muhammad Ra'd, Nasrallah's deputy, in summer 2001, according to which the Hizballah would take into consideration the tourist season in Lebanon before making any military moves against Israel.[38]

Thus, while Israel had not been able to stop all attacks by its withdrawal, it had created a political situation that at least constrained Hizballah and forced it to confine most attacks to one small part of the border area.

To conclude, the Israeli withdrawal from south Lebanon should be considered a big achievement for Hizballah. At the same time this achievement presents the organization with a difficult dilemma: whether to end its military struggle against Israel and become an ordinary Lebanese political party or to continue the struggle against Israel with all its consequences. Within this choice is embedded an equally hard, though less obvious, problem, forcing Hizballah to transform itself from a revolutionary to a reformist group in trying to make Lebanon an Islamic state.

Choosing armed struggle abroad and revolution at home would isolate Hizballah and reduce its base of support. But selecting an end to foreign struggle and reformism at home takes away Hizballah's past political advantages and opens it to splits and complaints that it has failed or become an establishment group. Thus, the possible "normalization" of Hizballah may become Israel's revenge on the organization that first helped force it to remain on the south Lebanon battlefield and then helped force it to withdraw from that area.

NOTES

1. *Ha'aretz*, May 25, 2000.

2. *Ha'aretz*, July 28, 2000.

3. See Hizballah's Secretary-General Hasan Nasrallah's interview with al-Jazira TV, May 27, 2000; see also: <http://www.moqawama.org> (Hizballah's official Web site).

4. For historical background on the Hizballah see Eyal Zisser, "Hizballah in Lebanon—At the Crossroads," in Bruce Maddy-Weitzman and Efraim Inbar (eds.), *Religious Radicalism in the Greater Middle East* (London: Frank Cass, 1997), pp. 90–110; Waddah Sharrara, *Dawlat Hizballah, Lubnan Mujtama'a Islamiyya* (*Hizballah's State, Lebanon—an Islamic Society*) (Beirut: Dar al-Nahar li-Nashr, 1996); Hala Jaber, *Hezbollah, Born with a Vengeance* (New York: Columbia University Press, 1997); Shimon Shapira, *Hizbullah bein Iran ve Levanon* (*Hizbullah between Iran and Lebanon*) (Tel Aviv: Am Oved, 2000).

5. For more see Foud Ajami, *The Vanished Imam—Musa Sadr and the Shia of Lebanon* (Ithaca: Cornell University Press, 1986), pp. 16–23.

6. Ibid., pp. 125-140; see also Richard Augustus Norton, *Amal and the Shi'a: Struggle for the Soul of Lebanon* (Austin: University of Texas Press, 1987).

7. See Shapira, pp. 77–133.

8. Hizballah, *Nass al-Risala al-Maftuha alati Wajahatha Hizballah ila al-Mustad'afin fi Lubnan* (*Hizballah's Open Letter to the Oppressed in Lebanon*) (Beirut: n.p., February 1985).

9. Zisser, pp. 99–107; see also William Harris, *Faces of Lebanon* (Princeton: Markus Weiner Publishers, 1996), pp. 237–326.

10. William B. Harris, "Lebanon," in Ami Ayalon (ed.), *MECS* (*Middle East Contemporary Survey*), Vol. 13 (1989), (Boulder: Westview Press, 1991). p. 524.

11. Harris, "Lebanon," in Ami Ayalon (ed.), *MECS*, Vol. 16 (1992), pp. 598–608; see also Harris, *MECS*, Vol. 20 (1996), pp. 490–495, and Vol. 22 (1998), pp. 414–416; Nizar Hamzeh, "Lebanon's Hizballah: From Islamic Revolution to Parliamentary Accommodation," *Third World Quarterly*, Vol. 14, No. 2 (1993), pp. 321–337.

12. Radio Nur, November 3, 1997.

13. Radio Nur, August 5, 1992.

14. See an interview with Hasan Nasrallah, *al-Sharq al-Awsat*, March 16, 1997; Da'irat al-'Alaqat al-'Amma wal-I'lam fi Mu'assasat Jihad al-Bina', *Sit Sanawat min al-Jihad wal-Bina'* (*Six years of Jihad and of Construction*) (Beirut: n.p., 1994).

15. Hala Jaber, *Hezbollah, Born with a Vengeance*, pp. 145–168; Shapira, pp. 140–149.

16. See Eli Hurvitz, *Ha-Dereg Ha-Tsva'i shel Ha-Hizballah, Diyukan Hevrati* (*The Military Wing of Hizballah: A Social Profile*) (MA Thesis, Tel Aviv University, September 1998), pp. 134–171.

17. See Shapira, pp. 205–213; Zisser, pp. 101–108; Richard Augustus Norton, "Walking Between Raindrops: Hizballah in Lebanon," *Mediterranean Politics*, Vol. 3, No. 1 (1994), pp. 81–102; Al-Muqawama al-Islamiyya, *Safahat 'Izz, 'Ard wa Tawthiq li'Amaliyyat al-Muqawama al-Islamiyya Khilal 'Amm 1994, 1995, 1996, 1997* (*Pages of Glory, The Islamic Resistance Operations during the Years 1994, 1995, 1996, 1997*) (Beirut: n.p., 1994, 1995, 1996, 1997).

18. See Nasrallah's interview with *Der Spiegel*, October 30, 1997; see also Mahmud Suwayd, *al-Islam waFilastin, Hiwar Shamil ma'a al-Sayyid Muhammad Husayn Fadlallah* (*Islam and the Question of Palestine, a Dialogue with Muhammad Husayn Fadlallah*) (Beirut: Institute for Palestine Studies, 1998).

19. See *Ha'aretz*, March 27, May 22 & 23, 2000.

20. Reuters, June 22 & 23, 2000.

21. See *al-Nahar*, July 20; *Ha'aretz*, July 28 & 30, 2000.

22. R. Beirut, July 16 & 17, 2000.

23. Harris, *MECS*, Vol. 22 (1998), pp. 415–416.

24. Harris, *MECS*, Vol. 21 (1997), p. 411.

25. See Waddah Sharrara, *Dawlat Hizballah, Lubnan Mujtama'a Islamiyya* (*Hizballah's State, Lebanon—an Islamic Society*) (Beirut: Dar al-Nahar li-Nashr, 1996); Hala Jaber, *Hezbollah, Born with a Vengeance* (New York: Columbia University Press, 1997), pp. 7–74; Shapira, pp. 134–171.

26. For more on Fadlallah see Martin Kramer, *Fadlallah, haMatspen shel Hizballah* (*Fadlallah: The Compass of Hizbullah* (The Moshe Dayan Center for Middle Eastern and African Studies, Tel Aviv University, 1998).

27. See Shapira, pp. 192–199.

28. Harris, *MECS*, Vol. 21 (1997), p. 411.

29. *Al-Nahar*, July 20, 2000.

30. See for example articles by *al-Nahar*'s editor, Ghassan Tuwayni, *al-Nahar*, June 5 & 8, July 10, 2000.

31. See declarations by Israeli Prime Minister Ehud Barak and Israel Defense Force Chief of Staff Sha'ul Mofaz, *Ha'aretz*, May 25, 2000.

32. Radio Nur, July 23, 2000.

33. *Al-Mustaqbal*, July 22, 2000.

34. See interviews with Nasrallah, al-Jazira TV, May 27, 2000; *al-Safir*, June 25, 2000; see also *al-Nahar*, July 20, 2000.

35. *Ha'aretz*, February 25, 2000; May 26, 2000.

36. *Ma'ariv*, October 10, 2000, November 19, 2000.

37. *Ha'aretz*, April 17, 2001, *al-Hayat*, April 18, 2001.

38. *Al-Hayat*, August 6, 2001.

7

Balancing State and Society

The Islamic Movement in Kuwait

Shafeeq N. Ghabra

The events surrounding the 1990–1991 Iraqi attempt to destroy the state of Kuwait created a societal vacuum. Everything Kuwaitis had believed during the preceding decades regarding the positive nature of traditional Arab nationalism suffered a blow. This crisis in belief created the conditions for a further Westernization of Kuwaiti society.

Conservative Islamic forces that sought to politicize Islam and impose strict Islamic practices and behavior on society and state felt the need to counter these moral and behavioral changes, while also taking advantage of the resulting ideological vacuum. In order to accomplish this task these forces relied on the strength and zeal of their historical experience and, in particular, the credibility they had gained in confronting the Iraqi occupation. They also exploited the sense of alienation among some sectors of Kuwaiti society.

This study will analyze the conditions that led to the Islamic revival in Kuwait, as well as the forces and ideas behind it. It will attempt to explain how a welfare society such as Kuwait's, with a per capita income of $14,772, can support a strong Islamic movement.[1] Also discussed are the regional shifts and influences that can play a role in the rise and fall of national political and cultural currents. Shedding light on Islamic groups in Kuwait should further the understanding of the dynamics affecting Islamic movements in the Arab world as a whole.

Contrary to popular thought, societal groups in Kuwait do hold state power in check. Formal and informal groups based on different affiliations (class, urban/rural, tribal, Islamic) bring to the government's attention their particular interests.[2] Kuwait has more than 60 voluntary associations representing political trends, religious, civic, and professional groups. The state plays each of these groups off against the others, informally shifting its alliances.

As the owner of the means of production (oil) and the country's main employer (92 percent of the work force), the state provides the ruling Sabah family with the power to influence and sometimes control political events.[3] The state elite in Kuwait assigns a constant flow of values and rules to the different players in society, while permitting a relatively wide margin of freedom of expression to individuals and the press, which allows for serious debate on political issues. State policies and the authoritative distribution of values were responsible, during the 1970s and 1980s (outside the normal parliamentary institutions), for the Islamic forces' access to state resources, privileges, and rights.[4]

The Kuwaiti model of politics can be seen as an experiment in flexible pluralistic corporatism, where the state legitimizes certain groups at the expense of others.[5] The complicated interaction between the state's ruling family, formal groups, and society with all of its informal underpinning, is a dynamic mix of fluid corporatism and restricted pluralism.[6] This multiplicity of interests makes older, more authoritarian methods of control outmoded. Attempts to use authoritarianism in such an environment would only complicate the political process and engender ongoing crisis.

Throughout the Middle East, the Arab defeat in the June 1967 war opened the door for the dormant Islamic forces that Nasserism and Arab nationalism had shut out in the early 1950s.[7] As a result, when states faced internal opposition from pan-Arab nationalist and leftist opposition forces, some in power felt that they could depend on the newly aroused Islamic forces to counter them. The Lebanese civil war starting in 1975 and the role of both Palestinian and leftist Lebanese forces in it were quite alarming to the Kuwaiti government, because of relations between the Lebanese left and some Palestinian groups on the one hand and the Kuwaiti opposition on the other. The existence in Kuwait of a large Palestinian community added to this fear.

In response, the government dissolved Parliament in 1976 and reached out to those who were not critical of its decision. This marked the beginning of an informal, undocumented government alliance with the then-passive, nonradical, and nonpolitical Islamic forces in Kuwait. The government rewarded the Islamic Social Reform Society (*Al-Islah al-Ijtima'i*), which had not condemned the dissolution of Parliament, by appointing its chairman, Yusef al-Hajji, to the position of minister of *awqaf* (religious endowments).[8]

The success of Iran's Islamic revolution also spawned waves of religious revival. While the Sunni Muslims of the Social Reform Society were deeply suspicious of Shi'ite Iran's intentions, they nonetheless found the Iranian model to be proof of the adaptability of Islam to the modern era.[9] It inspired them to become more vocal and aggressive in their attempts to Islamicize society and gain a share of power. Their ability to infiltrate the government bureaucracy increased, and they strengthened old ties with the Muslim Brotherhood in Egypt.

As in most Middle Eastern countries, in Kuwait prior to the mid-1970s few women wore the Islamic *hijab* (which permits only the hands and face to show). Many people prayed, but the elderly were the most religious. Restrictions on the mixing of the sexes were not rigidly observed, and regulations inhibiting women's participation in sports and many kinds of work were slowly loosening. In the 1970s, female students joined their male counterparts in classes at Kuwait University, opening the way for a coed university. Activities were jointly planned, regardless of sex.

In most Middle Eastern societies during the 1950s and 1960s, the majority of Muslims expressed their commitment to Islam through cultural and spiritual manifestations rather than in political forums. Belief in Islam underpinned the moral rectitude of the community, where followers were asked to remember God by doing good and caring for others.

After 1979 in Kuwait, Islamic forces seemed increasingly bold, as secular nationalist forces lost many of their traditional bases of power such as the teachers and students associations. In most nongovernmental organizations, every election after 1979 was characterized by an attempt on the part of Islamic forces to gain control.[10]

On the economic level, the movement was able to build a network in every mosque and neighborhood, and major institutions founded in the mid-1970s complemented their power. For instance, *Bayt al-Tamwil* (Finance House) became the second biggest bank in Kuwait. The movement built and solidified its base in the 1980s. Kuwaiti Islamists became key players in the financial support given to Islamic movements in Afghanistan, Egypt, Algeria, and Sudan.

Since 1980, Islamic forces have consisted of three main groups: the mainstream Muslim Brotherhood, whose base is in the Social Reform Society; the more marginal Ancestral *(Salaf)* Islamic group, which has its base in the Heritage group *(al-Turath)*;[11] and the Cultural Social Society *(Jam'iyyat al-Thaqafah al-Ijtima'iyah)*, which is under the influence of the forces inspired by the Iranian revolution and represents the interests of segments of the Shi'ite community (20 to 30 percent of the citizenry.)[12]

The strength of the Islamic movement, as expressed primarily in the Social Reform Society, was clearly demonstrated during the 1981 parliamentary elections, the first after the dissolution of Parliament in 1976.[13] In the elections, the secular pan-Arabist forces were defeated by the Islamists, who became the only organized political group in Parliament. Although a minority, they were influential, shrewdly focusing on strengthening their alliance with the state.[14]

The Kuwaiti government felt that co-opting the Islamic current in the bureaucracy would soften its appeal, while at the same time boosting government legitimacy. Such a boost was sorely needed following the second dissolution of

Parliament in 1986, which prompted both secularist and Islamic forces to confront the government on a host of issues, most of them dealing with government accountability.

By 1981, Islamist influence had spread to the teachers association and from there to the Ministry of Education. This laid the groundwork for the imposition of a more conservative school curriculum. Books in Arabic began citing parables from the Quran rather than from modern sources. The secular and 'open' poetry of the 1970s was increasingly replaced by that of a religious and conservative nature. First-grade Arabic primers were revised to include examples of children praying and eating, drinking, and thanking God for what they had. No examples were given of people working, producing, drawing, singing, dancing and so on.[15]

National day, on which boys and girls from all grades performed national songs and dances for parents, educators, officials and the media, was challenged on religious grounds. In 1986, it took a threat of resignation by the minister of education, Hassan al-Ibrahim, to prevent the cancellation of the government-approved ceremony. The celebration has since been abolished (though it was revived informally by teenagers after the Gulf War.)[16]

The Islamic movement's influence during the 1980s was also felt in the Ministry of Information. Television programs became more conservative and censorship increased.[17] The ministry censored all kinds of books, including those critical of the Islamic current. Conversely, books and tapes with narrow interpretations of Islam flooded the market.

Islamic groups including the mainstream Muslim Brotherhood controlling the Social Reform Association, the minority Salafi organization, and Jam'iyyat al-Thaqafah representing the Shi'ite community, have demonstrated exceptional organizational skills over the years. It seems natural that Islamic forces would target influential associational and professional groups and use them to further their cause. The amount of funding, equipment, and staffing available to the Islamic groups was much greater than what had previously been available to any political group in the Middle East.[18] These groups are responsible, by and large, for the introduction of more formal and organized politics in Kuwait and the region as a whole. The Islamic movement made the best use possible of the diffuse nature of informal groups based on such institutions as tribe and *diwaniyya* (traditional meeting place for men) in Kuwaiti society. As stated above, in the 1980s, the Islamic movement became the only organized mass-based political force in the country.

In addition to the state's leniency regarding interest groups furthering Islamic doctrines, cultural factors played an important role in the spread of the Islamists' doctrines. Mosques, organized prayer, and the various teachings of Islam helped make the population more accepting of narrowly-based political Islam. The overall conservative attitude of society toward women, dress codes, and religion exemplified the overlap between social conservatism and political Islam. By preaching the leading role of the elders over the young, of men over

women, and the right of men to have more than one wife, the Islamic message
attracted conservative and less-educated people, particularly among the Bedouin.

In the mid-1980s, the Islamic movement in Kuwait ceased to be an expression of disillusionment by the urban elite, and the marriage between Bedouin
conservative values and the movement matured. Society's change from traditional to modern, and from rural (desert) to urban, isolated the Bedouin and
made them more open to messages that would help them define the world,
simplify its meaning, and find (sometimes superficial) solutions to its problems.
The majority of the relatively deprived Bedouin tribes have moved from the
sidelines to the forefront in demanding societal recognition and equality, the
basis for which is found in Islam.[19] Several influential populist Islamists have
risen from among their ranks. A similar trend of outspokenness can be seen in
urban families of lesser influence seeking equal footing with the more cosmopolitan and traditionally powerful families.

This process of "desertization," as the Bahraini thinker Muhammad Ansari
labels it, is among the most destructive processes in the Middle East.[20] It under-
mines modern life by bringing into urban society the ultraconservative values of
the desert and mixing them with Islamist populism. The process destroys the
hope of a nation-state whose urban centers can assimilate and acculturate new-
comers. It puts the national civil framework at risk, and prevents it from ma-
turing. Desertization of the city and the state entails populism and an increased
urban-Bedouin divide. Religious fervor, in addition to creating a divisiveness
based on values, also builds a sectarian (Shi'ite-Sunni or Bedouin-urban) division
on the most limited and narrowly defined issues: prayer, time of prayer, style of
dress, and so on.[21] Short of authoritarian repression, in order to counter populism and Islamist radicalism the state has no choice but to undergo a process of
democratization, societal neutrality, and egalitarianism. In the new milieu, repression will work only on a temporary basis.

In Kuwait, the attitudes of the Islamists toward modernity are of a dual
nature. Somewhat ironically, the overwhelming majority of Islamists among
Kuwait University students are in the colleges of science; their conservatism is
somehow wedded to the fruits of modern technology. But just as the colleges of
science provide a technical view, the social sciences provide a global view. The
educational system at Kuwait University and in the rest of the country, as well
as the region, has failed to provide a convincing set of ideas packaged in an
indigenous social-science framework capable of assimilating students into more
modern and forward-looking ways of thinking in both religion and secularism.
The science and technical schools teach skills and techniques, not values or
concepts for comprehending these changes.

The college of *Shari'a* at Kuwait University, like those in many other Arab
universities, is a school of traditional religious indoctrination. This school also
produces Islamist activists since most of the professors tend to be either fundamentalist or orthodox. Then comes the question of what type of employment
will a "College of Shari'a" graduate get.

But in the world of Islam, flexibility is part of the process. In choosing between the doctrine and its historical application, practical considerations have always influenced its interpretation. This approach has developed a concept of allowing for a choice between the lesser of two evils, even if the decision taken would violate Islamic law. For instance, if forbidding alcohol would make more people consume it—profiting criminals—or encourage them to use drugs instead, such a law would be counterproductive.[22] This means that countries like the United Arab Emirates, Syria, or Egypt that allow the consumption of alcohol are not introducing an anti-Islamic practice. Interpretation can allow for much flexibility in Islam. However, this flexibility is not always observed. In the last two decades such flexibility has been lost to the conservative interpretation.

Further, the Islamic current carries with it a message of respect for the self and for Arab and Islamic history. It provides orientations for individuals, providing moral guidelines to the young in a society experiencing rapid change. However, the moment is also ripe for excess. Like any movement seeking power and influence and believing in the sole accuracy of its interpretations, it seeks full obedience by society to its version of truth.

Kuwait's relative wealth has had quite an impact on Islamic politics. Wealth by and large has defused the radical nature of the movement, and its moderating effect has helped Kuwait avoid the Algerian, Sudanese, and Egyptian experiences. In Kuwait, because of a combination of factors related to government policy on the one hand and relative wealth on the other, Islamists and liberals talk, debate, and vote against each other. But wealth also means that the Islamists have independent bases of power, which give them the ability to support other Islamists and also embark on larger social programs.

After its liberation in 1991, Kuwaiti society went through a searching self-evaluation. Many young Kuwaitis looked to the United States as a model for creating a new way of life. Their contact with the U.S. military, and its role in the liberation, had created among them a respect and fondness for Americans. Exiled Kuwaitis who had lived for almost a year in more open Western environments began to appreciate the need for change in their own society and values.

On the other hand, social conservatism also spread among equally large sectors. For example, Kuwaitis who had lived in Saudi Arabia during the invasion were impressed by the religiosity of the Saudis. Many religiously conservative Kuwaitis felt that the invasion and occupation were punishment from God for the Kuwaitis' lavish lifestyle. Only through Islam could the situation be rectified. During this period, Islamists needed to build on the confidence gained in confronting the Iraqi occupation and at the same time counter movements toward opening up society. The opportunity was at hand because the secular forces were weak and fragmented, and the government was less capable of dealing with new societal demands. The government's own legitimacy was at stake.

Three Islamist political groups appeared in this period. The Islamic Constitutional Movement (ICM) has its roots in the Muslim Brotherhood of Kuwait and in the Social Reform, an influential Islamic associational group that had been gaining strength since the 1970s. The Islamic Popular Alliance (IPA), better known as al-Salaf (Ancestral), has roots in the Society for the Rebirth of Islamic Tradition. This group, which has been attracting followers since the 1980s, is more literal than the Constitutional Movement in its interpretation of Islam. The Islamic National Alliance (INA) has roots in al-Jam'iyyah al-Thaqafiyyah, a group attractive to segments of Kuwait's Shi'ite population that was dissolved in 1989 after bombings in Saudi Arabia were linked to some of its members.

In addition, after Kuwait's liberation in 1991 a nongovernmental association was attempted by Islamists linked to the Social Reform Society in order to practice what can "direct the public to do good and refrain from evil," similar to what is done in Saudi Arabia. According to its general secretary, Fahid Abd al-Rahman al-Shwayyib, the group's goal was to enlist 1,000 men and establish a religious police with "a branch in every neighborhood to patrol and watch citizens, in order to spread the teachings of Islam."[23] The government responded by discrediting the practice, stating that "the police will not allow any group to harm any citizen or resident in Kuwait in any form, verbal or physical."[24]

Several incidents of violence involving radical Islamists took place in Kuwait City toward the end of 1991 and prior to the October 1992 elections. At the time, some extremists were caught holding large quantities of weapons and explosives. There were shooting incidents involving the Romanian circus, which was visiting Kuwait, due to the costumes worn by women performers, and explosions occurred in several video stores.[25] This wave of violence came to a halt as Parliament played its part in initiating appropriate legislation and state security sought weapons caches and made arrests.

In this context Abdallah al-Mutawa, director of the Social Reform Association, saw the need for an immediate application of Shari'a, including severing thieves' hands, outlawing interest rates, segregating the sexes, and enforcing the dress code for women. Al-Mutawa also announced the need to change the wording of the Kuwaiti constitution from "The State's religion is Islam, and the Islamic Shari'a is a source of legislation" to "Islamic Shari'a is the only and main source of legislation."[26] Likewise, Shayikh Jasim Muhalhal al-Yasin, secretary of the Constitutional Movement, called for the application of the Shari'a immediately.[27]

Because the constitution, written in 1962, made Islam the state religion and Shari'a a source (though not the only one) of legislation, Kuwait did not ban *awqaf* (Islamic foundations), nor did it follow anti-Islamic policies, as did many socialist and revolutionary Middle Eastern states. It interpreted its rules on the basis of reason and necessity rather than on a particular interpretation of the Shari'a. The application of the Shari'a in a literal sense is, therefore, a controversial and oft-debated issue in Kuwait.

The Shari'a is applied in laws governing personal matters such as marriage, divorce, inheritance, and *waqf*, but other laws strike a balance between the Shari'a and social and international practices. For example, alcohol is prohibited by law, but punishment is not administered according to the Shari'a. Those who trade in alcohol receive imprisonment, while a person consuming it in public can be fined and may at a maximum be imprisoned for a certain period. There is no punishment for consuming alcohol in the privacy of one's own home in Kuwait.[28] Furthermore, the state tends to turn a blind eye on this matter.

It is precisely such flexibility in Kuwaiti laws that Islamists want to change. Islamic groups have increasingly distributed cassettes in commercial centers and in front of mosques that preach the need to practice the Shari'a, in particular its more conservative orthodox interpretation. Since 1991, most of the Islamists' leading representatives have begun writing actively in the daily newspapers.

The emir of Kuwait, sensing the changing current, reacted immediately by establishing a higher consultative committee to work toward completing the enforcement of Islamic law. Established in December 1991, the committee was an attempt to institutionally co-opt the Islamists, many of whom were opposed to its formation. It had a long-term mandate but no enforcement capabilities; it has yet to issue a recommendation.

Despite the invigoration of the Islamist movement, relations between secular groups, intellectuals, and Islamists in Kuwait continued to be fairly positive. The main issue—the return to parliamentary life—dominated political discourse in the country throughout 1991 until the October elections in 1992. The Islamic groups continued, for political reasons, to be conciliatory toward non-Islamic groups.

The 1992 elections created a new atmosphere in Kuwait. The parliamentarians from Islamist groups believed that the vote could be interpreted as a mandate for the Islamicization of the country's laws and regulations. This led the assembly during its first year to introduce an array of measures, which ultimately failed, that can be characterized as contradictory to anything expected from a democratic institution.

At the time, the Parliament consisted of the religious right, the center, and the traditional left. The fourteen or so members of the religious right led the hesitant center—consisting of another fourteen or more members, who feared losing their local and tribal constituency—on most religious and conservative issues. The secular-oriented liberal group of former Arab nationalists, the Democratic Forum *(al-Manbar al-Dimuqrati)*, which was formed after liberation, and several other independent and liberal factions appeared fragmented.[29] Elected six years after the suspension of the previous Parliament—a period that included the Iraqi invasion—the members wasted a good deal of time on issues that should have been settled or dismissed quickly.

The suggestion by five Islamic parliamentarians to establish an "Authority to Direct the Public to Do Good and Refrain from Evil" is an example of the dominant trend.[30]

> The authority's main role would be to fight foreign behavior that infringes on Kuwaiti traditions and contradicts Islam. . . . This is done by planning and supervising public behavior. . . . In order to achieve its goals, the authority will hear complaints from citizens regarding any phenomena contradicting public decency. . . . It will also open offices in every area and district. . . . It will call Ministries such as Education and Information and Interior to inform them of non-Islamic behavior. The authority will study monthly reports that the Ministry of the Interior will commit itself to providing regarding cases of morality, regardless of whether it was transferred to court or was kept and pardoned. . . . The authority will give lectures, distribute pamphlets, and print books.[31]

Khalid al-'Adwah, a leading Islamist in parliament, called for making "Kuwait the state of belief and Quran."[32] Another leading Islamist from the Islamic Constitutional Movement said this was the only way to solve moral degeneration in Kuwait.[33] Another parliamentarian, Mufaraj Nahar al-Mutayri, explained that "police station files are full of moral crimes. . . . We are a country that went through a difficult crisis, and God put at our disposal all the countries of the world to defend us; our land has been liberated by those among us who contributed to the poor in the rest of the world."[34]

By extrapolation, it is time to thank God—not politics or politicians or even the Western coalition—by practicing Islam and returning to its doctrines.[35] The nongovernmental associations controlled by the Islamists released a statement calling for the application of the authority project.[36]

The suggestion to establish an authority to publicly enforce Islamic law initiated a major and divisive debate. In general, the Islamist deputies' assertions that government laws were non-Islamic—based, of course, on their narrow interpretation of Islam—led to the collapse of the alliance between the Islamists and liberals as opposition forces, an alliance forged during the years after Parliament was banned in 1986. During this debate, in some cases the differences between the branches of the opposition were greater than the differences between the opposition as a whole and the government. In the end, the minority of secular and liberal deputies realized to what ends the Islamic groups would use the coalition.[37] Columnists in major newspapers blasted the proposed Authority and succeeded in defeating it.[38]

Another divisive issue that captured the country's attention for several months was the *niqab*. The issue started with a November 1991 incident in which the dean of the faculty of medicine at Kuwait University attempted to prohibit medical students in laboratories, for reasons of safety, from wearing the *niqab*, which covers the entire body, including the face and hands. This matter, involving four students, was given priority by the Islamists later elected to Parliament. Month after month this issue took the Assembly's time. Parliamentary committees, such as those on education and legislation, were consumed with following the matter up. The Islamist parliamentarians tried to issue legislation nullifying the dean's decision prohibiting the *niqab*; university professors protested parliament's interference. Jamal al-Kindari, secretary of the educational committee, advised the university "not to challenge the Parliament."[39]

Furthermore, Islamic parliamentarians initially approved the segregation by gender of the coeducational Kuwait University, whose president was a woman. In December 1994, a vote for segregation failed to garner a majority by one vote. The government had lobbied heavily against the measure, as had liberal deputies and Minister of Higher Education Ahmad al-Rube'i, creating something of an alliance between liberals and the government. This alliance once again prevailed in February 1995, when the Islamists failed to push through a vote of no confidence against al-Rube'i.

Also in 1994, 35 members of Parliament signed and delivered a petition to the emir regarding the Shari'a and the changing of the second article of the constitution to make Shari'a "*the* main source of legislation" (instead of *a* main source).[40] In fact, all elected members of Parliament signed the petition, with the exception of six liberals, who were accused by Islamists of laxness in their faith. Despite this apparent support, such a measure would not pass easily, because it would require the agreement of two-thirds of Parliament (including the cabinet ministers) and the approval of the emir. Although the MPs signed the petition, no bill actually proposing the change was ever bought to the floor of Parliament.

However, the segregation law of Kuwait University did pass in 1996, and society, not only intellectuals, went through intense debates on the matter. Finally a compromise formula favorable to the Islamists was found that allowed Kuwait University to be coed for five years. The compromise also included noninterference in coed private schools. The passage of the law was a setback to liberal forces. Two days after the law was passed the university announced it could not apply the law for practical budgetary reasons, since Kuwait University had been coed for more than 20 years. However, five years have passed with the Islamic groups and representatives in Parliament continuously bringing up the issue making the work of the Minister of Education, Dr. Musaid Al-Haroun, quite difficult. Every year Parliament froze the university's budget and asked about steps towards segregation. The university segregated the cafeterias and some classes, hoping Parliament would forget the issue, but in the end, parliament had its way and the University had to segregate its classes in 2002.

Thus, some sectors of society considered certain activities to be heretical, while others viewed them as personal freedoms, and saw the Islamists' proposed laws as undemocratic and out of touch with the age. Journalists and opinion makers, and large elements of public opinion, attacked the suggested legislation, themselves putting pressure on parliamentarians to vote against these bills.

Thus while the Islamic movement won over many people, especially to greater religious observance, its more narrowly based interpretations of Islam—on issues of dress, modernity, East-West relations, personal freedom, and the need to control society and state behavior—alienated many who might have been sympathetic to a more moderate approach. Some saw the Islamists' claim that "Islam is the solution" for Kuwait today as a repeat of simplistic, ultimately unsuccessful, ideologies such as "Arab unity" or "the liberation of Palestine," heralded as the solution in earlier decades.

The Parliament elected in October 1996 was in some ways similar to the Parliament elected in 1992, though half the members were new. The main substantive difference was the presence of more members—21 percent—who tended toward cooperation with the government on at least some issues. But the hardcore support for the Islamic movement, including among some independents, continued to be high (14 percent). Now, however, more of them came from the Salaf movement and fewer from the Islamic Constitutional Movement. Other groups included eleven secular members critical of or opposed to the government[41] and four Shi'ite members who sometimes voted with the Islamists. Such a divided Parliament would have difficulty building consensus, yet the Islamists were able to get more than half the vote on any serious Islamic issue, such as gender segregation in Kuwait University or the application of the Shari'a.[42]

The new Parliament again sought the application of the Shari'a by suggesting a change in Article 2 of the constitution, though the opposition to this proposal rose from four members to nine.[43] Many others who voted for the suggestion did so out of concern for their image, knowing the emir would veto the legislation. A new issue was a parliamentary challenge to mixed-gender fashion shows, though the government paid little attention to the request. This added to the anger and mistrust between Islamic members of Parliament and the government.[44]

After the October 1996 election, the divisive atmosphere between liberals and Islamists increased, especially in the face of an Islamist-led campaign against several university professors and writers. For example, 'Alya Shu'ayb, a professor of philosophy at Kuwait University, was accused of spreading degenerate ideas when she stated in an interview with a Kuwaiti magazine that lesbianism was widespread at the university.[45] The reaction was intense, and the university rector had to form an investigating committee. The committee recommended expelling her from the university, but the university and the Ministry of Education did not act on the recommendation.

Likewise, Ahmad al-Baghdadi, the chairman of the political science department, and Sulaiman al-Badir, a former minister of education, were accused of insulting the Prophet Muhammad. Each had said in an interview with a Kuwaiti newspaper that in the early period of Islam the prophet "failed" in Mecca, which forced his move to Medina.[46] The word "failed" became an issue; several Islamists took it to Parliament and called for punishment and resignation. Some threatened Baghdadi's life, and others sued him in civil court, while yet others wanted to dissolve his marriage (as happened in a similar case in Egypt) by declaring he was not a valid Muslim. As a result of a lawsuit brought by Islamists, al-Baghdadi was sentenced to one month in prison in October 1999. Conservative Islamists hailed the decision; liberals were disappointed. The emir pardoned Baghdadi from all charges after he had served half the sentence.

The writer Layla al-'Uthman became subject to a court order in January 1997 because of short stories she had written 10 years before describing love relationships. The stories had long been on bookshelves when they came to the attention of the Islamists. Four Islamists pursued the author in the courts. Again there was a flare-up in the press, as liberal writers accused the Islamists of an organized campaign against freedom of thought. The association of artists held meetings, while journalists and nongovernmental organizations in the Arab world criticized the charges. This case, like similar ones, was buried in the court system and no decision is anticipated.[47]

The cases of dispute between the government and Islamists continued. The government may have considered on more than one occasion dissolving Parliament and calling new elections. The final decision, however, was to hope that time and politics would defuse the situation. A major confrontation took place in March 1998 when the National Assembly scheduled a vote of no confidence after the minister of information, Shaykh Sa'ud Nasser al-Sabah, allowed more than 160 banned books in Kuwait's Arab book fair in November 1998. Islamist deputies cross-examined the minister for nearly seven hours in a session that drew more than 2,000 spectators. The crisis ended when the government resigned one day prior to the vote, scheduled for March 17. When the new government was formed, Shaykh Sa'ud was appointed minister of oil. That ended the crisis but demonstrated how powerful Parliament and the Islamist bloc had become.

The Paladin Howitzer crisis was another dispute showing Parliament's renewed attention to accountability. Information reached Parliament that the Kuwaiti government had decided in May 1998 to purchase the U.S. Paladin artillery system but that the U.S. army was planning to purchase its successor, the Crusader. Press rumors of irregularities in the procurement process motivated members of Parliament to block the whole deal at the end of 1998. A confrontation took place with the Ministry of Defense and in March 1999 the government gave in, informing the National Assembly that it was freezing the procurement process.

While all these confrontations were taking place, the Islamists were also gaining strength by allying themselves with populace nationalist parliamentarians, a group led by the Assembly's speaker, Ahmad al-Sa'adoun. The skillful al-Sa'adoun used his oratorical abilities to build coalitions that led the 1985–1986 Parliament and the democratic movement in 1989. He was reelected speaker in

the 1992 and 1996 Assemblies. The loose alliance between the Islamic opposition and populace nationalists continued from one session to another. Populace
nationalists sometimes voted Islamist on conservative bills in order to gain Islamist support on other issues.

In certain ways, the lack of public political debate after 1986 contributed to the
Islamic groups' growing strength and popularity. During the long period between parliamentary elections (1985–1992), people turned to rigid interpretations of Islam as a protection against change, modern life, social inequality, state
differentiation between groups, etc. They sought Islam at a time of defeat, lack
of democracy, and failure and hardship in their personal lives.

In each Islamic grouping, trends are being pulled by the past and pushed
toward the future. Public debate and long-term experience with the democratic
process can be expected to create conditions for a more reasoned, forward-looking
view of Islam among the population. This process can help in the transformation
of Islam, allowing it to become more active, participatory, and modern. Yet such
a process has no future if the limited press freedoms and nondemocratic institutions prevalent in the region do not change.

A small, moderate trend already exists in the Islamic movement. While it is a
minority, it may, as a result of the losses of the Islamic mainstream, play a larger role
at another stage. Khalid al-Madhkur, the chairman of the government-appointed
committee to study the application of the Shari'a, is, for example, a leading scholar
among those who have a moderate and practical understanding of Islam.

Former Member of Parliament (ICM) Dr. Isma'il al-Shatti, a former editor
of *al-Mujtama'*, the weekly magazine of the Muslim Brotherhood, and one of the
most soft-spoken Islamic leaders, has called for a transition in stages toward the
application of the Shari'a. He has criticized attempts to apply it in other countries as failures. Time is important, according to al-Shatti:

> We did not solve the problem of the relation between Shari'a and music and
> theater, among other things. How can we create Islamic information? . . . It is
> wrong to start the application of the Shari'a with *al-hudud* [restrictions]. The
> origin in people is honor and goodness, not delinquency. . . . We must first
> provide good, honest lives for people and then ask them about restrictions
> and applications of rules in other matters.

He goes on to note, "The Quran came in stages." To further make his point, al-
Shatti cites the Sudanese experiment with the Shari'a as a failure. There, leaders
started with the sword, cutting off the hands of those who stole, whipping those
who committed adultery. They did not start with economic recovery or education and development.[48]

However, al-Shatti is indebted to the Islamic Constitutional Movement for his
place in Parliament (1992–1996). The ideologues of the movement do not trust

their politicians and constantly supervise their statements. It appears that the ideological leaders are also those most exposed to public debate and politics and experienced in dealing with problems that will be affected more by rational thought and secular approaches. In the long run, this will also have an effect on Islamist groups, shaping them toward rational, modern and democratic Islamic thinking.

Public debate equally helps in bringing to light those Islamic ideas most susceptible to modernity and change. There is a whole range of modern interpretations of Islam being expressed in books and articles. These interpretations link democracy with Islam and consider women's and individual rights to be compatible with Islamic beliefs and practices. The writings of Muhammad Shahrur, Muhammad Arkun, Hussain Ahmad Amin, Nasr Abu Zayd and al-Sadiq al-Nayhum are already stirring intense debate. Shahrur's *Al-Kitab wal Quran* (the Book and the Quran) was at one time banned in Kuwait, but today it can be found in bookstores.[49]

The friction between government and Parliament—which was also partly a conflict between government and the Islamist movement—came to a turning point in April 1999. The crisis began when a new edition of the Quran published by the Ministry of Religious Affairs was found to contain mistakes. The Islamists wanted an investigation and wanted to question government officials. When the government was on the verge of resigning in May, the emir dissolved Parliament and the government called for early elections in accordance with the constitution.

Then almost immediately the emir, in a rare interference in the political process, announced his wish to see a governmental decree that would give women the right to vote and be elected to Parliament. This announcement fell like a bombshell, and all of society reacted. The liberals and many women supported it; radical nationalists were taken by surprise. Although they supported the concept, which appealed to their urban, upper class, and semiliberal taste, they did not want to set a precedent of laws being made by decree.

But the Sunni Islamists reacted very negatively. Al-Mutawa, director of the Social Reform Association, warned the government, criticized the emir, and threatened to lead a demonstration at his palace. Preachers in at least 80 mosques also condemned the decree. The government responded by showing strength. It prevented the same 80 preachers from preaching on Friday, since preachers at Friday prayers must be licensed by the Ministry of Religious Affairs. The preachers demonstrated in protest.

The government, enforcing this law for the first time in years, announced that all Islamic money collection and associations must follow legal procedures, which include full accounting and reporting of income and expenditures. There was much speculation that unlicensed groups were misusing contributions, and that money may have been sent to illegal groups in Egypt and elsewhere. The Islamic associations had opened many chapters in Kuwaiti neighborhoods without permission, and the government now enforced registration requirements.

Even the National Union of Kuwaiti Students, dominated since 1977 by the Islamists, came under scrutiny. The government also said it was considering appointing its own boards to run cooperative supermarkets in Kuwaiti neighborhoods, since these cooperatives had become politicized and dominated by Islamists. Finally, the government hinted it would downgrade several official commissions run by Islamists, such as the "Committee for the Preparation for the Application of the Shari'a in Kuwait," headed by a leading cleric.

These government actions made the Islamists reduce their protests of the decree. The government had won the first round over women's rights, and the emir received widespread support from the population and the international community for his decision.

But the government carried the confrontation further, in an unusual show of zeal and decisiveness. While the election campaign was under way, the government established an interministerial committee chaired by the deputy prime minister and Foreign Minister Shaykh Sabah al-Ahmad al-Sabah. This committee produced 60 decrees, all approved by the Cabinet, chaired by Crown Prince and Prime Minister Shaykh Sa'ad al-Abdallah. The decrees included permission for foreign investments without a Kuwaiti guarantor; non-Kuwaiti participation in the stock market, private universities to be opened in Kuwait, privatizing the statist economy; and a law on the *Bidun* (stateless residents) that will make many of them citizens and settle their status. This was a major reform program promising to liberalize Kuwait's society and economy. While the decrees are considered effective laws, and took effect immediately, they had still to be either confirmed or vetoed by a parliamentary vote.

To a large extent, the election of July 3, 1999 became a referendum on the 60 decrees and, in essence, the country's future direction. The elections produced a bloc of 20 out of 50 Parliament members who were liberal and independent. The Islamist delegation shrank from 14 to 10 seats, while Shi'ite and tribal representation grew slightly.

The new situation gave the liberals a chance to set the agenda for the new Parliament, as the Islamists had done in the 1992 and 1996 sessions. This liberal, independent group was not united on all issues. Among them was a group of radical independents who saw relations with the government through the prism of confrontation and parliamentary power. However, the fact that the new speaker of the Assembly, Jassem al-Khorafi, was an independent moderate, gave an advantage to the centrists in the group.

In general, the liberal independents sought compromises with the government in order to institute the reform program. A second bloc, in which radical representatives joined with hard-core Islamists, continued to focus on the illegality of legislation by government decree and the need to block it. The main issue centered on a constitutional phrase that said decrees in the absence of Parliament must deal with urgent issues. Islamists in Parliament argued that the women's decree and most of the others were not urgent. These members of Parliament feared that the government might abuse its power in the future when Parliament is not in session. A number of members who belonged to neither bloc held the balance of power.

A good case study is the vote on the *emiri* decree enfranchising women. This decree became a law when it was instituted in May 1999. But it had also to be voted upon to make it permanent. The liberal bloc in support of women's rights had postponed the vote for fear that the Islamists and the radical independents would muster enough opposition to defeat it. The tactic of postponement was supported by the government, which had hoped to either schedule a vote when it felt it had a majority, or just keep delaying a vote until February 2000 when women would have registered to vote. But Parliament forced a vote, and the decree was rejected in November, 32 to 30, with two abstentions. The result was a clear setback to women's suffrage. But the defeat was a triumph for parliamentary power, and set a precedent for the separation and limitations of executive and legislative authority. Ten or fifteen years ago, an *emiri* decree would have passed easily in Parliament. Today, every decree is scrutinized, and no law is law until voted upon and approved by Parliament. Parliamentarians are using all their powers without any hesitation.

Those who support women's suffrage are drawing lessons from the setback. The issue of women's suffrage has been raised by the emir and will not disappear: it will continue to be on the table during the months and years to come. The vote in Parliament expressed the ambivalence of Kuwaiti society: 32 to 30 reflects how evenly the country is divided. It is clear today that women's activists ought to take the emiri decree as a starting point in order to open a wide debate and appeal to all forces, including conservative ones. The evolution of women's role in society speaks for itself. Today 35 percent of the Kuwaiti work force is composed of women and 67 percent of Kuwait University students are female. Establishing an organization dedicated to women's suffrage could be key to a process leading to women's enfranchisement.

Conclusion:
The rise of the Islamists has been a reaction to both internal and global trends.[50] The overall environment and the global reality of more open thinking, market economies, and democratization will continue to generate tensions with the Islamist trend. While global trends and liberalization at home can undermine radical Islam, mainstream Islamist forces will survive these pressures as they use these powerful institutions to stay ahead of the current.

Therefore Kuwait's journey into the global reality will not be an easy one. Kuwait could still fall hostage to a nonconclusive conflict with Islamists on every issue. Sometimes the conservatives will get their way; other times the liberals will get their way. The country could become more divided, with the government caught in the middle, one faction using the Islamists to further its agenda and another using the liberals. The history of the last decade testifies to how negative and frozen in time and space things can be.

But on the other hand, government resilience since the emiri decrees and the July 1999 election tells us that the country is experiencing pressures to reform in economics as well as politics and that Kuwait's membership in the WTO, the challenges of the new millennium, and the need to depend on an enfranchised population are serious factors in the process. This does not mean that change will be linear. In fact, to hold the peace among Kuwait's components, compromises must be made at every junction.

As the wind blows in the direction of reform, and as the world reacts in the wake of the radical Islamic terrorism that brought havoc to New York and Washington, D.C., on September 11, 2001, the survival of the Islamic movement will be a function of its ability to adapt. Reform, social change, and government policy may succeed in helping to transform Islamist radicalism into Islamist reformism and interest group politics. The constant challenges to the movement, from society and state, and from intellectuals and the modern world, can in the long run weaken its appeal in favor of a more 'compassionate' Islamic interpretation of both personal and political behavior. But if differences are not mediated, if reforms are not addressed, and if the economy is mismanaged, the division and radicalization can increase. This era is therefore central in deciding on the future path of the country, its relation to "Islam" and the world.

NOTES

1. State of Kuwait, Ministry of Planning, Central Statistical Office, *Statistical Review*, Issue 17, 1994.

2. See Jill Crystal, *Kuwait: The Transformation of an Oil State* (Boulder: Westview Press, 1992), pp. 65–89.

3. In 1998, out of a work force of 215,500 people, 202,500 worked in the government sector and 13,000 in the private sector. *Statistical Review*, 1999, 22nd edition.

4. Khaldun al-Naqib, *Al-Mujatama' wal Dawlah fi al-Khalij wal Jazirah al-'Arabiyya: Min Manzur Mukhtalif (State and Society in the Gulf and Arabian Peninsula: A Different Perspective)* (Beirut: Center of Arab Unity Studies, 1989), p. 152.

5. See Andrew Cox and Noel O'Sullivan (eds.), *The Corporate State: Corporatism and the State Tradition in Western Europe* (Hants, England: Edward Elgar Publishing, 1988).

6. On these concepts, See Robert Bianchi, *Interest Groups and Political Development in Turkey* (Princeton: Princeton University Press, 1984).

7. Shafeeq Ghabra, "Voluntary Associations in Kuwait: Foundations of a New Society?" *Middle East Journal*, Vol. 45, No. 2 (Spring, 1991), pp. 199–215.

8. Ibid., p. 206.

9. No author, *Jam'iyyat al-Islah al-Ijtima'i: 25 'Aman Min al Ta'sis (The Social Reform Society: 25 Years Since Its Establishment)* (Kuwait: The Social Reform Society,

1988), pp. 11–39.

10. See Ghabra, "'Voluntary Associations in Kuwait" pp. 199–215.

11. Ibid., pp. 206–211.

12. See James Bill, "Resurgent Islam in the Persian Gulf," *Foreign Affairs,* Vol. 63, No. 1 (Fall 1984), p. 120.

13. *Sawt al-Khalij,* March 5, 1981, p. 12.

14. See interview with Abdullah al-Mutawwa, chairman of the Social Reform Society and one of the founders of the Muslim Brotherhood in Kuwait, *al-Mujtama' Weekly Magazine* (Kuwait), December 15, 1981.

15. Based on a review of the school curriculum and on several interviews with teachers and members of the Kuwait Ministry of Education, spring 1994.

16. Discussion with Hasan al-Ibrahim, former Kuwaiti minister of education, spring 1994.

17. Comparisons between television programs in the 1980s and today reveal many differences. Today, although such pressures remain, they can be challenged.

18. On the previous dearth of organizational skills in Arab mass politics, see James Bill and Robert Springborg, *Politics in the Middle East,* 3rd ed. (New York: Harper Collins Publishers, 1990), p. 89.

19. Shafeeq Ghabra, *Al-Kuwayt: Dirasah fi Aliyyat al-Dawlah al-Qutriyyah wal Sultah wal Mujtama'* (*Kuwait: A Study of The Dynamics of State, Authority, and Society*) (Cairo: Dar Ibn Khaldun for Developmental Studies and Dar al-Amin lil-Nashr, 1995), pp. 53–60.

20. Muhammad Jabir al-Ansari, *Takwin al-'Arab al-Siyasi wa Maghzah al-Dawlah al-Qutriyya* (*Arab Political Formation and the Meaning of the State*) (Beirut: Center of Arab Unity Studies, 1994).

21. See *al-Qabas,* March 6, 1993, for the story of a Shi'ite child denied the right to pray in school.

22. Muhammad Sa'id al-'Ishmawi, *al-Islam al-Siyyasi* (*Political Islam*), 3rd ed. (Cairo: Sina lil Nashr, 1992), p. 59.

23. *Al-Qabas,* August 31, 1991.

24. Ibid.

25. *Majalat al-Majalah* (London), August 14, 1993.

26. *Al-Anba',* December 21, 1991.

27. *Al-Mujtama',* June 7, 1992.

28. Najib al-Waqayyan, a lawyer, quoted in *al-Anba',* December 22, 1991.

29. On the 1992 elections, see Shafeeq Ghabra, "Democratization in a Middle Eastern State: Kuwait, 1993," *Middle East Policy,* Vol. 3, No. 1 (1994), pp. 102–119.

30. *Arab Times,* October 27, 1993, p. 1.

31. From the original draft of the proposed law as published in *al-Anba',* March 1, 1993.

32. *Al-Qabas,* March 14, 1993.

33. *Al-Mujtama',* March 23, 1993.

34. *Al-Siyasah*, March 14, 1993.

35. See the column of Abdul Rahman al-Najjar, *al-Anba'*, March 12, 1993.

36. *Al-Watan*, March 18, 1993.

37. "Salah al-Hashim" ("The honeymoon is over"), *al-Qabas*, March 18, 1993.

38. *Al-Qabas*, March 4, 1993; *al-Tali'ah*, March 10, 1993; Sami Abud al Latif al-Nisif, *al-Qabas*, April 7, 1993, p. 11; Abdul Rahman al-Najar, *al-Anba'*, March 12, 1993; *al-Siyasah*, March 20, 1993.

39. *Al-Watan*, December 6, 1992, p. 1.

40. *Arab Times*, August 31, 1993; "MPs Seek Constitutional Change to Islamic Law," *Arab Times*, August 27, 1993, p. 1.

41. (Surprises in the Elections . . .), *al-Qabas*, October 8, 1996, p. 1.

42. "The Islamists control half the seats in Parliament," *al-Watan al-'Arabi* (weekly), October 18, 1996, p. 18.

43. "37 Udwan Yas'un Lil-taghyir al-Dusturi" (37 Members Seek Constitutional Change), *al-Siyyasah*, January 23, 1997, p. 5.

44. *Al-Qabas*, December 25, 1996, p. 1; December 29, 1996, p. 7.

45. Interview with 'Alya Shu'ayb in *al-Hadath* (monthly), November 1996, pp. 22–24.

46. Interview with Ahmad Baghdadi, *al-Shulah* (student monthly), July 1996; interview with Sulaiman al-Badir, *al-Anba'* (daily), December 10, 1996.

47. *Al-Siyyasah*, January 2, 1997, p. 1.

48. *Al-Anba'*, December 21, 1991.

49. Muhammad Shahrur, *Al-Kitab wal Quran* (*The Book and the Quran*), 3rd ed. (Beirut: Sharikat al-Matbu'at lil Tawzi' Wal Nashr, 1993).

50. Shafeeq Ghabra, "Kuwait and the Dynamics of Socio-economic Change" *Middle East Journal*, Vol. 51, No. 3 (Summer, 1997), pp. 361–372.

8

The Rise of the Islamist Movement in Turkey

Nilufer Narli

Beginning in the 1950s and peaking in the 1980s, a number of developments greatly advanced Turkey's modernization. These same events also transformed Turkish politics. The result was a confrontation between provincial/traditional and urban/modern cultures, new social classes, and the fragmentation of the conservative electorate from the 1970s onward.[1] This same situation provided the environment for the growth of Islamist parties in Turkey pilfering votes from their center-right competitors.[2]

Islamist political movements vary greatly among different states in their doctrines and strategies.[3] Turkey's groups have their own distinctive history. In Turkey, the Islamist movement emerged soon after the founding of the secular republic in 1923.[4] It was led by *tarikat* (religious order) shaykhs and professional men of religion who lost their status and economic power when secular reforms abolished religious institutions.[5] Trying to stage revolts against the secular state in the 1920s and 1930s, the movement failed to gain wide support and was crushed by the authorities.[6] In general, though, Islamist groups stayed underground during the era of one-party rule between 1923 and 1946.

With the transition to a multiparty system in 1946, Islamist groups formed covert and overt alliances with the ruling center-right Democratic Party (1950–1960).[7] After the Democratic Party won the 1950 elections, it softened its secularist policies. With the provision of civil liberties in the 1961 constitution, Islamist groups began to operate legally, though their activities were still technically banned.[8] Until Necmettin Erbakan established the National Order Party

(NOP) in January 1970, Islamists had either formed conservative factions in a center-right party or had remained underground. With the NOP, however, for the first time Islamists had an autonomous party organization through which they could campaign for their agenda. Since the NOP's founding, the same Islamist party has endured, albeit under different names: NOP (1970–1971), National Salvation Party (NSP) (1972–1981), Welfare Party (1983–1998), and Virtue Party (1997–2001).

The NOP largely represented Anatolian cities controlled by religiously conservative Sunnis, and the small traders and artisans (*esnaf*) of the hinterland.[9] These groups had long waited to benefit from the state's modernization policies but had rarely done so, partly due to their own resistance to modernization in the name of religion and tradition. For example, girls were not often sent to school. In addition to the frustrated periphery, the NOP also represented religiously conservative people who were informal members of outlawed religious orders. These people formed silent, but powerful, pressure groups with a large network.

The NOP was shut down by the Constitutional Court on May 20, 1971— due to military pressure—on the grounds that it violated the principles of laicism laid down in the constitution (the preamble and articles 2, 19, and 57) and in the Law of Political Parties (Law No. 648, articles 92, 93, and 94).[10] As a result, the National Salvation Party (NSP) was founded in October 1972 to succeed the NOP. With support from provincial merchants, the *esnaf*, and the covert network of two leading, informally organized religious groups, the Nakshibandis and Nurcus, the NSP achieved a surprising electoral success in the 1973 general elections, obtaining 11.8 percent of the total vote, mainly in central and eastern Anatolia.

After its solid showing in the 1973 general elections, the NSP became a coalition partner in successive governments. First, it formed a government with the staunchly secularist Republican People's Party (CHP) led by Bulent Ecevit. Soon after, it managed to place its members in the bureaucracy, particularly the ministries that it controlled. Moreover, it succeeded in passing a bill that made theological high schools (*imam-hatip*) equal to secondary schools and enabled these schools' often pro-Islamist students to attend universities. A large number of girls also enrolled in these schools. Many graduates have gone on to political power as Islamists in the 1980s and 1990s (as in the case of the mayor of Istanbul, Recep Tayip Erdogan) and have formed a powerful pressure group.

Ecevit's coalition government collapsed following Turkey's July 1974 military operation in Cyprus to protect the Turkish-Cypriot community. The NSP then became a coalition partner in a new "National Front" government on March 31, 1975, formed under the premiership of Suleyman Demirel's center-right Justice Party (JP). This coalition also included the ultranationalist National Action Party (NAP) led by Alpaslan Turkes.

In the June 1977 general elections, the NSP suffered a setback, winning only 8.6 percent of the vote, but was included in the second National Front

government formed by Demirel after the elections. In July 1977 Demirel resigned, but he returned to power in August at the head of an almost identical
coalition including the NSP, NAP, and JP. However, Demirel was forced to
resign again following defections from the JP in December. Ecevit formed a
coalition government in January 1978, promising to deal with the economic
problems and political violence that were increasing as a result of conflict between left and right as well as between Sunnis and Alevis. But the JP's victory
in the by-elections of October 1979 deprived Ecevit of his working majority, and
he resigned. In November 1979, Demirel formed an all-JP minority government
with the backing of the NAP and NSP. In short, the NSP had quickly grown
to become a regular member of government coalitions.

In the late 1970s, successive governments failed to solve the country's serious economic and political problems as antagonism between the radical left and
radical right escalated into violent clashes bordering on civil war. The armed
forces, led by General Kenan Evren, seized power in a bloodless coup on September 12, 1980 and restructured the political system with a new military-
drafted constitution in 1982. The leading parties, including the JP, NAP, and
NSP, were banned from political activity.

On July 19, 1983 the Welfare Party (RP) was formed under the leadership
of Ali Turkmen, in place of the banned Erbakan, replacing the NSP. Erbakan was
eventually reinstated into Turkish politics and became the Welfare Party's leader.
In the first general elections entered under Erbakan's leadership, in November
1987, the RP received 7.2 percent of the total vote. In the 1989 local elections
it polled 9.8 percent, showing signs of increased support in Istanbul and capturing municipalities in several districts. In the October 1991 general elections, the
RP formed an electoral alliance with Turkes' ultra-nationalist party and together
obtained 16.7 percent of the total vote. During this time the Islamist movement
drew support from larger segments of the population, the majority of which had
migrated from rural to urban centers.

One of the Islamist movement's important strategies was to develop an
educated counter-elite as a base of support, especially by strengthening the Islamic stream in the educational system. During the post-1980 coup period,
governments perceived Islamic education in the schools as a panacea against
extremist ideologies.[11]

As Islamist supporters moved from provincial towns and villages to urban
centers, they were more likely to gain access to formal education and opportunities for upward social mobility. Islamist groups responded to the needs and
aspirations of the newly urban who might be university students, professionals,
shopkeepers, merchants, or workers. The groups offered food to the needy,
scholarships and hostels to university students, a network for young graduates
looking for jobs, and credit to shopkeepers, industrialists, and merchants.[12] Self-
help projects conducted by women were particularly important to this endeavor.
Financial assistance came from a newly formed Islamist business elite.

In the late 1980s, a new urban middle class and business elite emerged whose members often came from provincial towns. Their parents were often self-employed small traders and shopkeepers, merchants, and agrarian capitalists. Some of them came from state-employed families. Many provincial youths from this background moved to big cities where they had access to higher education. After graduation, many joined the urban middle class through employment in the modern economic sector, which expanded in the 1980s as a result of reforms that replaced the statist economic model with a liberal approach.

The liberal and export-oriented economic development model adopted by then Prime Minister Turgut Ozal gave birth to a new business elite, also with a provincial background. This new model provided opportunities not only for the established business elite, but also for the small and medium businessmen in Anatolian towns. Some of them have developed their businesses there. Others moved to Istanbul, seeking opportunities for expansion in this newly invigorated commercial center.

Having their origins in Anatolian towns, the new business elite desired to assert its provincial identity and preserve its values and traditions. Consequently, its members—dubbed "Anatolian Lions" ("*Anadolu Aslanlari*")—differentiate themselves from the more urban, Westernized business elite represented by TUSIAD (The Turkish Businessmen's and Industrialists' Association, founded in 1971), whose members are the chief executives of Turkey's 300 biggest corporations. In contrast, the Anatolian Lions follow the leadership of the pro-Islamist MUSIAD (the Association of Independent Industrialists and Businessmen) and now challenge the established business elite.

MUSIAD was founded on May 5, 1990 in Istanbul by a number of young pro-Islamic businessmen: Erol Yarar,[13] who was the president until May 1999, Ali Bayramolu, who replaced Yarar, Natik Akyol, and Abdurrahman Esmerer. The first letter of its acronym is commonly perceived as standing for *Muslim* rather than for *mustakil* (independent). The founders of MUSIAD aimed to create an "Islamic economic system" as an alternative to the existing "capitalist system" in Turkey.

This goal, though, remained only a slogan. The group's membership reached 400 in 1991, 1,700 by 1993, and 3,000 in 1998.[14] In that year, its members' companies' annual revenue reached $2.79 billion. Members are active in most sectors of the economy, particularly in manufacturing, textiles, chemical and metallurgical products, automotive parts, building materials, iron and steel, and food products. There are also several powerful Islamist finance houses, some of which have been hit by the February 2001 economic crisis. In 1998 MUSIAD aimed to increase its membership to 5000 and the number of its branch offices from 28 to 40 by the year 2000.[15] However, this goal was not reached. In September 2001 its membership was 2300 and the number of branch offices was 27, showing an actual decrease in membership due to the anti-Islamist policies adopted after the February 28, 1997 National Security Council meeting.

The Islamist movement is an outlet to express political dissatisfaction with the existing order on the part of the geographical periphery and specific social groups with grievances or different interests. At least five types of relationships are represented here: center-periphery conflict,[16] class cleavages, regional cleavages, Islamist-secularist conflict, and sectarian antagonism (that is, Sunnis vs. Alevis).

The country's central government and main institutions are led by military officers, senior bureaucrats, notables, and industrialists. Those living in, or belonging to groups based in peripheral areas have traditionally been distanced from power.

Thus, we see a progression in which specific socioeconomic and peripheral regional groups have backed a succession of parties in order to voice their grievances. During the 1950s, the Democratic Party, in opposing the centralist elite represented by the Republican People's Party, represented the periphery, including peasants and the provincial bourgeoisie as well as Islamists and religiously conservative people dissatisfied with secular policies.

In the 1960s and 1970s, its successor, the Justice Party, was also sensitive to Islamic demands in the electorate, while representing newly emerged bourgeois elements—agrarian capitalists, big capital, the provincial bourgeoisie—as well as peasants and petty traders. Thus, it was different from the center-right political parties that represented big capital and the urban middle class in Western Europe.

While peasants and petty traders had voted for the Justice Party until the mid-1970s, by the 1973 general elections the Anatolian *esnaf* and some segments of the religiously conservative provincial lower and middle classes switched to the National Salvation Party. Clashes between the left and right in the 1970s, however, became the central feature of political life in that era and led to military intervention in 1980. The Justice Party and other parties were outlawed.

In the post-coup period, the Motherland Party came forth to represent the center-right. Rather than representing only bourgeois classes, it had to represent a diversified electorate. It included a conservative faction representing the religiously conservative provincial bourgeoisie and new urban classes, and a liberal faction representing an urban managerial class expanding as a result of Ozal's liberal economic model. In this coalition, the Motherland Party represented Islamists and moderate ultranationalists on the one hand, and adherents of liberal democratic values on the other.

The Motherland Party was able to keep such an ideologically diversified constituency together until the late 1980s when the True Path party, which had a strong hold on some rural sectors, challenged its base. In addition, Motherland was subverted by the Islamist and ultranationalist parties. Consequently, the Motherland membership was fragmented. The culmination of this political change came in the 1999 election with a reduced Motherland and True Path vote, and enhanced support for the pro-Islamist Virtue Party, ultranationalist MHP (Nationalist Action Party), and a small but growing pro-Kurdish HADEP (People's

Democracy Party). Emerging victorious from the fragmented political scene was the Democratic Left Party (DSP), combining nationalist rhetoric with liberal democratic values.

The migration of many people to cities—in search of upward social mobility—since the 1950s has often meant merely transforming rural poverty into urban poverty. In the cities, immigrants suffer from substandard housing conditions and a lack of infrastructure. They constitute a new periphery whose members are often economically disadvantaged, culturally disintegrated, and politically isolated. Their social rage has fostered extreme political tendencies since the beginning of the 1970s. In the 1970s the revolutionary left articulated its political discontent and anti-regime sentiments. In the 1980s and 1990s, the Islamist movement took on this role.

Conflict caused by regional economic imbalances in the 1990s and the sectarian antagonism between the Sunnis and Alevis[17] have further complicated the political tension. Corruption allegations have aggravated social rage and mobilized people to turn to radical parties and groups challenging the system. The result has been political polarization and radicalization and a progressive decline in backing for the center-right and center-left parties since the late 1980s.[18]

The socioeconomic background, political aims, and interests of those supporting the Islamist movement are diverse.[19] Its supporters include the large university student population, especially upwardly mobile youths who must compete with the established urban middle and upper-middle classes; members of the unskilled young urban subproletariat, whose numbers have increased with migration and a higher level of unemployment;[20] and some of the state-employed petit bourgeoisie, proletarianized by falling real wages and high inflation, particularly since the early 1990s. In addition, there are bourgeoisie factions including some from the relatively privileged new middle and upper classes: rich merchants, businessmen, and industrialists of humble *esnaf* origins, as well as several rural agrarian capitalists.

In Anatolia, among the religiously conservative Sunni Turks who have perceived modernization as an attack on their family values and tradition, there are also sectors of ultranationalists who have embraced Islamist attitudes and a sizeable number of religiously conservative Sunni Kurds[21] who assume that an Islamic order could possibly bring solutions to the conflict in their region, which has cost more than 35,000 lives since the early 1980s.[22]

As a result of these different developments, which furnished a base for Islamist politics, the Welfare Party scored a success in the March 1994 local elections. The RP won 28 mayorships including six major metropolitan centers, and leadership of 327 local governments. Nationwide, the RP received 19 percent of the vote. In the 1995 general elections, it obtained 21.4 percent.

The RP joined in July 1996 with Tansu Ciller's True Path Party to form a coalition government which lasted one year. Legislative disputes between the two partners were intensified by a crisis created by Welfare Party mayors and deputies, whose anti-secular rhetoric and activities agitated secular public opinion. Erbakan's relationship with Muammar Qadhafi also made some suggest the Turkish prime minister might owe ultimate allegiance to Libya's dictator, who headed a secretive organization called the Islamic People's Command, to which Erbakan also belonged.[23]

These developments exacerbated tensions between the military and the Welfare Party, which had been building due to a number of factors, including: disagreement over the expulsion of Islamist officers from the army in December 1996; the Welfare Party's attempt to sign a defense cooperation agreement with Iran; Welfare's call for lifting the ban on head-covering for female university students and civil servants; the dispute over building a mosque at Istanbul's Taksim Square; the Iranian-inspired Jerusalem Night (January 31, 1997) in the Welfare-controlled Sincan district of Ankara, where anti-regime slogans were shouted; and Erbakan's reluctance to endorse the National Security Council's February 28, 1997 meeting that called for curbing Islamist activities.[24]

The Welfare Party's anti-democratic position on several issues also disappointed secular public opinion. For example, Erbakan and Justice Minister Sevket Kazan made critical and insulting comments about people who took part in the "One Minute of Darkness for Enlightenment" civil protest in February 1997.[25] Welfare's support for constitutional changes made some worry that it was trying to dilute the secular state. Women worried about the reduction of their rights.[26] The party's allegiance to democracy was also called into question. Islamist dailies including *Akit* and *Yeni Safak* were also severely critical of the January–February 1997 protest. Finally, there were many allegations that the Welfare Party had connections with militant Islamist groups.[27]

As a result, tension between the military and the Welfare Party, as well as antagonism between the Islamists and secular public opinion, escalated. This provided a legitimate framework to bring the Welfare Party to court in May 1997. Consequently, the Constitutional Court outlawed the Welfare Party in January 1998, banning Erbakan from politics, on the grounds that the party violated the principles of secularism and the law of the political parties. Moreover, on June 28, 1998, Erbakan was charged with defaming the Constitutional Court by saying that the Court's ruling had no historic value and would eventually rebound against those who had made it.[28] By dissolving the party, the ruling left more than 100 seats vacant in Parliament and orphaned local administrations.

A new party, the Virtue Party (FP), was founded by thirty-three former RP deputies under the leadership of Recai Kutan on December 17, 1997. At the time it had 144 seats in Parliament, which it obtained as a result of the switchover of former RP deputies. The party's conservative wing, controlled by Erbakan, elected the parliamentary group leaders before the reformist wing, led by then Istanbul Mayor Recep Tayip Erdogan, could pull itself together. But the struggle for power between the party's young reformists and those loyal to Erbakan was not over. It eventually resulted in the resignation of four of the reformists (Cemil

Cicek, Ali Coskun, Abduallah Gul, and Abdulkadir Aksu) on July 26, 1999. Their resignation was interpreted as the start of a new party given the fact that since the April 1999 elections, the Constitutional Court had been deliberating about closing down the Virtue Party on charges that it was carrying out anti-secular activities and was the successor to the RP. However, the parliamentarians denied any plan to form a new party.

Prior to the 1999 local and general elections, the Virtue Party set up organizations in all districts of the country and began recruiting new members and renewing its membership profile.[29] The party has also tried to soften its anti-women, anti-democracy image. It recruited a number of highly educated, upper-middle class modern women such as Nazli Ilicak and Professor Doctor Oya Akgonenc. Women from lower social classes carried the party to power, and were able to participate in public life as result. But, despite their contribution, they were not represented at the higher ranks. The Virtue Party appointed Ilicak, Akgonenc, and Gulten Celik to its Central Decisionmaking Board. Only Celik wears a head-covering.

Both Turkey's leaders and the party's own supporters ask how the FP differs from the RP. The Virtue Party has signaled that it takes some new approaches. For example, the FP declared support for Turkey's European Union membership, a step the RP opposed for three decades. Virtue's appointment of two women who do not wear head-coverings to its Central Decisionmaking Board stands in clear contrast to the Welfare Party's demand that its supporters observe an Islamic dress code. Indeed, the FP has downplayed the head-covering issue altogether. Third, instead of mentioning the old party's "Islamic mission," Virtue's rhetoric emphasizes democracy, human rights, and personal liberty.[30] The FP presents the head scarf ban as a human rights violation and a suppression of personal liberties, rather than as a matter of religion.[31]

Another change in the Virtue Party's rhetoric is its highlighting of the theme of *millet* (nation), as opposed to the RP's strong organic link between millet and *devlet* (state). The implication in the Virtue Party's stance is that the state should be in the service of the people rather than—as in the RP's view—a holy entity that stands far above the people.[32] The FP pledges to create a democratic and humanitarian state that meets the millet's needs. This issue has become a dominant topic in *Milli Gazette*, a religious newspaper, since January 1998. Moreover, the FP co-opted the Western concept of human rights and democratic norms, and leftist criticism of income inequality in its rhetoric.[33]

Another interesting development is the FP's position on the "Kurdish issue." The RP had not been hesitant to talk about the Kurds' identity and cultural rights without seeming to go further in backing bigger demands. The FP's chairman, Recai Kutan, spoke in favor of "cultural rights," announcing in August 1998: "It would be necessary to recognize some of the rights of Turkey's Kurdish identity. The right to educate and publish in the Kurdish language would have to be considered after discussions and a normalization period."[34]

However, the FP became more cautious after the capture of outlawed PKK leader Abdullah Ocalan in February 1999.

The FP has tried to change its image in a number of ways. For example, rather than holding social gatherings segregated by gender, as it did in the past, it now organizes dinner parties where men and women mix freely. (Nazli Ilicak and Recai Kutan sang together at a dinner party in 1998.) While such an endeavor alienates religiously conservative supporters, party leaders understand the necessity of improving the party's image and making concessions.

Islamism in Turkey has grown as a response to social, economic, and political discontent, the causes of which include foreign influences, urbanization, modernization, and secularization. The Islamist movement's upsurge, the growth of ultranationalism, and Kurdish ethno-nationalism have eroded the center in Turkey. The center-right parties have declined because they did not meet their constituency's needs or expectations and also failed to absorb the compromising spirit of democratic liberalism.

In the context of modern Turkish political history, the Welfare and Virtue parties must be understood not only in terms of their specific Islamist ideology but also as representative of specific social sectors reacting to circumstances. Equally, and partly as a result of this fact, the erosion of the center-right and increased support for the Islamist and ultra-nationalist parties have not yet created the danger of regime instability.[35] The nationalist secular majority in Turkey,[36] supporters of the DSP and other parties, act as a counterweight to the Islamist and ultranationalist groups both in public life and in Parliament.

While anti-Islamist forces counterbalance Islamist politics, the Islamists are divided over the strategies to be adopted in response to certain developments, including the military's initiative to curb Islamist activities by formulating an eleven-point plan in February 1997, and the failure of the Islamist state in Iran reflected in the election of a moderate president, Mohammed Khatami, and the overwhelming victory of moderates in the 2000 parliamentary elections in Iran. The eleven-point plan played a major role in compelling the Turkish Islamists to alter their program, while the developments in Iran had a minor effect in motivating them to reconsider their theory and political action plan.

It is possible to foresee three major trends in the future evolution of the Islamist movement in Turkey by analyzing the current inclinations.[37] First, some of the radical groups that formerly resorted to political violence, such as Hizballah's Ilim faction, the IBDA-C (Islami Buyuk Dogu Akincilari-Cephesi—Islamic Great Eastern Raiders' Front), and the Muslim Youth, will choose to stay outside the system and continue to pursue their radical political agenda without considering reconciliation with the system. Other radicals who did not formerly adopt armed struggle as a strategy will ally with the second set of Islamists, consisting of nonmilitant groups and political parties that have worked within the system to gain a share in political power.[38] While many in the second group continue to

employ constitutional political means to obtain political power, some have begun to withdraw from the political arena in response to the state's intolerance
of political Islam since the 1997 February National Security Council meeting.
Instead they discover new areas of Islam that will insure the survival of their
Islamic program. One of their options will be to target the individual and
nurture his religiosity and piety by means of Islamic education and cultural
activities with an aim of creating a highly religious society that could be politicized at the right time.[39] Their new rhetoric emphasizes that Islam is a religion,
not a political ideology. For many of them, even some of those who were
inspired by the Iranian revolution and its ideology, Tehran is not a guide for the
future. On the contrary, they criticize Tehran on grounds that it uses Islam as
a political instrument to build and sustain a nation state. They believe that the
Iranian Islamic system has failed but not the Islamist cause and that theory of
the latter is valid in all spaces and in all times. The third group chooses to pursue
political Islam and work within the existing system by revising its Islamic rhetoric and party program and co-opting the Western concepts of human rights and
universal democratic norms. This group has become less averse to Western
modernity and norms after admitting that its resistance is futile.

Despite taking different paths and employing diverse plans of action ranging from political undertakings to cultural projects, the different groups still
share the same goal: to rebuild the individual and society and revise the nation's
thought and politics based on Islam.

The Islamist movement is not likely to lose popular support because Islam has
spread to the cultural and political mainstream, and social discontent, which has
been one of the key factors sustaining its growth, is not likely to decrease. On the
contrary, economic problems, which generally fuel popular disappointment, continue to hit salary and wage earners due to a fall in real wages. Should the
government trim agricultural subsidies in an effort to bring Turkey's economy in
line with European Union norms, the agricultural sector might also voice its
dissatisfaction.[40] Such a situation could lead to a large-scale migration from rural
areas to urban areas in a very few years, and in turn, is more likely to increase the
number of the unemployed urban poor. This new wave of rural-urban migration
would complicate the problem of social dislocation that resulted from migration
from rural areas in the Black Sea region and troubled southeastern and eastern
provinces from the mid-1980s until the late 1990s. The Islamists or other groups
whose members have an antithetical attitude towards the existing system would
exploit the likely expansion of the discontented ally, comprising the newly urbanized and economically disadvantaged social classes referred to above.

As a result of the party's own electoral shortcomings and the government's
pressure against it—capped by the Virtue Party's closure by the Constitutional
Court on June 22, 2001—the Islamists split into two separate parties. Erbakan's
supporters created the Saadet Party (The Party of Blissfulness) on July 20, 2001.
But on August 11, 2001, Tayyip Erdogan, the former mayor of Istanbul, formed

the Akparti (Adalet ve Kalkinma Partisi, The Justice and Development Party). Erdogan had been convicted of making a seditious statement after a speech which suggested that Turks had to choose between God and Ataturk. He was temporarily banned from politics.

This development resulted essentially from two factors. On the one hand, there had been intensive external pressure for the Islamists to turn toward a more moderate ideology and strategy. The February 28, 1997 National Security Council meeting had sent a serious warning that the state and armed forces would move against Islamist forces deemed too radical in seeking to change the basis of the Turkish state. The fall of Erbakan's government had sent a strong warning signal to the Islamists, reinforced by the banning of Virtue four years later.

On the other hand, there were also genuine conflicts within the party over its doctrine and goals. There was a clear generational aspect of this struggle, with some relatively younger leaders rebelling against Erbakan's heavy-handed control. To some extent, too, the battle was one for personal power among several contenders and factions.

Each side would argue that it has the proper formula for winning the voter's support. Erdogan represents a more modernization-oriented democratic approach which, it could be contended, is more likely to be acceptable to the power structure and to Islamists who want to be in tune with the Turkish mainstream. Yet Erbakan's supporters can claim that by watering down traditional stances, the moderates will lose the backing of the old base of social conservatives and religious devotees.

Only time will tell whether either approach can produce a party that can survive both the voter's scrutiny and the state's response. After many decades, Islamist politics have not yet found their place in Turkey's society and political structure.

NOTES

1. For the voting behavior of the Turkish electorate, see Ersin Kalaycioglu, "The Turkish Political System in Transition in the 1980s," *Current Turkish Thought*, Vol. 56. (Fall 1985), pp. 2–38; Ersin Kalaycioglu, "Elections and Party Preferences in Turkey: Changes and Continuities in the 1990s," *Comparative Political Studies*, Vol. 27, No. 3 (1994), pp. 402–424; Ergun Ozbudun and Frank Tachau, "Social Change and Electoral Behaviour in Turkey: Toward a Critical Realignment," *International Journal of Middle East Studies*, Vol. 6 (1975), pp. 460–480; Ergun Ozbudun, "Turkey," in J. M. Landau, E. Ozbudun and F. Tachau (eds.), *Electoral Politics in the Middle East: Issues, Votes and Elites* (London: Croom Helm, 1980), pp. 107–143.

2. Turkish modernization began in the nineteenth century with the Tanzimat reforms. The Young Ottomans' ideas of constitutionalism, parliamentary government and secular education and the ideas of the Young Turks on a modern nation state provided the intellectual framework of the Turkish modernization.

3. For the definition of the Islamist and the differences between the radical and moderate Islamists, see Nilufer Narli, "Moderate Against Radical Islamicism in Turkey,"

Zeitschrift Fur Turkeistudien, Vol. 1, No. 96 (Zentrum Fur Turkeistudien. Essen University, 1996), pp. 35–59.

4. The history of the Islamist movements goes back to nineteenth century Ottoman rule. The author focuses here on Islamist movements in the Turkish republic.

5. Tarikats were banned in 1925. They then went underground and were organized as secret brotherhood groups. In the 1980s they discovered new strategies to organize themselves as legal entities. They have established foundations under various names, which enable them to operate legally and have avenues of fund raising.

6. For example, Kozanli Ibrahim and his friends revolted to demand Arabic Ezan on February 1, 1933 in Bursa; Shaykh Halit' declared himself as Mahdi in December 1935 and a series of bloody insurgencies led by his son Shaykh Kudus ensued; and Kayserili Ahmet Kalayci proclaimed a new religious order in Iskilip and consequently incited the public in 1936. See Cetin Ozek, *Devlet ve Din (State and Religion)* (Istanbul: Ada Yayinlari, 1986), p. 498.

7. Particularly, the Nurcus adopted the strategy of forming an alliance with a center right political party. They approached Adnan Menderes, the chief of the Democratic Party. Seeing his responsiveness to their overtures, they called him "Musluman Menderes" and supported him in the 1950 general elections. They expected Menderes to restore Islam and even include Said-i Nursi's Risalei Nur articles in the school curriculum. See Cetin Ozek, *State and Religion,* p. 544.

8. For further details on the strategies of the Islamist groups, see Narli, "Moderate Against Radical Islamicism in Turkey," pp. 35–59.

9. The support of the provincial merchants and the *esnaf* (small shopkeepers, artisans), and the covert network of the two leading informally organized religious groups, the *Nakshibandi*s and *Nurcu*s, played a role in the surprising electoral success of the National Salvation Party in the 1973 general elections. It obtained 11.8 percent of the total vote while collecting over 15 percent of the vote in twenty provinces of central and eastern Anatolia but not in the urban centers. For a profile of Islamists who voted for the National Salvation Party in the 1973 elections, see Ergun Ozbudun, "Islam and Politics in Modern Turkey: The Case of the National Salvation Party," in Barbara Freyer Stowasser (ed.), *The Islamic Impulse* (Washington, Center for Contemporary Arab Studies, Georgetown University, 1987), pp. 142–156; and Binnaz Toprak, *Islam and Political Development in Turkey* (Leiden: E. J. Brill, 1981). Similarly, in Iran the bazaari class was an ally of the Islamic Revolution. See Nikki Keddie, "Iranian Revolutions in Comparative Perspective" in Edmund Burke and Ira M. Lapidus (eds.), *Islam, Politics and Social Movements* (Berkeley: University of California Press, 1988), pp. 293–313.

10. Bihterin Dinckol, *1982 Anayasasi Cercevesinde ve Anayasa Kararlarinda Laiklik* (Laicism in the Constitutional Context and in the 1982 Constitution) (Istanbul: Kazanci Hukuk Yayinlari, 1992), p. 179.

11. For the Islamist student movement and associations, see Elizabeth Ozdalga, "Civil Society and its Enemies: Reflections on a Debate in the Light of Recent Developments within the Islamic Movement in Turkey" in Elizabeth Ozdalga and Suna Persson (eds.), *Civil Society, Democracy and the Muslim World* (London: Curzon, 1997), pp. 73–84.

12. For the mobility of the perpherial groups to urban centers and their gaining access to secular education, see Yilmaz Esmer and Muge Gocek, "Boundaries of Religious

Fundamentalism in Turkey," survey conducted in Istanbul and Konya in 1994; paper presented at Bogazici University, May 1995. For the Welfare Party's mobilization of this newly urbanized social group by providing it moral and material support, and in turn, obtaining its electoral support in the 1994 local and 1995 general elections, see Sencer Ayata, "Patronage, Party and State: The Politicisation of Islam in Turkey," *Middle East Journal*, Vol. 50, No.1, (1996). pp. 40–58.

13. On May 25, 1998 the State Security Court (DGM) prosecutor demanded the closure of MUSIAD for violating the laws governing societies and associations. The court also charged MUSIAD Chairman Erol Yarar, a 36-year-old U.S.-educated businessman, with "inciting hatred amongst the people" in a speech he made on October 4, 1997 criticizing a law that brought restrictions on religious education. See *Turkish Probe*, May 31, 1998, p. 18. According to the Turkish penal code, article 312-2, inciting hatred by making reference to class, race, religion, sect, or regional differences is a crime punishable by a jail sentence of one to three years. It is worth mentioning that the Virtue Party introduced a bill asking for the abolition of Article 312–2. In his speech, Yarar called for a "liberation struggle," and that constituted a crime according to the prosecutor. Yarar also likened to "dogs" the proponents of the law, which extended compulsory education from five to eight years. He also described the new education law as the work of "non-believers" by saying, "uninterrupted education is certainly unreligious education" ("kesintisiz egitim kesin dinsiz egitim"). Yarar's hearing was held on June 29, 1998 in the State Security Court in Ankara. The prosecutor asked for a one- to three-year prison term. At the hearing on July 29, Yarar denied his opposition to eight-year compulsory education. *Turkish Probe*, May 31, 1998, p. 12. However, MUSIAD was highly critical of the new arrangements in the education system and the closure of the middle section of the imam-hatip schools in its March 31, 1998 press bulletin. MUSIAD *Basin Bulteni*, March 31, 1998, Istanbul; see <http://www.musiad.com>. In May 1999 the court convicted Yarar, and he resigned.

14. *MUSIAD Bulteni*, May–June 1998, No. 29, p. 37. For the membership profile and activities of MUSIAD, see "MUSIAD in the U.S." Special Supplement of the *Turkish Daily News*, May 21, 1997. For further information, see Nilüfer Narli, "The Tension between the Center and Peripheral Economy and the Rise of a Counter Business Elite in Turkey," *Islam en Turquie. Les Annales de L'Autre Islam*, No. 6 (Paris: INALCO, 1999), pp. 50–72.

15. It has branch offices in Ankara, Konya, Izmir, Kocaeli, Kayseri, Bursa, Balikesir, Gaziantep, Denizli, Kahramanmarai, Adana, Karadeniz Eregli, Samsun, Corum, Malatya, Sanliurfa, Cankiri, Bandirma, Diyarbakir, Bartin, Gebze, Elazig, Icel, Inegol, Adapazari, Eskisehir, and Antalya.

16. For the center-periphery conflict and its significance in the rise of the Islamist movement, see Serif Mardin, "Center-Periphery Conflict: A Key to Turkish Politics," *Dedalus*, Vol. 102, No. 1, (1973) pp. 169–190.

17. For example, the Sivas incident on July 2, 1993, when 37 Alevis were burned as a result of an alleged arson attack by Islamists agitated by a speech delivered by Aziz Nesin. According to press reports, Nesin, speaking at an Alevi cultural festival, proclaimed the reign of the 1,000-year-old Quran over. See *Turkish Daily News*, July 5, 1993. (Nesin had previously angered the Islamists by publishing excerpts from British author Salman Rushdie's *The Satanic Verses*.)

18. Nilufer Narli and Sinan Dirlik, "Turkiye'nin Siyasi Haritasi" ("The Political Map of Turkey"), *Yeni Turkiye Dergisi*, Vol. 2, No. 9 (May–June 1996), pp. 125–151.

19. The profile of the Islamists is based on an empirical study by the author: Nilufer Narli, *The Islamist Movement, University Students and Politics in Turkey* (unpublished report presented to the Ford Foundation, 1996).

20. It has been observed that the young urban subproletariat is vulnerable to the radical Islamist movement in Middle Eastern countries as well. See Saad Eddin Ibrahim, "Crises, Elites, and Democratization in the Arab World," *Middle East Journal*, Vol. 47, No. 2 (Spring 1993), pp. 293–305. The growing youth population, its lack of access to education and professional opportunities and its potential to turn to extremist movements in the Middle East have been a concern to the students of Middle East politics. See Gad. G. Gilbar, *Population Dilemmas in the Middle East* (London: Frank Cass, 1997); and Alan Richards, "Economic Imperatives and Political Systems," *Middle East Journal*, Vol. 47, No. 2 (1993), pp. 217–227.

21. Most Kurds are orthodox Sunni Muslims who belong to the Shaafi School, whereas the majority of Turks subscribe to Hanefi doctrine as classified by Islamic law. Kurds have traditionally been religious and involved in the various *tarikat*s that have flourished in eastern Turkey. Tarikat leaders and shaykhs have always had a great influence on the Turkish Kurds owing to their feudal tradition. Shaykhs have been able to dictate decisions of great importance in people's lives. Along with being a key element in social life, Islamic elements have a political function too. Religious elements can be instrumental in political action. There are cases confirming this hypothesis. The first two decades of the republic witnessed several Kurdish rebellions (for example, the Shaykh Said Revolt in 1925, Agri, Zile and finally Dersim in 1937) led by religious shaykhs and tribal leaders. Islamic as well as ethnic sentiments triggered these revolts.

22. For information on Turkey's separatist Kurdish party, the PKK (Kurdistan Workers' Party), led by Abdullah Ocalan (recently captured, tried, and sentenced to death), see Ismet Imset, *The PKK: A Report on Separatist Violence in Turkey 1979–1992*. (Istanbul: Turkish Daily News Publications, 1992); and Henri J. Barkey and Grahan Fuller, *Turkey's Kurdish Question*, Carnegie Commission on Preventing Deadly Conflict, Carnegie Corporation of New York (New York: Rowman and Littfield Publishers, 1998).

23. For details, see "As If Troubles at Home Were Not Enough . . . ," (no author indicated), *Briefing*, April 2, 1997, No. 8 (Ankara).

24. MGK *(National Security Council)* is a constitutional body. Article 118 of the 1982 constitution establishes the MGK as a body evenly divided between five civilians (the president, prime minister, and ministers of defense, internal affairs, and foreign affairs) and five military officials (the chief of the general staff, the commanders of the army navy, and air force, and the general commander of the gendarmerie). The recommendations of the MGK are given priority during legislative procedure. Article 118 states: "the Council of Ministers shall give priority consideration to the decisions of the National Security Council concerning the measure that it deems necessary for the preservation of the existence and independence of the State, the integrity and indivisibility of the country, and the peace and security of society."

25. The "One Minute of Darkness for Enlightenment" civil protest was a response to the public perception of corruption and injustice in Turkey. In 1997 it began with a call for citizens to turn their lights off at 9:00 PM every night. The scope of the protest

got larger as thousands of people took to the streets carrying candles, putting them out at exactly 9:00 PM, and holding meetings to discuss ways of attaining their goal, an "enlightened" Turkey. It was largely supported by the center-left parties, but was criticized by the Welfare Party, the ultranationalist party, and the True Path Party.

26. For example, the Welfare Party opposed a bill passed by the Parliament on January 14, 1998, to protect women and children against domestic violence. For the law (No. 4320), see *Resmi Gazete*, (*Official Gazette*), January 17, 1998, No. 23233.

27. For example, there is an accusation that the former RP minister Uevket Kazan and RP deputy Sevki Yilmaz organized sending 150 Turkish students to Islamic countries, 30 of them to Egypt to receive "Shari'a commando" training. *Yeni Yüzyil* reported that a number of students connected with the now defunct RP had made confessions about being sent to Cairo's Al-Azhar University with false papers. These young people recount that in Egypt they stayed in houses belonging to the National View Organization and that they received armed training at Hizballah camps in Lebanon. They stress that their aim was an armed struggle to set up an Islamic state in Turkey. See *Yeni Yüzyil*, March 1, 1998, p. 10. An article in the daily *Cumhuriyet* (March 1, 1998) cited an "RP-linked foundation" as the focal point in the investigation extending from Al Azhar to Hizballah." *Cumhuriyet* (March 4, 1998) also reported that Istanbul State Security Court prosecutor Nuh Mete Yuksel indicated that investigators were looking into possible links with Turkish Hizballah and the European National View Organization (AMGT), which was considered to be a subsidiary of the now defunct Welfare Party (RP). *Cumhuriyet* also reported that the police were seeking three more AMGT officials. AMGT has many hostels and associations in Turkey and in Western Europe, as well as in the Middle East. For the unconstitutional activities of the militants groups, see Ely Karmon, "Islamic Terrorist Activities in Turkey in the 1990s," *Terrorism and Political Violence*, Vol. 10, No. 4 (Winter 1998), pp. 101–121.

28. Erbakan made this statement on January 18, 1998, soon after the closure of his party by the Constitutional Court. See *Turkish Daily News*, June 30, 1998.

29. For more on the organization of the FP, see M. Recai Kutan's press conference, *Turkiye'nin Oncelikleri ve Temel Goruslerimiz* ("Priorities of Turkey and Fundamentals of the Party"), (Bilkent, Ankara: Semih Offset, December 17, 1998).

30. University rectors agreed in 1998 to enforce a secular dress code that bans the wearing of head scarves in all universities. In January 1998 a government decree banned religious clothing, including the head scarf, for teachers, officials and students in all schools and universities. Universities and schools refused to register female students unless they submitted ID photographs showing an uncovered head and neck.

31. Virtue Party Chairman Recai Kutan said, "The headscarf ban was not a matter of religious belief but rather a human rights issue." Quoted in *Turkish Daily News*, September 11, 1998.

32. This analysis is based on an examination of the leading deputies' speeches and the articles in *Milli Gazete*, an organ of the Welfare Party/Virtue Party.

33. Observers have noted that many Islamist groups have adopted the Western concept of human rights as a new strategy to draw larger support and to criticise the state. See Bruce Maddy-Weitzman and Efraim Inbar (eds.), *Religious Radicalism in the Greater Middle East*, (London: Frank Cass, 1996).

34. Quoted in *Turkish Daily News*, August 13, 1998.

35. Roy Macridis, *Modern Political Systems: Europe* (New Jersey: Prentice Hall International, 1987).

36. A recent survey conducted by Binnaz Toprak and Ali Carkoglu shows that even religiously conservative people tend to support the separation of the state and Islam and are not for an Islamic state. See Toprak and Carkoglu, *Turkiye'de Siyasi Islam* (*Political Islam in Turkey*), a survey report submitted to the TESEV Foundation, Istanbul, May 1999.

37. The analysis of future trends in the Islamist movement and of changes in the theory and action plans of the Islamists is based on in-depth interviews with Islamist intellectuals and reading discussions from the mid-1990s on in *Hikmet ve Bilgi* quarterly and Yasin Aktay's book *Turk Dininin Sosyolojik Imkani* (*Sociological Feasibility of Turkish Islam*) (Istanbul: Iletisim, 2000).

38. Islamists in many Middle Eastern countries have abandoned the old strategy of toppling the state and moved in the direction of following legitimate political avenues. Ibrahim A. Karawan, *The Islamist Impasse* (Adelphi Paper no. 314, London: The International Institute for Strategic Studies, 1997).

39. While the Toprak and Carkoglu study shows that some religious people support separation of state and religion, religious people have a higher tendency to support political Islam and political parties representing Islamist causes, like the RP/FP. Toprak and Carkoglu, *Turkiye'de Siyasi Islam.*

40. The agriculture sector accounts for 14 percent of GDP and employs about half (43 percent) of the labor force. This sector, which is largely excluded from the customs union, continues to be subject to extensive and costly government intervention. Support for the sector has increased in recent years. According to OECD estimates, total transfers almost doubled in the period 1994 to 1997, reaching the equivalent of 7.5 percent of GDP. Support price interventions and the fertilizer subsidy continue to be serious drains on the budget. This is why the government has chosen to restrict and gradually eliminate agricultural subsidies.

9

Fethullah Gulen and His Liberal 'Turkish Islam' Movement

Bulent Aras and Omer Caha

The community that has developed under the influence of Fethullah Gulen, a prominent religious leader in Turkey, simultaneously has Islamic, nationalist, liberal, and modern characteristics. Its ability to reconcile traditional Islamic values with modern life and science has won a large, receptive audience. The group has even brought together divergent ideas and people, including the poor and the rich, the educated and the illiterate, Turks and Kurds, and Muslims and non-Muslims. Gulen's movement could be a model for the future of Islamic political and social activism.

In comparison to so-called 'fundamentalist' Islamic groups, Gulen's movement's views on Islam are surprisingly liberal and tolerant of non-Islamic lifestyles. However, this approach may be the result of the long-term, specific experience of the Anatolian people and the unique historical dynamics of Turkish sociocultural life. For example, the movement is influenced by the concept of 'Turkish Islam' formulated by some nationalist thinkers, and also the *Nurcu* or *Nur* (Light) movement that developed around the writings of Said Nursi.

The main premise of 'Turkish Islam' is moderation. Since people of Turkish origin first accepted Islam, they perceived and practiced it under the influence of Sufi ideas. Sufi-oriented Islamic movements kept a certain distance from the politics of their times in contrast to other Islamic movements. For example, the Shi'ites or Haricis defined themselves according to an imagined other (those who do not support the truth) and became associated with specific political stances over the proper nature of the state and who should hold power. Sufi tradition, however, has described itself as being based on the philosophy that all creatures should be loved as God's physical reflection and objects of the Creator's own love. There is no place for enemies or 'others' in this system.

Islam in Turkish political history, during the reigns of both the Seljuks and the Ottomans, remained under the state's guidance but as a private matter. The dominant belief was that a truly religious sultan would govern the state according to the principles of justice, equality, and piety. This approach of keeping religion apart from worldly affairs led to a collective memory that regarded Islam as a flexible and tolerant belief system. Thus, it was assumed that religious institutions should adopt flexible attitudes toward the changing situations of their times. In the Ottoman era, there was never a full-fledged theocratic system.

While the principles of Shari'a (Islamic law) were applied in the private sphere, public life was regulated according to customary law formulated under the authority of the state.[1] This aspect of the Ottoman political system made religion's role less rigid. Moreover, the empire accepted that it would be a multireligious state, in which Christian and Jewish subjects would continue to be governed by their own laws.

While Western domination of the Islamic world during the nineteenth century led some Muslims to reject Western ideas, the Ottomans adopted many Western innovations. For example, they opened Western-style schools (including women's schools), promulgated major programs for reform and human rights (the *Tanzimat Fermani* in 1839 and *Islahat Fermani* in 1856), developed a constitution, and opened a parliament in 1876. Said Nursi became one of the most insistent supporters of the parliamentary system at that time and later of the republican regime in Turkey.

In addition to this history of a Turco-Islamic heritage, another influence on Gulen's movement was the Nur movement (also known as the *Risale-i Nur* movement). The movement was organized around Said Nursi (1877–1961), a prominent religious authority, and his writings, the *Risale-i Nur* (Letters of Light). It spread throughout Turkey after 1950, despite the state's efforts, and had special success among the young and those educated in Turkey's secular education system mainly because Nursi argued that there was no contradiction between religion and science.[2] The *Risale-i Nur* is well thought of by religious moderates because of its emphasis on the links between Islam and reason, science, and modernity. It also rejects the idea that a clash between the 'East' and 'West' is either necessary or desirable and advocates the use of reason in issues related to Islamic belief.

Born in Erzurum in eastern Turkey in 1938, Gulen learned Arabic and religion from his father.[3] In 1953 he began his career as a government preacher (the only legal position a preacher can hold in Turkey), and in 1958 he took a teaching position at a mosque in Edirne. Four years later, he transferred to Izmir, where his movement began and came to be known by some as the "Izmir Community." During the era of military rule starting in 1971, he was arrested for clandestine religious activities (organizing summer camps to disseminate Islamic ideas) and spent seven months in prison. In the early 1980s, the police initiated a case against him, but he was not arrested due to the ruling military junta's relative tolerance of Islam. During the premiership of Turgut Ozal, Gulen gained official protection. He is now retired and living in both Izmir and Istanbul in modest homes given to him by followers, while continuing to write extensively.[4]

Throughout his career, Gulen, addressed by his followers as "respected teacher" (hocaefendi), has traveled the width and breadth of Turkey. He has also lectured abroad on such subjects as the Quran and contemporary science, the Islamic perception of Darwin, and social justice in Islam.

Gulen has knowledge of both traditional Islamic sources and Western philosophy, and is especially interested in Immanuel Kant.[5] He is an effective speaker in person and on television. His books have become bestsellers in Turkey. As Nuriye Akman, a senior Turkish columnist, concedes:

> He is like that "old-style gentleman" we read about in old books and see in old films. He says "estagfurullah" [I beg the pardon of God] in every other sentence. He speaks in delicate and polite phrases. He is extremely modest . . . He speaks in an even tone knowing what he will say and uses correct grammar and an Ottoman vocabulary.[6]

Gulen does not favor the state's applying Islamic law, the Shari'a. He points out that most Islamic regulations concern people's private lives and that only a small portion of them concern the state and government. These latter provisions need not be enforced because religion is a private matter, and its requirements should not be imposed on anyone.[7] He looks at Islamic regulations bearing directly on the government—such as those related to taxation and warfare—in the context of contemporary realities.

Concluding that the democratic form of government is the best choice, Gulen is very critical of the regimes in Iran and Saudi Arabia. He accepts Said Nursi's argument that the idea of republicanism is very much in accord with the idea of "consultation" discussed in Islamic sources. Moreover, he fears that an authoritarian regime would impose strict control on differing ideas. At the same time, though, Gulen views the state's role as important in "protecting stability."

Gulen's goals are simultaneously to Islamicize the Turkish nationalist ideology and to Turkify Islam. He hopes to re-establish the link between religion and state that existed in the Ottoman era, when leaders were expected to live their private lives based on Islamic regulations. Such an approach, he argues, would strengthen the state, and thus protect society by widening the state's base of legitimacy and enhancing its ability to mobilize the population.

Gulen holds that the Anatolian people's interpretations and experiences of Islam are different from those of others, especially the Arabs. He writes of an

"Anatolian Islam" based on tolerance and excluding harsh restrictions or fanaticism and frequently emphasizes that there should be freedom of worship and thought in Turkey. He proposes two keys to provide peace in society—tolerance and dialogue. "We can build confidence and peace in this country if we treat each other with tolerance."[8] In his view, "no one should condemn another for being a member of a religion or scold him for being an atheist."[9]

His ideas about tolerance and dialogue are not restricted to Muslims but also extend to Christians and Jews. Gulen met twice with Patriarch Bartholomeos, head of the Greek Orthodox Fener Patriarchate in Istanbul, and has also met several times with Christian and Jewish religious leaders to promote interreligious dialogue. In February 1998, for example, he visited the pope in Rome and received a visiting chief rabbi from Israel. The meeting between the pope and Gulen was not received positively by some circles in Turkey. Some argued that this meeting created the impression that Gulen wanted to become the leader of Islam in the world. Others argued that the meeting was a plot to portray him and his community as embracing all sections of society and as enjoying a status higher than the state.

On the question of women's rights, Gulen has progressive views. He believes that the veiling of women is a detail in Islam, and that "no one should suppress the progress of women through the clothes they wear." Gulen also states that "no one should be subject to criticism for his or her clothing or thoughts."[10] Furthermore, he says, "Women can become administrators," contradicting the views of most Islamic intellectuals. Despite these views, modern professional women in Turkey still find his ideas far from acceptable.

Gulen favors education that leads to integration into the modern world. According to Mehmet Ozkaragoz, a U.S.-educated devotee, "A basic principle of Islam is seeking knowledge. We recognize the West as the best source of technology at the moment although, of course, we would prefer the Muslim world to be the leader."[11] Moreover, Gulen wishes to merge Islam into the international economic and political systems, and supports Turkey's bid for membership in the European Union.

Here, too, Gulen is influenced by Said Nursi. While Nursi believed that some actions of nonbelievers harmed humanity's future, he advocated cooperation among believers of all religions as a countermeasure. Gulen goes a step further and extends his tolerance toward secularists and nonbelievers in Turkey. He sees this approach as a way to revive the multiculturalism of the Ottoman Empire, secure Turkey's stability, and prevent conflicts such as those between Sunnis and Alevis.

Gulen has had considerable success advancing his aim to create a Muslim community that opposes politicized Islam. No one knows the actual size of Gulen's large group of sympathizers (known as *Fethullahcilar* or "the followers of Fethullah," a name Gulen strongly opposes) but guesses range between 200,000 and 4 million people influenced by his ideas.[12] This community draws much of its support from young urban men, with a special appeal to doctors, academics, and other professionals. It has grown in part by establishing student dormitories, summer camps, high schools, universities, educational and cultural centers, and publications. Although Gulen is its sole leader, a number of his longtime devotees run the community.[13]

Gulen has considerable political weight on the right of the political spectrum, which explains why party leaders are eager to maintain close contacts with him. Since 1994, he has met with a president, a prime minister, the leaders of many parties, and important businessmen. He regularly gives interviews to the country's leading media outlets. In 1997, Turkey's President Suleyman Demirel accepted an award from one of Gulen's organizations and praised the movement's educational activities. Gulen also met with Bulent Ecevit, the longtime leader of Turkey's left and the current prime minister, after which Ecevit reported that their meeting involved a "conversation that focused entirely on religion and philosophy. The meeting had no political dimensions. I found Gulen to be a sincere and candid person. Our meeting was useful."[14] This exchange was remarkable in that it showed Gulen's ideas could also find a receptive audience on the left.

To promote their views, Gulen's followers have set up a wide range of organizations. The Turkish Teachers' Foundation, for example, publishes a monthly journal, *Sizinti* (Disclosures), and two academic journals, *Yeni Umit* (New Hope) and *The Fountain* (published in English). It also organizes national and international symposiums, panel discussions, and conferences. Another foundation, the Journalists' and Writers' Foundation, brings secularist and Islamist intellectuals together in what are called *Abant* meetings, putting forward the view that no individual or group has a monopoly on interpreting Islam and that secularism does not mean being anti-religious.[15] The foundation has organized conferences and has invited prominent intellectuals to talk on various issues such as on dialogue among civilizations.

An American expert on Islam, Dale F. Eickelman, calls Gulen "Turkey's answer to media-savvy American evangelist Billy Graham . . . In televised chat shows, interviews and occasional sermons, Gulen speaks about Islam and science, democracy, modernity, religious and ideological tolerance, the importance of education, and current events."[16] The Gulen community also has its own media, including the daily newspaper *Zaman*, the television channel Samanyolu, and the radio station Burc. In addition, it distributes video- and audiotapes. Those involved in its campaigns include prominent intellectuals from Turkey's prestigious universities.

The Gulen community owns and runs about 100 schools in Turkey. These institutions use the same curriculum as state schools and are under tight state control, but they also emphasize conservative values such as good manners and respect for elders. The schools are funded by the community and instructors are graduates of some of the best Turkish universities. Once the schools began functioning, they became the focus of further fund-raising efforts and are regarded as providing a high-quality education.

In keeping with his Turkish orientation, Gulen encourages paying attention to the Turkish-speaking republics of the former Soviet Union, where he has gained many loyal followers. In October 1996, Gulen's followers financed a noninterest-bearing bank, Asya Finans, backed by sixteen partners and $125 million in capital, which aims to raise funds for investments in the Turkic republics. In this way, Gulen hopes to draw the attention of Turkish business-men to these new countries, and in doing so, solidify links to them.

Followers of Gulen have also founded more than 200 schools around the world from Tanzania to China, but mostly in the Turkic republics. The schools in the Turkic republics support a philosophy based on Turkish nationalism rather than on Islam. As one reporter has stated, "From the Balkans to China, he wants to see elites formed with Turkey as their model."[17] In Gulen's view, Turkey's virtues include its Ottoman heritage, secularism, market economy, and democracy. These schools also admit non-Muslim students, and because of their high quality, and perhaps the use of English as the primary language of instruction, they attract children of the elite and of government officials in various countries. The commu-nity supports a secular state model in both Azerbaijan and Central Asia.[18] The Turkish analyst Sahin Alpay noted that graduates of these schools go on to hold important positions in all walks of life in these newly independent states.[19]

Arguing that Gulen's group fosters the idea of an Islamic *umma* or a commu-nity of Muslims in this region would probably be wrong. The authoritarian leaders of the new republics are highly intolerant of Islamic activities and Gulen's group is very careful not to provoke these rulers. Small groups are organized to hear a follower of Nursi read and interpret his books. Ideas are also spread through personal relationships. As has been observed by Elisabeth Ozdalga: "The main objective [of the education provided in these schools] is to give the students a good education, without prompting any specific ideological orientation. One basic idea of Gulen's followers is that ethical values are not transmitted openly through persuasion and lessons but through providing good examples in daily conduct."[20] Actually, this way of conveying messages in a subtle manner is no different from the early Islamicization of this region at the hands of Ahmed Yesevi and Bahaeddin Naksibendi. Some analysts describe the community's efforts in this region as Islam blended with Turkish nationalism.[21] However, the Gulen community has also opened schools in non-Muslim areas. More accurately, the community is trying to create the idea of Turkey as a role model and leading power in this region.[22]

This does not mean that Gulen's community has advanced without setbacks or even that it enjoys support from the Turkish state. For example, prosecutors investigated statements made by Gulen on a June 18, 1999 television broad-cast.[23] Prime Minister Ecevit, who said he saw the program, urged that the government look into the matter rather than having a debate in the media about it. He also made a supportive statement about the movement's educational sys-tem: "These schools spread Turkish culture and information about Turkey to the world. They are under the continuous supervision of our state."[24]

What was the problem? Gulen had made some vague statements that were somewhat critical of the Turkish establishment. He apologized publicly, but some secularists remained suspicious that he was seeking to gain political power over state institutions, including the army.[25] About a week after the broadcast, President Suleyman Demirel sent a warning to Gulen by saying: "I think that a man of religion should not have political targets. Being a man of religion is a hard task, but being a respected man of religion is only possible by being in compliance with the rules of our religion; that is, it is possible by giving good advice to humanity rather than by being involved in worldly affairs."[26]

Clearly, Gulen and his community could again face such allegations in the future. Some segments of the Turkish bureaucracy will continue to hinder the activities of Gulen's community. For example, YOK, the Higher Education Council, has decided not to recognize universities opened overseas by foundations and corporations that support the Gulen community. According to this decision, students will not be allowed to transfer from universities abroad run by the Gulen community to Turkish universities. Moreover, YOK will not grant any "equivalency degrees" for degrees conferred by such universities.[27]

Public concern about the Gulen community was raised again after allegations were made shortly after the videotape controversy that the community was behind tension that arose between Uzbekistan and Turkey. This led to the closure of some of the schools run by the community in Uzbekistan. However, Ecevit urged calm: "The Uzbek president has several unjust concerns about Turkey. . . . Turkey does not intervene in the domestic affairs of other countries. I attribute great importance to relations with Uzbekistan. We cannot allow these relations to be damaged by unnecessary touchiness."[28]

The Turkish military has staged three coups—in 1960, 1971, and 1980—to restore stability and order in the country. But in June 1997, rather than stage a fourth coup, the army maneuvered the Refah (Welfare) Party, Turkey's largest vote-getter in the 1995 parliamentary elections, out of office. It did so on the grounds that Islamic radicalism was poised to cause a civil uprising which it would be legally obliged to resist, "by force if necessary."[29]

Gulen takes particular care not to antagonize the army. In fact, he tries hard to persuade the military leadership that his activities do not challenge the status quo and should not be regarded as reactionary (a code word for Islamist). For example, he says that, if need be, he would turn over his community's schools to the state.[30] When asked about the threat of reactionaryism being on the agenda of the army-dominated National Security Council (MGK), he replied: "The MGK is a constitutional institution. It is a part of the state. I have never believed that a threat of reactionaryism exists in Turkey. Turkey needs enlightenment. Reactionaryism means going backward. In an enlightened era which has experienced democracy and secularism, it is impossible for the Turkish people to go back."[31]

While the Turkish army appears to accept Gulen and his followers as a domestic movement, not inspired by any foreign influence such as Iran or Saudi Arabia, the suspicion still exists that he may seek to subvert the military from within by sending his followers to the military academies. If this is true, it means that the community will have a difficult relationship with the military leadership. This may already be the case since it is known that the West Working Group in the office of the chief of the General Staff, has prepared a file dealing with the activities of Gulen's followers focusing on their educational institutions abroad. Members of the military have also visited most of these schools in Asia. Furthermore, the military leadership has shown no desire to be seen with Gulen, unlike secular politicians and intellectuals. Ismail Hakk Karaday, the army's chief of staff, did not even reply to an invitation to an *iftar* (a breaking of the Ramadan fast) dinner.

A split in the government over Gulen and his community has potentially significant political consequences, for Gulen has found civilian support even while the military has looked askance at his activities. In a dramatic move, as reports circulated that the military leadership planned to discuss Gulen's activities at a National Security Council meeting, both Suleyman Demirel and Bulent Ecevit endorsed him.[32] Despite the fact that Gulen himself has expressed respect for the military, the military is generally opposed to him. Since conservative circles in Turkey hold the military above all other state institutions and never criticize it, if the military were to oppose Gulen strongly, he would lose his civilian support.

Islamist intellectuals who supported the Refah Party and now support the Fazilet (Virtue) Party (formed by Refah supporters when Refah was closed), generally stay clear of Gulen's movement, limiting their remarks to the nature of the curriculum at the community's schools or to assessing Gulen's intentions. Relations with Refah supporters are tense given that Refah supporters widely believe that the secular establishment uses Gulen's community to obstruct their path. Necmettin Erbakan, Refah's longtime chairman, even accused Gulen of accepting government support to threaten Refah.[33]

In turn, Gulen frequently criticized Refah Party policies and activities. Keeping his distance from the Refah Party contrasted sharply with Gulen's efforts to carry out a dialogue with the secularist parties. Gulen did acknowledge Refah's impressive organization and growth in membership but noted that if other parties had worked as hard, Refah would not have received 21 percent of the vote in the December 1995 elections. He also concluded that the vote for Refah was larger than its actual base of support when he said that "Our friends in Refah may be annoyed, but I think that Refah's electoral share is still around 15 percent—maybe not even that. The great majority of those who vote for Refah are people who are dissatisfied because there is no strong government that inspires confidence in Turkey."[34]

Gulen held the Refah Party itself responsible for the crisis in Turkish politics that pitted it against the secularist military. He has also deemed Refah's removal from office in June 1997 not unfair. "Hopefully, and God willing, no one will come out and try to drag the nation into a vicious circle [like the one in the 1970s] from which we extricated ourselves with much difficulty."[35] Indeed, he sees Turkey as having barely missed entering a deep conflict along the lines of Algeria.

Since 1996, prosecutors have argued that statements such as those of Istanbul's former Mayor Recep Tayyip Erdogan, read from a poem, that "the minarets are our bayonets, the domes our helmets, and the mosques our barracks,"[36] which led to his criminal prosecution in May 1998, prove the party's anti-secular intentions. Thus, they sought to shut down Refah as a threat to Turkey's constitutionally enshrined secular system. They got their way in January 1998, when the chief judge of the Constitutional Court, Ahmet Necdet Sezer, announced Refah's closure on the basis that it had engaged in "actions against the principles of the secular republic."[37]

Gulen rejected comments like those of Erdogan, holding that they "are not binding on believers who respect God in Turkey."[38] He supported the closure of Refah, given his emphasis on the preservation of order, but said it would be more sensible, for tactical reasons, not to close Refah. Instead, he urged continuing the lawsuit against the party until the next round of elections:

> "If a trial is on when the election campaign gets under way, public trust in Refah would be shaken. It would be viewed as a party that will be closed. People would not vote for it. Its votes would move, more democratically, largely to the parties that are most closely aligned with the Refah Party. That would achieve the desired objective."[39]

Gulen predicted the Islamists would not gain from having suffered the closure of Refah, and he rejects the idea that Turkey's new Islamist party, the Fazilet Party, would emerge with more strength among voters. Interestingly, during the media campaign against Gulen in June 1999, the leader of the Fazilet party, Recai Kutan, and some other prominent figures in the party defended Gulen publicly and tried to counter arguments against him. The Islamist media also adopted the same attitude and supported Gulen and his movement when serious questions about him were raised.

Gulen's June 1999 emergence upon the political scene triggered much controversy among secularist intellectuals, a considerable number of whom have suspected him of using different tactics to reach the same goal as the Islamists. They worry that behind his benign facade, Gulen hides ambitions to turn the country into an Iranian-style Islamic state. The insecurity and intolerance of some secularists cause them to accuse Gulen's community of being the enemy of the Turkish republic. They also worry that secularist parties have offered Gulen support in exchange for a promise on his part not to endorse the Refah Party.

Rusen Cakir, author of a book on the rise of Islam in Turkey, finds that "the [secularist] parties are promoting him as an alternative to Welfare. They're using their enemy's weapon against their enemy."[40] Another expert on Islamists, Iskender Savasir, made similar remarks, saying that "I cannot say that Fethullah Hoca is not collaborating with the state."[41] A "radical socialist" weekly, whose sometimes sensationalist and unreliable allegations have been used by the Turkish military, claims that the Gulen group "acquired financial support from the state, particularly from the Ministry of Foreign Affairs" and points to Tansu Ciller's having transferred "large sums from her ministry's secret budget" to his schools, seeing this as "one of the reasons for the close relations he has with her."[42]

On the other hand, Gulen has obtained the support of a number of well-known liberal intellectuals, such as the journalists Mehmet Altan, Ali Bayramoglu, Mehmet Barlas, Etyen Mahcupyan, Mehmet Ali Birand, and Cengiz Candar, who argue that the solution to Turkey's problems depends on reaching a consensus. Thus, they like the 'soft' face of Islam he presents. Birand, for example, recently argued that Gulen has original ideas and that *all* segments of Turkish society, implying the military, should pay attention to his vision. Gulen's critical stance toward the Refah Party also won him the support of some nationalist-conservative intellectuals like Altemur Kilic. As a symbol of this support, Gulen's Turkish Journalists and Writers Foundation hosted an *iftar* dinner in February 1996, at which about a thousand distinguished politicians, businessmen, artists, and intellectuals turned up.

A discussion of the significance of Gulen's movement requires considering both the organizational structure of the movement itself, the movement's place in Turkey's political and economic system, and its influence beyond Turkey.

First, the organizational structure of the movement is seen as hierarchical and somewhat undemocratic, which is somewhat unexpected given the community's liberal attitudes and tolerance of differences. Gulen is the sole leader of the movement and the hierarchical order extends from the top to the bottom through an increasing number of *abiler* (elder brothers). The ranking is very strict, and each rank's *abi* (elder brother) obtains only a certain amount of knowledge of the activities occurring or under discussion while agreeing to refrain from asking questions or seeking more knowledge about the higher ranks. An abi or someone under his supervision may, however, talk to other abis informally and also talk to those assigned to overseeing the activities. Although this sort of structure may be helpful if the members of the community were to face persecution by the government, it does raise serious problems for the development of democracy within the group and creates the likelihood that many followers are left out of the decision-making process. Of course, those entering into this structure do so of their own free will.

As for the movement's standing in Turkish society, it does occupy a special place given the new cultural space created after the liberalization attempts of the 1980s in Turkey. Its tolerant Islamic discourse that seeks consensus aims to integrate its followers into the existing political system. The Gulen movement does not encourage bringing down the government or even challenging the status quo. In fact, because the Gulen movement is highly sensitive about being involved in any controversy, it avoids taking up controversial issues or even entering into public debates. This cautious stance constitutes a self-imposed restriction, and it may prompt more radical Islamic movements to do likewise.

Further, as already noted, Gulen's movement seeks integration with the modern world by reconciling modern and traditional values. This attempt to create a synthesis of ideas resembles the efforts of the last nationalist thinkers of the Ottoman Empire. For example, Ziya Gokalp emphasized the necessity of creating a synthesis based on combining elements taken from Turkish culture (*hars*) and from Western science and technology. Gulen and his devotees go a step further, accepting Western civilization as a suitable foundation for material life while considering Islamic civilization suitable for spiritual life. It should be noted, though, that given the movement's conservative character, it does appeal to those who find that the Turkish political system is overemphasizing secularism and modernization.

Another way of viewing the movement's place in Turkish society is to consider Gulen's community one among many other civil society organizations, despite its hierarchical structure, given that the community has achieved autonomy from state power and has been able to play a significant role in society— the main characteristics of civil society organizations. The movement does mobilize a large segment of society, a segment not tied to the state.

The movement must be seen in contrast to a sector that has long been tied closely to the state. A strategy began as early as the 1920s aimed at creating a native bourgeoisie. The result was a social group that received special incentives and protectionist measures. Some enormously wealthy industrialists emerged with strong links to part of the state bureaucracy. Given the state's willingness to give these wealthy industrialists control over the Turkish economy, competition has been prevented from developing and the political will of the people has been rendered ineffective and even meaningless with respect to influencing economic policy.

In the 1990s, however, policies oriented towards greater liberalization and a shift to export-oriented industrialization have led to the emergence of new, dynamic, export-oriented, small and medium-sized businesses, many based in traditionally conservative Anatolian cities. This segment of society has been mobilized by Gulen's movement. The newly emerging export-oriented economic class is likely to challenge the existing economic structure and pressure the state bureaucracy to end the unequal treatment. It might also be said that the economic activities linked to Gulen's movement as well as the educational activities of Gulen's community have become part of an alternative economy.

This aspect of Gulen's movement, with its focus on disciplined work and efforts motivated by national-religious values, makes comparing it to the Protestant movement of the sixteenth century fitting. As Weber argued in his classic book *The Protestant Ethics of Capitalism*, religious-spiritual values can motivate people to work hard and accumulate wealth. In Turkey's case, given the current insistence upon a strict secular model of government, citizens may be choosing to worship "safely" by working hard to achieve economic modernization and development, or they may view the "self-discipline" Islam encourages as being attained when they work hard. In fact, Gulen uses the term *hizmet* or service, stating that there is no end to the service that can be carried out to build a peaceful society. At the same time he argues that a person's energy to serve comes from belief and that serving one's society is the most important way to gain God's favor and a place in paradise. This resembles what Weber called "in-worldly asceticism," which was significant in the development of capitalism.

As for the significance of Gulen's movement beyond Turkey, its best potential is in the Turkic countries in the Caucasus and Central Asia, where Gulen's emphasis on Turkish Islam will probably weaken the appeal of the message coming out of Iran. In the larger Muslim world, Gulen's movement does pose a potential challenge to Islamism, for its ideas may find receptive audiences among those with access to the outside world—those generally the most prone to Islamism. This said, Gulen's ideas have a much better chance than his organization, for authoritarian states and a general intolerance for new interpretations of Islam could impede it.

The unique character of Gulen's movement lies in its attempt to revitalize traditional values as part of modernizing efforts such as the Turkish state's official modernization program. Thus far, it has had some success as it attempts to harmonize and integrate the historically diverse lands of Turkey and reconcile hundreds of years of tradition with the demands of modernity, not easy tasks. In brief, Gulen seeks to construct a Turkish-style Islam, remember the Ottoman past, Islamicize Turkish nationalism, re-create a legitimate link between the state and religion, emphasize democracy and tolerance, and encourage links with the Turkic republics.

Gulen's movement seems to have no aspiration to evolve into a political party or seek political power. On the contrary, Gulen continues a long Sufi tradition of seeking to address the spiritual needs of people, to educate the masses, and to provide some stability in times of turmoil. Like many previous Sufi figures (including the towering thirteenth-century figure Jalal al-Din Rumi), he is wrongly suspected of seeking political power. However, any change from this apolitical stance would very much harm the reputation of his community.

Ultimately, the future of the Gulen group will be determined by its ability to evolve into an open-minded, flexible, and democratic community and improve its relations with the Turkish military leadership and secular elites. If these endeavors are successful, then the group could have a major impact on both the Turkish state and Turkish society and on the changes that take place in Turkey in the coming decades. As for Gulen himself, in a new Turkey he would become an even more important religious figure.

NOTES

1. See Niyazi Berkes, *The Development of Secularism in Turkey* (London: Routledge, 1998).

2. For further information, see Serif Mardin, *Religion and Social Change in Modern Turkey: The Case of Bediuzzaman Said Nursi* (Albany: State University of New York Press, 1989).

3. Erzurum's location near the border between Turkey and Iran, and the large number of immigrants from the Caucasus there, are said to render its Islam state-oriented and nationalistic.

4. Some of Gulen's writings are available in English: *The Infinite Light*, *The Lights of the Way*, *Questions*, *Towards the Lost Paradise*, and *Truth through Colors* [no reference information for these publications]. In addition, the second half of the 1990s witnessed numerous (speculative, popular, and scholarly) studies of Gulen's life and his community. For example, see Oral Calislar, *Fethullah Gulen'den Cemalettin Kaplan'a* (*From Fethullah Gulen to Cemalettin Kaplan*) (Istanbul: Pencere Yayinevi, 1998); Eyup Can, *Fethullah Gulen Hocaefendi ile Ufuk Turu* (*A Tour of New Horizons with Fethullah Gulen*) (Istanbul: AD Yayinevi, 1995); Nevval Sevindi, *Fethullah Gulen ile New York Sohbetleri* (*Conversations with Fethullah Gulen in New York*) (Istanbul: Sabah Yayinevi, 1997); Mehmet Ali Soydan, *Fethullah Gulen Olayi* (*The Case of Fethullah Gulen*) (Istanbul: Birey Yayinevi, 1999); Osman Ozsoy, *Fethullah Gulen Hocaefendi ile Mulakat* (*An Interview with Fethullah Gulen*) (Istanbul: Alfa Yayinevi, 1998); (n.a.) *Medya Aynasinda Fethullah Gulen* (*Fethullah Gulen as Portrayed by the Media*) (Istanbul: Gazeteciler ve Yazarlar Vakflar Yayinlari, 1999).

5. For example, see M. Fethullah Gulen, *Varligin Metafizik Boyutu* (*The Metaphysical Dimension of Existence*) (Istanbul: Feza Yayinevi, 1998).

6. Nuriye Akman, "Hocaefendi ile Roportaj" ("Interview with Hocaefendi") *Nokta*, February 5–11, 1995, pp. 16–18.

7. Fethullah Gulen, *Fasildan Fasila 1* (Izmir: Nil Yayinevi, 1995), p. 223.

8. Alistair Bell, "Turkish Islamic Leader Defies Radical Label," *Reuters*, August 7, 1995.

9. *The Turkish Daily News*, February 18, 1995.

10. Ibid.

11. Bell, "Turkish Islamic Leader."

12. "Hocaefendi Cemaati," *Tempo*, February 7, 1997, pp. 46–50.

13. See the series in *Milliyet*, August 10–13, 1997.

14. Ibid.

15. *The Turkish Daily News*, July 21, 1998, and *Milliyet*, July 21, 1998.

16. Dale F. Eickelman, "Inside the Islamic Reformation," *Wilson Quarterly* 22, No. 1 (Winter 1998), pp. 84–85.

17. Wendy Kristianasen, "New Faces of Islam," *Le Monde Diplomatique* (English edition), July 1997, pp. 11–12.

18. *Hurriyet*, November 3, 1996.

19. *Milliyet*, November 4, 1996.

20. Elisabeth Ozdalga, "Entrepreneurs with a Mission: Turkish Islamists Building Schools along the Silk Road," (Paper delivered at the Annual Conference of the North American Middle East Studies Association, Washington, D.C., November 19–22, 1999).

21. For example, see M. Hakan Yavuz, "Societal Search for a New Contract: Fethullah Gulen, Virtue Party and the Kurds," *SAIS Review,* Vol. 19, No. 1 (Winter/Spring 1999), pp. 114–143.

22. During a series of interviews with students of the community's high schools in Azerbaijan and Turkmenistan (who were brought to Turkey for a vacation) in August 1999, the students expressed their gratitude and appreciation for their teachers' attempts to educate them. Their perception of Turkey consisted of the projected image of their teachers—that is, they attributed to all Turkish people the good conduct of their teachers.

23. *Anatolia*, June 19, 1999.

24. *Anatolia*, June 22, 1999.

25. *TV News Bulletin*, June 24, 1999.

26. *Anatolia*, June, 24 1999.

27. *Hurriyet,* June 27, 1999.

28. *Anatolia*, June 21, 1999.

29. *The Hindu*, February 19, 1998.

30. *Milliyet*, December 30, 1997.

31. Ibid.

32. Nicole Pope, "Generals Get Their Way," *Middle East International,* No. 571 (March 27, 1998), p. 14.

33. *The Turkish Daily News*, February 18, 1995.

34. *Milliyet*, August 31, 1997.

35. Ibid.

36. *Milliyet*, December 27, 1997.

37. *The New York Times*, January 17, 1998, and *The Washington Post*, January 17, 1998.

38. *Milliyet*, December 30, 1997.

39. *Milliyet*, August 31, 1997.

40. Bell, "Turkish Islamic Leader."

41. Nadire Mater, "Rise of Secular Priest Seen as a Threat by Islamicists," *Inter Press Service*, February 22, 1995.

42. *Aydinlik*, March 23, 1997.

10

Islam and Democracy

Ali R. Abootalebi

The study of the role of Islam in politics, society, and the economy since the early 1970s, and particularly after the Iranian revolution, has produced a wide range of academic and policy debates and conversations. The relationship between Islam, civil society, and democracy especially has been of interest to Islamic activists, Islamic clerics (the *'ulama*), intellectuals, and state policymakers. At the heart of the question is whether Islam is compatible with democracy, and, if so, what then accounts for the authoritarianism and absence of democracy in most, if not all, Muslim countries.

Scholars of various persuasions have offered different cultural, economic, social, and political explanations.[1] Historically, the Orientalists' view emphasized Islam's cultural essentialism, proposing that Islam was responsible for the sociopolitical ills of Middle Eastern societies, including the absence of democracy. That is, Islam is the independent variable that can explain the major characteristics of Muslim societies, including the lower level of socioeconomic and political development. Such culturally grounded explanations have been seriously discredited by the neo-Orientalists' arguments that the structural underpinnings of societies can better account for socioeconomic and political inadequacies in the Middle East and elsewhere in the developing world.[2]

Islamic doctrines and beliefs pose no serious opposition to democracy, understood as a political system where the political and civil rights of the individual are guaranteed and practiced through institutional and legal arrangements. The Islamic doctrine holds the state partly responsible for the welfare of society, but ultimately it is through individual participation and the development of civil society that democracy can emerge. And to this end, Islam does recognize the

155

sovereign rights of the individual to promote his or her own self-interest as well as contribute to the welfare of society as a whole.

To understand the relationship between Islam and democracy, one cannot overlook the distinctions among the message of Islam, the diversity of the Islamic movements in ideological composition and tactics, and the power struggle over ideological and political interests among traditionalist *'ulama* and Islamists in various Islamic communities. It would be a gross mistake to generalize about the behavior of Muslims and their leaderships across the Islamic world. It would also be a mistake to categorize Muslims as "fundamentalists," "Islamists," or other such types without considering the ideological overlaps among members of such groupings.[3] Indeed, the very nature of Islamic law and its application for the creation of an 'Islamic society' has necessitated different interpretations of law and Islamic leadership from the very beginning. It is therefore quite feasible for an Islamic cleric to simultaneously have conflicting 'conservative' and 'progressive' views on the extent of the individual's rights and duties, as opposed to the state's, in social, economic, and political affairs.

Islamic movements have been diverse in their approaches to propagating the message of Islam. The Islamic movements in Tunisia, Algeria, Egypt, the Sudan, Saudi Arabia, Iran, Afghanistan, Pakistan, and elsewhere in the Muslim world have had different experiences in their dealings with the state. But the diversity of Islamic movements in ideological tone, political posturing, and success or failure in challenging the state can largely be explained by differences in preexisting social, economic, and political contexts. Islamic leaders now realize the success of their movements as alternatives to the politics and ideology of the state is conditioned by their ability to deliver material gains to their followers, in addition to the promise of a more spiritually fulfilling life. The appeal by Muslim leaders to the public for political support without actual material benefits cannot succeed in the long run. Thus, the Islamic movements' preoccupation with public welfare programs in Egypt, Jordan, Lebanon, and elsewhere in the Muslim world. Similarly, no 'Islamic' state can, in light of persistent socioeconomic problems, hope to survive indefinitely through ideological rhetoric and the application of coercive policies.

The debate between traditionalist *'ulama* and reformist clerical and nonclerical 'civilian' intellectuals on the proper role of Islam in state-society relations has made the Islamic movements of the late twentieth and early twenty-first centuries potent alternatives to the secular and predominantly authoritarian state. The nineteenth-century wave of Islamic movements, for example, was preoccupied with anti-colonialism and the search for reviving Islam in modern times. A century later and in light of socioeconomic, political, and global challenges facing Muslim societies, Islamic movements are reinventing Islam in fundamental ways.

The debate on the proper role of Islam emphasizes either the direct political role of Islamic clerics in running state affairs, thus bridging the political and religious divide, or the presence of Islam as a sociocultural variable in promoting socioeconomic justice, the rule of law, and political toleration, without direct participation by clerics in the temporal realm of politics, which can corrupt all those involved, religious or not. Either solution has immediate and long-term consequences for the development of civil society and democracy in Muslim countries. But ultimately the success or failure of Islamic movements, whether in charge of the state or in opposition, is largely contingent upon their ability to establish themselves as well organized and institutionalized movements, with clear sociopolitical and economic agendas for dealing with the ills of their respective societies.

In light of the above, this chapter will argue that prospects for democracy in Muslim countries (and in non-Muslim countries, for that matter) are contingent upon the extent of the distribution of socioeconomic resources and political power within society and between the state and society. Islamic movements must be understood not merely on the basis of their declared religious convictions, but also on their interest articulation and participation in the broader struggle between state and society over socioeconomic resources and political power. Islam is no more or less antithetical to democracy than Christianity or Judaism, and the behavior of Islamic movements and their leadership in different Muslim countries must be understood within the larger context of a struggle for power by various groups, including religious groups. Islamic movements, whether ruling the state as in Sudan, Iran, and Afghanistan, or in opposition, as in most Muslim countries, have offered different visions of an 'Islamic solution' to the ills of their respective societies. But, as with their secular counterparts, the ultimate goal for these movements has been gaining popular support and control of the state to implement their 'Islamic' agendas. Despite the ideological underpinnings of Islam, the behavior of Islamic movements' leaderships has not fundamentally differed from other political movements in many non-Islamic developing countries.

The wide range of Islamic movements—in social make-up, structure, and program—has left many observers baffled. Since the Iranian revolution there has been a sharpened distinction between two approaches which might be called "fundamentalism" and "Islamism."

Islamism can embrace both progressive *'ulama* and those urban intellectuals who believe Islamic tenets are compatible with such modern values as freedom and democracy. The Islamist view stands in sharp contrast to that held by the fundamentalist, traditionalist *'ulama* who have had an historical monopoly over the right to interpret Islam and its tenets.[4]

There has been much confusion, especially over the term *fundamentalist*, which implies a return to the past in recapturing the roots of Islamic religion. There is also an implication here that other readings of Islam are illegitimate, since they supposedly neglect traditionally accepted concepts in favor of innovations that are often imports from non-Islamic societies.

Robin Wright shows one side of this approach in pointing out that fundamentalist movements also incorporate a great deal of modernity and innovation. Thus, she denies that most Islamic movements today are:

> 'fundamentalist': The various Islamic movements are often called 'fundamentalist' in the West, but most are in fact not fundamentalist in their agendas. Fundamentalism generally urges passive adherence to literal reading of scriptures and does not advocate change of the social order, instead focusing on reforming the lives of the individual and family. Most of today's Islamic movements resemble Catholic Liberation theologians who urge active use of original religious doctrine to better the temporal and political lives in a modern world. Islamist or Islamism more accurately describes their forward-looking, interpretive and often even innovative attempts to reconstruct the social order.[5]

Ibrahim Yazdi, who claims that all truly Islamic movements are "fundamentalist," conveys the opposite standpoint. As Yazdi puts it, there are:

> . . . two major trends in Islamic movements. One, we call the traditionalist. (The term 'fundamentalism' does not reflect the true facts. All of us are fundamentalists according to the definition in Western culture, that whoever believes the Bible is the word of God is a fundamentalist.) There are the tradition-oriented Muslim intelligentsia, the so-called *'ulama*. Then there are the reformist or modernist Muslim intellectuals.[6]

Both Islamic *fundamentalism* and *traditionalism* are used here interchangeably as referring to opposition to Islamic reformists, or 'Islamists,' who are less rigid in their views of Islamic law (Shari'a) and of non-Islamic cultures. In any case, the classification of Muslim movements into traditionalist/fundamentalist and Islamist/reformist can be confusing, since Islamic doctrine itself allows for different interpretations and therefore different opinions on Shari'a and its principles. It is quite possible for a traditionalist religious leader (*'alim*) to share similar Islamic values with a reformer on the overall position of Islam in society, the economy, and politics. The late Ayatollah Taleqani, who played an important role in Iran's revolution, for example, had an activist vision of Islam and an Islamic state much closer to Islamist views than to those of Ayatollah Khomeini. The current ideological and political gulf between the 'moderates' led by President Muhammad Khatami, and 'conservatives' headed by Ayatollah Ali Khamene'i and other conservatives in the Iranian parliament (*Majlis*), has been widening. The two camps recognize that the Iranian regime's survival hinges upon their unity, but despite the symbiotic relations that exist between them, differences in ideological interpretations of Islam and its tenets have put them on a collision course.

Indeed, the differences are over more than just moderate or conservative interpretations of Islam, but over a question of practical Islam versus stagnant Islam. Muslim societies will forge ahead with reforms needed for both material gains as well as spiritual uplifting, inspired by Islamic values, with or without the *'ulama*. In other words, the future role in Islam of the *'ulama*, or at least the more rigid *'ulama*, as sole interpreters of the Shari'a and legitimate heirs to the legacy of the Prophet of Islam himself is being challenged.[7]

Thus, it should be stressed that fundamental disagreements remain even among traditionalists over divine versus popular sovereignty. Some, like Abul A'la Mawdudi, founder of the Jamaat-i Islami in India, have argued that if democracy is conceived as a limited form of popular sovereignty, restricted and directed by God's law, there is no incompatibility with Islam, but Mawdudi concluded that Islam is the very antithesis of secular Western democracy based solely on the sovereignty of the people.[8]

On the other hand, Sayyid Qutb, a leading traditionalist theoretician of the Muslim Brotherhood executed by the Egyptian government in 1966, objected to the idea of popular sovereignty altogether. Qutb believed that "the Islamic state must be based on the Quranic principle of consultation or *shura* [consultation, on the interpretation of *Shari'a*], and that the Islamic law or *Shari'a* is so complete a legal and moral system that no further legislation is possible or necessary."[9]

Yet the rapidly unfolding events of the 1980s and 1990s have helped popularize the message and broaden support for moderate Islamists, compared to the revolutionary fundamentalists who flourished following Iran's revolution. The more radical forces have been somewhat discredited by criticism of the Iranian model, their use of violence, and their failure to seize power. The current trend is for Muslim political leaders who favor participation in the electoral process as the way of taking control of the state, and intellectual reformists, who have been engaging in a lively debate on Islam and modernity (e.g., the outlook of Islam on democracy, equality, and human, minority, and women's rights). The *'ulama* have historically preoccupied themselves with literal interpretation of the Quran and development of Islamic Law that relies basically on the Quran and *Sunna* ("path" or "tradition," referring to the traditions about the conduct of the Prophet).[10] In this undertaking, a great deal of analysis has been written on the contributions by such Muslim thinkers as al-Shafi'i (767–820), Ibn Hanbal (780–855), al-Ghazzali (1058–1111), Ibn-Taymiyya (1263–1328), and others. These thinkers paid less attention in their writings to the political dimension of Shari'a than to its theological aspects. Vital questions, such as the right of the individual versus the community (*umma*), the right to rule and the source of political legitimacy, and the right or duty to rebel against unjust government, have been left underdeveloped. Thus, the scholars have not examined the duties and functions of an Islamic government in detail. As a result, no concrete political philosophy based on Shari'a has ever developed, and Islamic political thought has remained purely speculative.[11] Some have even gone so far as to argue that Shari'a never developed as a system of law in the sense it is understood nowadays, and thus invoking Shari'a to enforce autocratic rule by clerics is not legitimate.[12] As Fazlur Rahman has noted, "Islamic law . . . is not strictly speaking law, since much of it embodies moral and quasi-moral precepts not enforceable in any court. Further, Islamic law, though a certain part of it came to be enforced almost uniformly throughout the Muslim world (and it is primarily this that bestowed homogeneity upon the entire Muslim world), is on closer examination a body of legal opinion or, as Santillana put it, 'an endless discussion on the duties of a Muslim' rather than a neatly formulated code or codes."[13]

In short, while a detailed theological discussion of the relationship between Islam and democracy is outside the scope of this study,[14] Islamists argue that *shura* can be interpreted as a democratic principle since it demands open debate among both the *'ulama* and the community at large on issues that concern the public. But traditionalists' unilinear and rigid view of society and politics has also come increasingly under question among Muslims. Fundamentalist militant groups like the Egyptian al-Gama', Algeria's Islamic Salvation Front (FIS), or the Palestinian Hamas have neither been able to expand their bases of support beyond a certain point nor been able to gain power. Their views on Islam and politics are too rigid and outmoded for modern problems, and are even, some would say, un-Islamic. The Taliban movement in Afghanistan in the 1990s under the religious guidance of some *'ulama* imposed such restrictive 'Islamic' laws in provinces under their military control, they made both conservative and radical *'ulama* in Iran look like liberal reformists. And Islamic militants in Egypt, Algeria, and elsewhere may be praised as martyrs by some clerics but are denounced as terrorists by others.

Not only are traditionalists everywhere under scrutiny in terms of what they say and do, but the foundation of their power as the only legitimate interpreters of the Shari'a has been shaken. The Arab fundamentalists have even been accused of a false representation of Muslim history, the presentation of a biased and incoherent account of Islamic thought, to further their position and interest.[15] And of course, their historically close association with the state further weakens the credibility of some fundamentalists.

The political and economic turmoil in the Middle East has sharpened people's image and expectations of Muslim groups and their leadership. Increasingly, the capacity to deliver tangible economic goods and basic political rights has become more important than the politics of ideology and rhetoric, Islamic or not. The Islamic governments of Iran and Sudan, for example, remain somewhat isolated in the international community and face tremendous domestic problems that have led to popular discontent and even uprisings. Saudi Arabia, a self-proclaimed Islamic state, faces increasing economic problems, and while the monarchy claims legitimacy through fundamentalist Wahhabi Islam, it denies the population fundamental political and civil rights that are respected in Islam.

The latest phase of the Islamic movement that began in the 1980s varies distinctly from the Islamic experience in Iran in 1979, in Lebanon after 1982, and among a host of small groups in Egypt, Saudi Arabia, Kuwait, Syria, and elsewhere during the late 1970s and early 1980s.[16] The most conspicuous difference is the tactics of the new Islamists. If extremism characterized the first phase of the fundamentalist movement, the new Islamic movements attempt to work within the state system rather than outside it. Islamists, in other words, have not failed to recognize that pluralism and interdependence are the catchwords of the present day.[17]

Historically, Islam as a religion remained on the periphery of state politics, overshadowed by authoritarian states that propagated secular ideologies and values. Furthermore, the overall structure of the post-World War II international political economy helped consolidate state power over most Muslim societies. The rent collected from oil and gas exports, and external support in the form of military, economic, and financial aid, for example, helped Middle Eastern states monopolize domestic power during the Cold War. The Arab-Israeli conflict also bolstered the Arab states' political hegemony by legitimizing their authoritarianism and providing an excuse for inadequacies in socioeconomic performance.[18]

It is clear to all Muslims that in the Quran and Shari'a, Allah is the ultimate sovereign and everything on Earth and in heaven is under His command. Yet, there is nothing in either source to deny Muslims freedom of action to improve their individual and communal lives; nor does Shari'a promote subservience to the state as a proof of proper Muslim behavior. On the contrary, individuals are regarded as responsible for the salvation and well-being of themselves, their families, and their communities.[19] Thus, blind obedience to a self-proclaimed Islamic state can be as anti-Islamic as open defiance of such a state. If a government rules in the name of Allah, then it must respect the fact that Allah regards individuals—and not the state—as responsible for their actions, for it is they who will be punished or rewarded accordingly on Judgment Day.[20] On this basis, the Islamists dismiss the idea that further legislation beyond Shari'a is impossible, as confusing the boundary between the overall sovereignty of Allah and the particulars of popular sovereignty.

The debate among Islamists and among some progressive traditionalists— be it in Iran, the Sudan, Egypt, Algeria, or elsewhere—is over the old question: how to reconcile the tenets of Islam with the modern notions of democracy, liberty, justice, and gender equality. In terms of democracy, the traditional meaning of the concept of *shura* is outdated, according to Islamists. After years of debate, according to Yazdi, "Many [Islamists] have come to the conclusion that general elections and a parliament properly serve that concept of consultation."[21] It is the extent of popular sovereignty and not its existence that is debated. Because of economic, technological, and environmental changes, further development of Shari'a seems inevitable to the Islamists. The development of Shari'a, they argue, need not be looked upon as a move away from Islamic principles, but, on the contrary, as a necessary stepping stone toward reaching an ideal Islamic society— a materially and spiritually developed utopia. An indispensable element in building such a society is freedom of thought and expression, including freedom from government control and suppression. In short, accepting the sovereignty of Allah does not necessarily contradict popular sovereignty.

Thus, Islamic traditionalists' reevaluation of their historical position on socioeconomic and political values is necessary to bring them more in line with the ongoing social and economic transformations in Muslim societies. Indeed, religious personalities such as Ayatollah Taleqani cautioned Iranians on relations between Islam and politics and on the position of the *'ulama* in society and polity. As Hasan Turabi puts it, Islam exists in society "as a matter of norms and laws. It is an integrated and total way of life. Therefore government must be limited, because Islamic government would be omnipotent. Government has no business interfering in one's religion or religious practices."[22] So, when it comes to dress codes in Muslim countries, for instance, society would definitely exercise a measure of censure and encouragement for one form of dress over another. But no organization, such as the Saudi *amr bil-maarouf wal-nahi an al-munkar* (the injunction "to command the good and forbid evil"), has legal authority to stop women or harass them. Segregation of women is definitely not a part of Islam. This is just conventional, historical Islam. It was totally unknown in the model of Islam or the text of Islam and is unjustified.[23] As for the relation of civil society to the state, according to Turabi, "In general civil society should be left alone, but if a societal function fails, government should step in. Once society picks up the function, then it [the state] should withdraw once more to its limit of security, organizing those aspects of society which must be legally organized."[24]

The founder of the Nurcu movement in Turkey, Said Nursi (1876–1960), argued that democracy and Islam are not contradictory and indeed democracy and freedom are necessary conditions for the existence of a just society. The individual, he argued, "needs freedom to realize the power of God and, through this realization, the individual will be free from man-made oppression and persecution."[25] Nursi further stressed the significance of popular sovereignty and asked for the rule of law in society. The Nurcu (or as it is known in Turkey, Nur) movement "seeks to move Islam from an oral-based tradition to a print-based medium and to raise religious consciousness through education and reason, . . . [updating] Islamic vocabulary in terms of the global discourses of science, democracy, and human rights."[26] The Nur movement today has the support of an estimated two to six million followers.

So, as one scholar of Islam has put it, "[A] major issue in democratization in Muslim societies is whether or not scholars and leaders have successfully made the transition from listing 'democratic doctrines of Islam' to creating coherent theories and structures of Islamic democracy that are not simply reformulations of Western perceptions in some Muslim idioms."[27] But the absence of a constructive dialogue between the traditionalist *'ulama* and the reformist Islamists has widened the gap between the two. The debate on creating legal codes dealing with political, human, and minority rights, civil liberties, gender equality, and the overall relationship of state to society is thus lacking.

One recent premise about state-society relations in the Middle East is that states there are weak and societies strong—the opposite of what was long argued. The Iranian revolution, the rise of Islamist movements in the 1980s, and declining oil prices are cited as proof for this viewpoint. This is taken as grounds for optimism and has led to an increasing interest in state-society relations and in prospects for the emergence of civil society in the region.[28] Thus, "today most scholars confidently affirm that the bases of civil society—both intermediate powers and autonomous social groups—exist in the Middle East."[29] Even traditional social formations based on blood and marriage, or tribal ties (as in the Gulf monarchies and Yemen), or bonyads—the semi-independent trusts (as in Iran)—are thought to be a part of civil society in the Middle East.[30] The mere presence of such groups, it is argued, deters the power of the state and leads to increased prospects for democratization.

But this position rests on shaky ground. Even the appearance of political parties and formal groups and associations in the Middle East does not by itself necessarily mean a fundamental move toward democracy by state or society. The augmentation of political parties in the region may be more a sign of the state's adjusting to pressure from Islamic groups and their allies than a genuine political opening on either side. Political parties in the Middle East remain mainly ineffective and play a mostly ceremonial role that serves to legitimate the state and its policies, without change in the composition of the ruling elites. For example, in all national elections in the Middle East since 1980, only in Iran (1989, 1997, 2001), Turkey (1991, 1995) and Israel (1992, 1996, 1999) did a change in the government actually occur. In all other cases, the ruling parties maintained their control over the state.[31] Even in Iran, where the ruling religious elite has affirmed the sovereignty of the people, the new elite has been reluctant to share power with its political opposition.

Although the formalities of a democratic state are in place (for example, elections and debates), the people remain politically and economically without much functional power. What civil society there was in Iran is fading, although intellectual and associational life continues to resist the state, which has come to dominate most aspects of life there.

Moreover, embryonic associations, although they exist in Muslim countries, are poorly organized and remain dependent on patrons within the state. As Carrie Rosefsky Wickham puts it in discussing Egypt: "The emergence of independent sites of social and political expressions within an authoritarian setting is not the same as the emergence of civil society, at least not in its liberal conception."[32] The emergence of state-controlled quasipluralism in countries such as Egypt and Jordan should not be seen as a shift from one-party rule to pluralism (ta'addudiya) involving numerous political parties and associations.[33]

The real basis of state power in Middle Eastern countries is largely informal and not institutional, for personal, family, and group ties help sustain the executive power of the ruling elites. The pattern of patrimonial leadership is not confined to the Middle East, of course, as many developing countries display the same phenomenon.[34]

The extent of ruling elites' autocratic power varies among the developing countries. Kuwait and the Persian Gulf shaykhdoms, along with Saudi Arabia and Oman, are perhaps the primary examples of highly traditional autocratic rule. On the other hand, South Korea, Taiwan, Malaysia, Turkey, Tunisia, and Brazil are examples that testify, to various degrees, to the changing balance of state-society relations in favor of society, as institutionalization of independent power relationships is gradually undermining informal and arbitrary state power associations.

The dominant position of the state in the Middle East has meant the dominance of politics by powerful families, elites, and military and bureaucratic officers. The slow emergence of independent groups and associations has been significant. For example, organized labor by itself, or through an alliance with the middle class, can be an effective force capable of checking the power of the state and promoting democracy, although most analysts ignore the role of organized labor in the civil society debate. But in any case, labor unions, a primary agent of civil society, in the Middle East remain either nonexistent or are repressed by the state.

Rachid al-Ghannouchi, the founder of the Tunisian Islamic movement al-Nahda, believes:

> Once the Islamists are given a chance to comprehend the values of Western modernity, such as democracy and human rights, they will search within Islam for a place for these values where they implant them, nurse them, and cherish them just as the Westerners did before, when they implanted such values in a much less fertile soil.[35]

That is to say, Islam need not go through a process of secularization as did the West, but must face one of the foremost challenges it has encountered yet: "to outline a regime that is Islamic but also representative and accountable."[36] Ghannouchi advocates "an Islamic system that features majority rule, free elections, a free press, protection of minorities, equality of all secular and religious parties, and full women's rights in everything from polling booths, dress codes, and divorce courts to the top job at the presidential palace. Islam's role is to provide the system with moral values."[37]

Others, like the Iranian Islamic reformist Abdul Karim Soroush, have argued that there is no contradiction between Islam and the freedoms inherent in democracy. "Islam and democracy are not only compatible, their association is inevitable. In a Muslim society, one without the other is not perfect."[38] Soroush believes that the will and beliefs of the majority must shape the ideal Islamic state, and that Islam itself is evolving as a religion, which leaves it open to reinterpretation: sacred texts do not change, but interpretation of them is always in flux because the age and the changing conditions in which believers live influence understanding. Furthermore, everyone is entitled to his or her own understanding. No one group of people, including the clergy, has the exclusive right to interpret or reinterpret tenets of the faith. Some understanding may be more learned than others, but no version is automatically more authoritative than another.[39]

Abdul Karim Soroush differs from Rachid al-Ghannouchi on how to free Muslims from their present dilemma. For Ghannouchi, the principle question is how to free the community from backwardness, while for Soroush, "the basic reality and objective is the person, the individual believer, making him a true reformer." He is interested in showing Muslims how to dwell with the complexity of traditions that for long prevented them from the free implementation of reason and science for the good of the individual. At any rate, "taken together, Soroush and Ghannouchi illustrate the broad alternatives offered by the situation in which Muslim societies now find themselves as they face the inescapable challenges of secularization in the modern world."[40]

Islam does not have a final authoritative spokesperson for all Muslims, and the Islamic world today is:

> in a state of disarray and confrontation between extremist religious movements that see themselves as the 'defenders of Islam' and authoritarian political regimes that claim to be 'defenders of modernity.' Yet, neither Islam nor modernity can be imposed on the people. This dichotomy warns of terrible consequences if the voices of reason and moderation—on both sides—are not allowed to prevail. Democracy offers a practical solution, and, possibly, the only way out of this dangerous situation.[41]

The prospect for the emergence of civil society depends on the characteristics of the people who form that society. The better educated, and the healthier, wealthier, and more organized the people, and the more broadly resources are spread, the stronger the society will be in protecting itself from domination by the state. Moreover, these resources allow for the formation of institutions that act as the focus of activity where differences in opinions and policies can be debated and resolved without resort to violence. Thus, institutionalization is essential for political stability—for the systematic and orderly channeling of the demands of contesting elites for political leadership. To be democratic, political parties, whether religious or not, must function within an independent institutionalized organizational network where final decisions are made and executed without constant interference from various layers of their country's state bureaucracies.

Associations and formal institutions that have played a critical role in Western political systems, however, have been considerably fewer in less developed countries.[42] Chances for a crisis from their nonparticipation increase where the opposition lacks an institutional basis for exerting pressure for participation (for example, religious opposition to the shah prior to the Iranian revolution) or where the state and its participants fail to adapt to changing social and economic forces (for example, Lebanon prior to 1975). On the other hand, institutional-ized opposition, whether religious or not, can be successfully incorporated into the political process (for example, Jewish religious opposition parties in Israel and to some degree Islamic opposition in Jordan, Turkey, Pakistan, and Egypt).

In fact, Samuel P. Huntington's pessimistic view of the incompatibility of Islam and democratic norms is undermined by his own argument for the desta-bilizing effects of modernization itself and for the stabilizing effects of institu-tionalization. He points to the revival of Islamic fundamentalism and the poverty of many Islamic states as the fundamental reasons for his pessimism.[43] Yet the revival of Islam and the rise of fundamentalism in Iran and elsewhere in the Middle East has not been an anti-democratic movement aiming at the destruc-tion of democratic values. Given the wide range of responses by Muslims to the West and to one another, the appeal in Muslim countries to unconventional forms of political conduct, including mass uprisings and rioting, is not due to any inherent intolerance of Islam toward democracy and the peaceful settlement of disputes. Islam in its various denominations has always been a source of both social protest against, and social support for, given regimes. The hostility toward the West by some—though not all—Islamic religious groups is aimed not at democratic values but at Western domination and interference in the domestic affairs of these countries.

There seems to be no immediate resolution to the debate among traditional-ists, Islamists, and intellectual reformers on Islam and democracy. However, the attempt to develop the political doctrine of Islam by Islamists, intellectual reformists, and some traditionalists need not necessarily be viewed by other traditionalists as an attempt to entirely undermine the legitimacy of the reli-gious establishment in Muslim countries.[44] Traditional religious leaders in the Muslim world, whether in power (Iran, Saudi Arabia, and the Sudan) or in opposition, must face the fact that, in light of complex socioeconomic and political problems facing Muslim societies in the twenty-first century, their position as legitimate religious/political leaders is bound to erode. The greatest threat to the traditional 'ulama comes from either their own meager perfor-mance as heads of state (for example, in Iran and the Sudan) or their failure in political opposition to formulate and propose comprehensive agendas for resolving socioeconomic and political problems (as in Egypt, Jordan and Kuwait), or from their sectarian fighting, which has resulted in violence and acts of terrorism. Further rifts among traditionalist 'ulama can be expected, as in Iran, as religious leadership in Muslim states finds itself under pressure to deal with modern problems. The progressive 'ulama will benefit from an open dialogue with the Islamists in streamlining the tenets of Islam to take into account modern values without abandoning the fundamentals of Islam itself.

As Laith Kubba notes, "The experience of Iran and the Sudan has shown that fundamentalism-in-power cannot solve every problem, and actually complicates the challenge of implementing Islamic values in public life."[45]

The potential for religious debate and political dialogue between traditionalists and Islamists, including the reformists, can be promising. The Islamists' pragmatic view of Islam and the traditionalists' recent popularity can be mutually beneficial in their common struggle for political sovereignty and development. This, however, can occur only when the religious establishment itself favors a fundamental socioeconomic and political restructuring of the status quo.

While it is not easy to predict the behavior of Islamist groups in their quest for power, it is possible to enhance cooperation between Islamists and secular groups in their common struggle against the state and in their future plans for their country. Thus, the question is whether the secular state can pursue a policy of political inclusiveness and allow Islamists to take part in the political process, given widespread concerns over the long-term fate of individual rights and liberties should the Islamists take control of the state. Some scholars have argued that where the popular will dictates it, Islamists must have the opportunity to rule, even if the future of such rights are not guaranteed. Some have advocated a slow and partial political inclusion of the Islamists. But, as Jerrold Green has argued, some sort of a "national pact must be devised as the best way to secure the democratization process, although devising a means to enforce the pact remain[s] unresolved."[46]

Muslim countries, like other developing countries though in varying degrees, suffer from acute socio-economic and political problems (e.g., strong and dominant states; weak associational opposition to the state, and an overall distribution of socio-economic resources and power that need to be addressed). Inauguration of democratic elections in Muslim countries without addressing the fundamental problem of uneven distribution of socio-economic and political resources in these countries will not succeed. The religious debate on Islam and democracy must then deal with not only the question of justice and freedom, but also with developing mechanisms necessary to remedy the structural problem of mal-distribution of resources.

An "Islamic" democracy will not embrace all the secular values adopted in the West. However, the initial steps taken toward such an end will need to include a process of institutionalization in Islam. The incorporation of an institutionalized Islam in the process of development will help the cause of democracy should Islamists successfully challenge the hegemony of the traditionalists in both the religious and political arenas. To play the democratic game, religious leaders will have to better organize themselves, to propose alternative plans for socio-economic and political issues facing the country. This in turn can help them maintain legitimacy and popular support, facilitating their struggle for political power. Organization is the key to the success of any group seeking to achieve its goals.

NOTES

1. For example, see John L. Esposito and John O. Voll, *Islam and Democracy* (Oxford: Oxford University Press, 1996); Rex Brynen, Bahgat Korany, and Paul Noble (eds.), *Political Liberalization and Democratization in the Arab World: Theoretical Perspectives*, Vol. 1 (Boulder: Lynne Rienner Publishers, 1995); John L. Esposito (ed.), *Political Islam: Revolution, Radicalism, or Reform?* (Boulder: Lynne Rienner, 1997).

2. For a brief overview of Orientalist and neo-Orientalist views, see Yahya Sadowski, "The New Orientalism and the Democracy Debate," *Middle East Report*, Vol. 23, No. 4 (July–August 1993), pp. 14–21. See also Ali R. Abootalebi, "Democratization in Developing Countries: 1980–1989," *Journal of Developing Areas*, Vol. 29, No. 4 (July 1995), pp. 507–530.

3. The often contradictory ideological and political posturing by both "moderate" and "conservative" religious leaders in post-Khatami Iran stands as a clear example. The conservative and moderate religious *'ulama*, as well as secular and religious democrats, continue to hold inconsistent views on issues with important religious and national implications. For example, even Ayatollah Khamene'i and conservatives in Parliament have not seriously resisted the increasing role of women in politics, society and the economy, despite their orthodox views of women.

4. The difference between traditionalism/fundamentalism and Islamism is in their views of Islam's relation to the state, society, and the economy. Admittedly, the classification of religious leaders into these two broad categories may not suit everyone, but for the general purpose of this study this classification should be sufficient. Others have made a similar distinction between fundamentalists and Islamists. See Robin Wright, "Islam, Democracy and the West," *Foreign Affairs*, Vol. 71, No. 3 (Summer 1992), pp. 131–145.

5. Robin Wright, "Islam, Democracy, and the West," p. 144.

6. Dr. Yazdi, a university professor and political activist who served as deputy prime minister and foreign minister under the Ayatollah Khomeini, is now Secretary General in the opposition political party the Liberation Movement of Iran. The status of the Liberation Movement of Iran as opposition party must be viewed with caution, since officially no political parties exist in the Islamic Republic of Iran. See interview conducted by Geoffrey Kemp, "A Seminar with Ibrahim Yazdi," *Middle East Policy*, Vol. 3, No. 4 (April 1995), pp. 15–28; quote from p. 16. On December 7, 1998, however, a new party was established by the supporters of President Khatami, called the "Islamic Iran Participation Front." The Islamic Revolution Tribunal officially banned the Liberation Movement of Iran party on the eve of the Iranian New Year in March 2001 as part of its ongoing crackdown on religious-nationalist leaders that began in summer 2000.

7. For reformists' views on the role of Shi'ite *'ulama* in Islam and Shari'a, see a collection of articles and speeches by leading Iranian reformists, including, among others, Abd al-Karim Soroush, Mohsen Kadviar, and Hasan Yusefi Eshkevari, organized by the Islamic Engineers Association and delivered in a seminar in Tehran, in: Islamic Engineers Association, *Din va Hukumat (Religion and Governance)*, (Tehran: Rasa, 1378 [2000]).

8. Quoted in John L. Esposito and James P. Piscatori, "Democratization and Islam," *Middle East Journal*, Vol. 45, No. 3 (Summer 1991), pp. 427–440. See also Abul A'la Mawdudi, "A Political Theory of Islam," in John Donohue and John Esposito (eds.), *Islam in Transition: Muslim Perspectives* (New York: Oxford University Press, 1982), pp. 253–254.

9. Quoted in Esposito and Piscatori, "Democratization and Islam," p. 436. For more on Qutb's views on Islam, see John L. Esposito (ed.), *Voices of Resurgent Islam* (New York: Oxford University Press, 1983).

10. Both Sunni and Shi'ite *'ulama* accept the authority of Sunna, although there are some differences in interpretation and the significance of the Prophet's Sunna. The Shi'ite *'ulama* also rely on the traditions of the Imams, "the rightful heirs of the Prophet," the last of whom, the Mahdi, remains hidden until his return to rule the Earth.

11. On this and related issues, see Sami Zubaida, *Islam: The People and the State: Political Ideas and Movements in the Middle East* (London: I. B. Tauris, 1993).

12. For a discussion of Islam, Muslims, secularization, and democracy, see Abdou Filali-Ansary, "The Challenge of Secularization," *Journal of Democracy,* Vol. 7, No. 2 (1996), pp. 76–80.

13. Fazlur Rahman, *Islam and Modernity: Transformation of an Intellectual Tradition* (Chicago: University of Chicago Press, 1982), p. 32. Cited in Filali-Ansary, "The Challenge of Secularization," p. 23.

14. For a recent discussion of various Islamic concepts with implications for democracy (for example, *tawhid, shura, khilafa,* etc.), see John L. Esposito and John O. Voll, *Islam and Democracy* (New York: Oxford University Press, 1996).

15. As'ad Abukhalil, "The Incoherence of Islamic Fundamentalism," *Middle East Journal,* Vol. 48, No. 4 (Autumn 1994), pp. 677–694.

16. Robin Wright, "Islam, Democracy and the West," p. 131. Wright believes that this second phase of the Islamist movement is marked by a different constituency as well.

17. Wright, "Islam, Democracy, and the West," p. 132.

18. See Simon Bromley, *Rethinking Middle East Politics* (Austin: University of Texas Press, 1994).

19. *The Quran* (N. J. Dawood, trans., New York: Penguin, 1993), Surah (chapter) 10, Aya (verse) 108.

20. *The Quran* (Dawood, trans.), Surah 38, Aya 26.

21. Geoffrey Kemp interview with Ibrahim Yazdi, "A Seminar with Ibrahim Yazdi," p. 18. Yazdi claims his interpretation of *shura* is correct, based on years of debate among Muslim scholars such as Rashid Reza, Maulana Maududi, Ali Shariati, Ayatollah Naini, Mehdi Bazargan, Ayatollah Taligani, and Ayatollah Mutahhari.

22. Quoted in Louis J. Cantori and Arthur Lowrie, "Islam, Democracy, the State, and the West," *Middle East Policy,* Vol. 1, No. 3 (1992), pp. 49–61.

23. Cantori and Lowrie, "Islam, Democracy, the State, and the West," p. 58.

24. Cantori and Lowrie, "Islam, Democracy, the State, and the West," p. 54.

25. M. Hakan Yavuz, "Search for a New Social Contract in Turkey: Fethullah Gulen, the Virtue Party and the Kurds," *SAIS Review,* Vol. 19, No. 1 (1999), p. 120. On Nursi's ideas on democracy, See Said Nursi, *Risale-I Kulliyat I-II* (Istanbul: Yeni Asya Yayinlari, 1996).

26. M. Hakan Yavuz, "Search for a New Social Contract in Turkey, " p. 120.

27. Esposito and Voll, *Islam and Democracy,* p. 31.

28. See for example the article by Emmanuel Sivan for the Social Science Research Council project on Civil Society in the Middle East, entitled "The Islamic Resurgence:

Civil Society Strikes Back," *Journal of Contemporary History*, Vol. 25, (1990), pp. 353–364. See also Michael C. Hudson, "After the Gulf War: Prospects for Democratization in the Arab World," Middle East Journal, Vol. 45, No. 3 (Summer 1991), pp. 407–426; Esposito and Piscatori, "Democratization and Islam," pp. 427–440.

29. Yahya Sadowski, "The New Orientalism and the Democracy Debate," *Middle East Report*, Vol. 23, No. 4 (July–August 1993), pp. 14–21; quote from p. 17.

30. Richard Augustus Norton and Farhard Kazemi (eds.), *Civil Society in the Middle East*, Vol. 2, (New York: Brill, 1996), p. 8.

31. National elections have been held since 1980 in Algeria, Bahrain, Egypt, Iran, Iraq, Israel, Jordan, Kuwait, Lebanon, Libya, Morocco, Oman, Saudi Arabia, the Sudan, Syria, Tunisia, Turkey, and Yemen, as well as in the Palestinian territories. For a discussion of elections and electoral laws in the Arab world, see Marsha Pripstein Posusney, "Behind the Ballot Box: Electoral Engineering in the Arab World," *Middle East Report*, Vol. 28, No. 4 (Winter 1998), pp. 12–16.

32. See Carrie Rosefsky Wickham's analysis of the case of Egypt, "Beyond Democratization: Political Change in the Arab World," *PS: Political Science and Politics*, Vol. 17, No. 3 (September 1994), p. 507.

33. Michael Hudson, "After the Gulf War," pp. 427–440.

34. On 'patriarchalism' and 'patrimonialism,' see Max Weber, *The Theory of Social and Economic Organization* (New York: Oxford University Press, 1947); and Reinhard Bendix, *Max Weber: An Intellectual Portrait* (Garden City: Doubleday, 1962), pp. 330–360. For patterns of patrimonialism in the Middle East, see James Bill and Robert Springborg, *Politics in the Middle East*, 4th ed. (New York: Longman, 2000).

35. From a lecture by Shaykh Rachid al-Ghannouchi, Chatham House, London, May 9, 1995, in Robin Wright, "Two Visions of Reformism," *Journal of Democracy*, Vol. 7, No. 2 (April 1996), p. 74.

36. Mohamed Elhachmi Hamdi, "The Limits of the Western Model," *Journal of Democracy*, Vol. 7, No. 2 (April 1996), p. 85.

37. Robin Wright, "Two Visions of Reformism," p. 73.

38. Soroush expressed his views in one of several interviews in Tehran and Washington, D.C., in 1994 and 1995, quoted by Robin Wright "Two Visions," p. 68. For more on Soroush's views, see *Din va Hukumat (Religion and Governance)*, 1378 (2000).

39. Wright, "Two Visions," p. 70.

40. Abdou Filali-Ansary, "The Challenge of Secularization," p. 78.

41. Ali Mazrui et al., "Preamble," of *Muslim Democrat*, Vol. 1, No. 1 (Burtonsville, MD: Center for the Study of Islam and Democracy, May 1999), p. 4.

42. On the role of groups and associations in the Middle East, see Bill and Springborg, *Politics in the Middle East*, p. 88.

43. Samuel Huntington, "Will More Countries Become Democratic?" *Political Science Quarterly*, Vol. 99 (Summer 1994), pp. 193–218.

44. The writings of Hasan Turabi, Mehdi Bazargan, Ali Yazdi, and Abd al-Karim Soroush, as well as the late Ayatollah Taleqani, are some examples. Mehdi Bazargan, for example, in response to Samuel Huntington's assertion of "the clash of civilizations," commented, before his death, on the positive relationship between Islam and individual

rights, peaceful coexistence with non-Muslims, economic development, freedom of action, and democracy. See Mehdi Bazargan, "Is Islam a Global Threat?" (Aya Islam yek khatar-i Jahani Ast?), *Rahavard*, No. 36 (Tir 1373 [1994]), pp. 48–57.

45. Laith Kubba, "Recognizing Pluralism," *Journal of Democracy*, Vol. 7, No. 2 (April 1996), p. 88.

46. Jerrold Green, *Civil Society and the Prospects for Political Reform in the Middle East* (New York University Press, 1994), p. 13. The conference was sponsored by the Civil Society in the Middle East Project, convened at the Aspen Institute Wye Conference, Queenstown, Md., Sept. 30–Oct. 1, 1994. Green was among the minority who advocated inclusion without reservation if commanded by popular will, but others such as Graham Fuller and Richard Norton have mixed feelings and more reservations about the inclusion of Islamists in the process of democratization.

11

Mediating Middle East Conflicts

An Alternative Approach

George E. Irani

Many Middle Eastern scholars and practitioners trained in the United States have returned to their countries of origin, ready to impart what they learned about Western conflict resolution techniques. But, in Lebanon, Jordan, Egypt, and other countries in the region, the reaching and practice of conflict resolution is still a novel phenomenon. Conflict resolution is viewed by many in the Middle East as a false Western panacea that is insensitive to indigenous problems, needs, and political processes. Others see it as a U.S.-concocted scheme intended primarily to facilitate and hasten the processes of peace and normalization between Israel and its Arab neighbors.[1]

In assessing the applicability of Western-based conflict resolution models to non-Western societies, professionals have only begun to realize the importance of acknowledging native ways of thinking and feeling, as well as local rituals for managing and reducing conflicts. As a region with a long history of conflict and Western intervention and mediation, the Middle East makes an interesting case study for students of conflict resolution. Western-style peace-making in the region has been rather superficial. Diplomatic agreements have not "trickled down" to the grassroots precisely because Western mediation models have not taken into account the deep cultural, social, and religious roots that underlie the way Arabs behave when it comes to conflict reduction and reconciliation.

This chapter will discuss Arab-Islamic modes of conflict reduction as an alternative to Western techniques in the Middle East, with a focus on Lebanon.[2] In contrast to U.S.-style mediation, local rites of reconciliation take into consideration the socioeconomic, cultural, and anthropological background in which conflicts erupt and are managed in the Middle East. They also factor in religious beliefs and traditions, and distinguish among different causes and types of conflicts such as family, community, and state conflicts, in mediating disputes.

The first section of this chapter looks at Western and non-Western approaches to conflict resolution and points to important cultural differences in approaching conflict management, including the role of the individual in society, attitudes towards conflict, styles of communication, expectations of mediators, understandings concerning victimization and forgiveness, and the usefulness of governmental (and/or non-governmental) programs and institutions—such as truth commissions—for national reconciliation. The second section considers the geographical, sociological, and cultural influences on the Arab Middle East. It highlights the importance of relationships based on family, patriarchy, gender, kinship, and clientism, and points to the underlying code of honor (and its counterpart, shame) in conflict and conflict management. The third part considers the concept of ritual and its role in conflict control and reduction (as opposed to conflict resolution) and focuses on the rituals of *sulh* and *musalaha* as examples of indigenous Arab modes of settling disputes. The final section considers the implications for policymakers and practitioners and suggests an alternative approach to national reconciliation in Lebanon.

Although conflict is a human universal norm, the nature of conflicts and the methods of resolving them differ from one sociocultural context to another. For instance, in contemporary North America, conflict is commonly perceived to occur between two or more individuals acting as free agents pursuing their own interests. Conflict is often thought of as a symptom of the need for change, and while it can lead to separation, hostility, civil strife, terrorism, and war, it can also stimulate dialogue and produce more socially just solutions. In addition, it can lead to stronger relationships and peace.[3]

A basic assumption made by U.S.-based conflict resolution theorists is that conflict can and should be fully resolved.[4] This philosophy, whereby virtually every conflict can be managed or resolved, clashes with other cultural approaches to conflict.[5] Many conflicts, regardless of their nature, may be intractable, and can evolve through phases of escalation and confrontation as well as phases of calm and a return to the status quo. For this reason, this chapter adopts the idea of conflict control and reduction to depict the processes of settlement and reconciliation in the Arab-Islamic tradition, rather than conflict resolution.

Another basic assumption is that conflict usually erupts because of different interpretations regarding data, issues, values, interests, and relationships.[6] According to the prominent anthropologist Laura Nader: "Conflict results from competition between at least two parties. A party may be a person, a family, a lineage, or a whole community; or it may be a class of ideas, a political organization, a tribe, or a religion. Conflict is occasioned by incompatible desires or aims and by its duration may be distinguished from strife or angry disputes arising from momentary aggravations."[7]

Conflict in Western perspectives is also viewed as having a positive dimension, acting as a catharsis to redefine relationships between individuals, groups, and nations. Such a perception makes it easier to find adequate settlements or possible resolutions.

During the last ten years, more and more voices within the field of conflict resolution have emphasized the importance of acknowledgment and forgiveness in achieving lasting reconciliation among conflicting parties. Many of the world's most intractable conflicts involve age-old cycles of oppression, victimization, and revenge. Racism and ethnic cleansing are only the most dramatic manifestations of such cycles.

These cyclical conflicts, which can have dangerous and long-lasting political repercussions, are rooted in a psychological dynamic of victimization. Usually, acts of violence, whether inflicted on an individual or a group, are the results of deep feelings of being victimized, regardless of who is the victim or victimizer. One of the guiding principles of U.S.-inspired conflict management and resolution is to help conflicting parties acknowledge one another's psychological concerns and needs so that they will be able to overcome their historic sense of victimization.[8] Overcoming feelings of victimization, which, unfortunately, are endemic to the human condition, is the most important step toward healing in the case of nations and ethnic groups in conflict.

According to Western psychologists, conflict usually erupts because some basic needs have not been fulfilled, such as the needs for shelter, food, self-esteem, love, knowledge, and self-actualization.[9] Indeed, the nonfulfillment of these needs may eventually lead to war if the conflict is not resolved. Conflicting parties must actively listen to each other to be able to mutually acknowledge each other's emotions, views, and needs. Thus, communication skills are fundamental to conflict resolution. In many cultures, the art of listening is drowned out by arguments and the never-ending struggle to get one's point across first. The opposite of listening is not ignoring; rather, it is preparing to respond. Active listening is a method that ensures that the whole meaning of what was said is understood.

Actively listening to all sides of a dispute is a specialty of mediators, who are often employed in Western conflict resolution. The mediator confronts two basic tasks when settling a dispute. First, he or she has to encourage people to negotiate in such a way as to reach an equitable outcome. Second, he or she has to be completely neutral and place the power of decision-making in the hands of the conflicting individuals or groups themselves. Negotiation is another important Western tool. 'Interest-based' negotiation focuses on people's long-term interests, rather than on short-term perspectives, and does not encourage 'hard' or 'soft' bargaining (such as occurs when one of the parties has to give in or compromise), which usually leads to unsatisfactory 'positional' compromises.[10]

Truth and justice commissions have also emerged as popular Western means of national healing. Following the collapse of various dictatorial regimes in Latin America and Central Europe (for example, Chile, Argentina, Brazil, East Germany, Czechoslovakia, and Poland), such commissions were formed to "police the past"—that is, to investigate the extent of human rights violations committed against civilians by the former military juntas and communist governments. These efforts encouraged atonement and remorse for past crimes, which, in turn, helped citizens and governments alike to rebuild democratic institutions. A similar commission was also established in South Africa following the dismantling of apartheid and the election of Nelson Mandela as president.

Lebanon shares some of the problems affecting societies in transition, though it should be noted that the country is not fully sovereign. In April 1994, as a contribution to the ongoing efforts at intercommunal reconciliation in postwar Lebanon, the Lebanese American University assembled on its Byblos campus a group of government officials, NGO activists, students, and lawyers for a three-day conference titled "Acknowledgment, Forgiveness, and Reconciliation: Alternative Approaches to Conflict Resolution in Post-War Lebanon."[11] The conference focused primarily on the psychological and interpersonal aspects of the Lebanese war, especially the politics of identity and the vicious circle of victimization and vengeance that fueled the long conflict.

Conference participants were initially uncomfortable with and suspicious of Western conflict resolution theory and methods. Participants expressed mixed feelings about the applicability of conflict resolution in the Lebanese social context. A U.S.-educated Christian banker noted that conflict resolution theory was initially forged in labor-management relations in the United States, later applied to business, and then to community relations and academia. He raised an important methodological question: "How can a theory which is supposed to be dealing with definite, programmed, institutionalized relationships deal with the unprogrammed, informal, and random relationships characteristic of social and political contexts in a totally different society?"

A Muslim academic and social activist declared that a better concept would be "conflict management" because "it is impossible completely to solve conflicts; the existence of conflicts goes together with human existence." He raised the point that conflicts were interrelated: the resolution of one conflict was contingent upon the resolution of other conflicts. "The crisis of Lebanon and the Middle East are the best proof of what I am saying," he concluded.[12]

The conference also revealed interesting insights into Lebanese conversational culture. The National Director of the Young Women's Christian Association-Lebanon (YWCA) commented that in Lebanon, when individuals are engaged in "heart-to-heart" conversations, they often interrupt with expressions of empathy and support. "It is not like interrupting rudely. The process of the discussion shows our concern because we are a very emotional people. That is the problem: we usually talk all together. We are active talkers and active listeners!"

While active listening involves remaining silent when the other person is talking, especially in cases of intense argument, in Lebanon, remaining silent is sometimes interpreted as meek acquiescence or agreement. A government representative from the Ministry of Education stated that "in the rural areas of Lebanon, if you do not talk, it means you are dull; the more you talk, the more it is assumed you know. People want to show that they know, especially those who go to town and come back to the village. They always talk."

The conference also addressed the key role of third-party mediators in disputes. In Lebanese culture, as in Arab culture in general, the mediator is presumed to have all the answers and solutions. He therefore has a great deal of power and responsibility. As one participant put it: "If [the third party] does not provide the answers, he or she is not really respected or considered to be legitimate." Finally, a number of conference participants expressed their expectations that conference organizers and facilitators would provide ready-made solutions to Lebanon's woes. This expectation was not unusual in the context of Lebanese culture and politics.

For several centuries, politics in Lebanon have been repeatedly penetrated by outside powers, either to foment strife or to impose solutions. The phenomenon of relying on outsiders for answers and solutions reveals one of the fundamental blind spots in Lebanese political thought: a lack of responsibility for one's actions and behaviors. At a more practical level, many Lebanese have opted to forget about the war and get on with their lives, even if the wounds and consequences of the war are still very much alive in the collective and individual Lebanese psyches.

If the role of the individual is crucial in Western theory, Lebanon is at a disadvantage. A Lebanese woman educator, while acknowledging the value of the Western concepts of acknowledgment, victimization, communication skills, and interest-based negotiation, pointed out that Western conflict resolution tools in the Lebanese context are hindered by the paradox that Lebanon is a "very individualistic society, but unfortunately, we do not have individuals." She went on to explain that "in order to have conflict management or conflict resolution, you have to recognize the other. But, you do not have the other if you do not have the individual. That is why there is no reconciliation, forgiveness, and conflict resolution [in Lebanon]. The existence of the individual is essential in this process."

This trenchant observation neatly summarizes the state of society in postwar Lebanon. Rather than a cohesive group of individuals bound together by an agreed-upon set of rights and obligations, (that is, citizens), the Lebanese instead comprise an agglomeration of competing communities, each of which requires absolute allegiance and obedience from its members. Every one of these communities feels victimized by the others, so the process of acknowledgment, forgiveness, and reconciliation has to begin at the community level, rather than at the individual level.

The conference also addressed the issue of government accountability for crimes committed during the Lebanese war. In Lebanon's case, the state's apparatus was noticeably absent during the long civil war. Thus, the central government and its institutions bear little, if any, direct responsibility for the atrocities committed between 1975 and 1990. Instituting war tribunals or truth and justice commissions in postwar Lebanon without some form of external, third-party intervention would undoubtedly be perceived as an affront by one community against another.[13]

It is important to understand the sociopolitical, cultural, and historical background of the Middle East in order to comprehend why conflict continues to plague the region. The influences shaping the characters and views of the conflicting parties must be considered if any resolution is to have a lasting effect.

Geography impacts people's behavior and interactions in terms of protection of scarce resources. The Arab Middle East is distinguished geographically by a variety of landscapes. The Arabian Peninsula is characterized by a large desert and other arid landscapes, and a scarcity of water. In the Levant, environmental conditions are more clement. Jordan and some areas of Israel are semiarid and poor in water while Lebanon and Syria are blessed with milder climates and numerous springs and rivers. Lebanon has a rugged mountainous terrain but also the fertile Biqa'a Valley and is self-sufficient in water.

The reality of Middle East ecology historically resulted in three key modes of subsistence: nomadic, village, and urban. Although communities of pastoral nomads, village farmers, and city-dwelling merchants and artisans were historically distinct from one another, they were nonetheless economically interdependent. Their lives and interests were always in actual or potential contact, and quite often in conflict. Although pastoral nomadism has become increasingly rare as a viable mode of subsistence due to the advent of nation-states with closed borders and the rapid and dramatic urbanization of the region's population, nomadic peoples and their traditions have nonetheless left a very deep imprint on Middle Eastern culture, society, and politics. One anthropologist hypothesizes that the characteristic form of pastoral nomadism that developed in this semiarid zone accounts for the strikingly similar cultural orientations found throughout the vast area of the Middle East:

> In the Near East today we find a remarkable similarity among the traditions of many people throughout a large region. . . . Islamization, the spread of a religious faith, is often offered as an explanation for this uniformity. But could Islam by itself have become so deeply-rooted among the diverse peoples of such a vast area, unless it was somehow a response to a life experience which all of these people shared in common? . . . Extreme arid conditions resulted in independent little herding groups dispersed across the desert and steppe. . . . This situation is reflected in the atomistic form which political alliances tended to take.[14]

Kinship ties are key to understanding social and political behavior in the Middle East. Despite the creation of modern states following the collapse of colonial rule, the basic unit of identification for the individual is not the state, the ethnic group, or the professional association, but the family.

Sociologically, the peoples of the Middle East remain famous for their loyalty to their families, distinctive rituals of hospitality and conflict mediation, and effective and flexible kin-based collectivities, such as the lineage and the tribe, which until quite recently performed most of the social, economic, and political functions of communities in the absence of centralized state governments.[15]

Patriarchal decision-making plays a powerful role in Middle Eastern family dynamics.[16] The father's supremacy in his family is an integral part of the more general authority system and maintains not only the genealogical cohesiveness of the family but also the cohesiveness of social life. This patriarchal pattern of power takes shape in the primacy of the *za'im* (leader) of the family. The *za'im* controls and defends the unity of the family both inside and outside of the group and acts as the family referee, managing conflicts that erupt within his family, while controlling solidarity and support between family members. He also acts as the family's ambassador toward outsiders. Each family in a given village is headed by a *za'im*, who collectively form the assembly of the village *zu'ama'*.[17]

Several writers on the Arab Middle East have underlined the fact that the only nation-state in the contemporary Arab Middle East is Egypt.[18] Egypt has an homogeneous population that identifies itself first and foremost as Egyptian. The only sizeable 'minority,' the Copts, who number about 6 million, consider themselves to be the descendants of the original Egyptians from Pharaonic times. Their allegiance is to Egypt as both government and country.

In Saudi Arabia, on the other hand, a family—the House of Sa'ud—dominates the body politic, as is the case in the other shaykhdoms of the Arabian Gulf. In Syria and Iraq, families from minority communities rule their respective societies.[19] Since Lebanon obtained independence in 1943, it has been ruled by a few prominent families—both Christian and Muslim—such as the Maronite Catholic Gemayel and Chamoun families, the Sunni El-Solh and Salam families, and the Druze Jumblatt family. As a strategy for survival, the patrilineal kinship system of the Middle East has certainly proved flexible and effective over many centuries under a variety of social, economic, and political conditions. Kinship is implicit in nearly every aspect of life and most social institutions, including religion and morality.

Religion also plays a very important role in both private and public interactions in the Middle East. The sociocultural and historic environment that saw the birth and spread of the world's three monotheistic religions—Judaism, Christianity, and Islam—encouraged a close relationship between the private and public in the individual's life in the Middle East.

In Judaism, the land (*eretz*), the people (*'am*), and the book (*torah*) cannot be separated. The same applies to Islam, which is a code of conduct, both temporal and spiritual. The Quran dictates the faithfuls' relations with God and people of other faiths living within the framework of the Islamic nation (*umma*). Christianity in the Arab world is very similar to Judaism and Islam in defining people's identities. For example, for some Christians in Lebanon, religious values are superseded by the fight for survival. Religion is thus used in an ethnic sense.[20]

Middle Eastern societies are defined by a variety of ethnic identities. Armenians, Kurds, Jews, Copts, Circassians, and Maronites are only some of the minorities in the contemporary Middle East. The existence of ethnic and ethnoreligious groups predates the rise of Islam and the creation of modern states in the region. In the Quran, "Peoples of the Book" (Christians and Jews) are treated as "protected peoples," (*dhimmis*), which literally means those on the conscience (*dhimma*) of the Islamic community.[21]

Under Ottoman rule, individuals living in the empire did not identify as Ottomans, Turks, Persians, or Arabs, but rather, as Muslims, Christians, Jews, and Druze. The Ottoman administration was controlled by Sunni Muslims and converts from other religions. Under the Ottomans, Islamic tolerance of Christians and Jews was defined by the *millet* (nations) system. "Under the system local communities of a particular sect were autonomous in the conduct of their spiritual affairs and civil affairs relating closely to religion and community, such as church administration, marriage, inheritance, property, and education."[22]

Ethnic groups thus identified with their religious leaders more so than with any abstract notion of the state. The *millet* system estranged Arab Christians from political life and deepened suspicions between them and Muslims, a legacy that eventually exploded in Lebanon. Christians were treated as foreigners and suspected of being agents of foreign powers; their loyalty was often in doubt. After the fall of the Ottoman Empire and in reaction to their plight, Middle Eastern Christians were at the forefront of the new movement for Arab nationalism, the secular movement in the Arab world, and some among them founded socialist parties, such as the Ba'th (Renaissance) Party now in power in Syria and Iraq.

Political scientist Bassam Tibi notes that:

> unlike the imperial and the territorial dynastic states that were familiar in Middle Eastern history, the externally imposed new pattern of the nation-state is defined as a national, not as a communal, polity. . . . In varying degrees, all states of the Middle East lack this infrastructure. . . . In most of the states of the Middle East, sovereignty is nominal.

> The tribal-ethnic and sectarian conflicts that the colonial powers exacerbated did not end with the attainment of independence. The newly established nation-states have failed to cope with the social and economic problems created by rapid development because they cannot provide the proper institutions to

alleviate these problems. Because the nominal nation-state has not met the challenge, society has resorted to its pre-national ties as a solution, thereby preserving the framework of the patron-client relationship.[23]

Social relationships in the contemporary Middle East thus require a melting of the individual's identity and personality within the framework of his communal group. A Maronite Catholic in Lebanon belongs to his community from birth to death whether he or she likes it or not. In addition, the confessional system, which is pervasive in Lebanon and other countries in the Middle East, means that the individual citizen must be part of a patronage network. Although patron-client relations "play an important role in facilitating the distribution of goods and services among the population and harnessing popular support behind leaders," patronage ties are essentially asymmetrical: perpetuating these relationships also perpetuates and reinforces the unequal power structure in the starkly stratified societies of the contemporary Middle East.

Patron-client ties ensure that people are kept 'in their place': the rich and powerful maintain their dominant positions, from which they have the advantage of becoming even more rich and powerful, while the less fortunate are kept in their position of dependency, remaining virtually powerless over the decision-making processes and larger forces that shape their lives.

Clientelism and the absence of citizenship in the Western sense have profound implications for reconciliation and processes of conflict reduction in the Middle East. Private justice is meted out through a network in which political and/or religious leaders determine the outcome of feuds between clans or conflicts between individuals. Notions of honor and shame also play a key role in this context. Most of the blood feuds among Lebanese, Jordanians, and Palestinians originate from incidents where family honor has been harmed. Usually, women are the direct victims of such tragedies. More and more Arab women are struggling to lessen the impact of honor crimes and fight for the abolition of this feudal tradition.[24]

British sociologist Anthony Giddens wrote that rituals are crucial to both an individual's emotional well-being and communal harmony and social integration:

> Without ordered ritual and collective involvement, individuals are left without structured ways of coping with tensions and anxieties. . . . Communal rites provide a focus for group solidarity at major transitions as well as allocating definite tasks for those involved. . . . Something profound is lost together with traditional forms of ritual. . . . Traditional ritual . . . connected individual action to moral frameworks and to elemental questions about human existence. The loss of ritual is also the loss of such frameworks.[25]

This very important observation brings to the fore the malaise that exists in Western society, where anomie and atomistic modes of living have relegated customs and rituals to the trash heap of premodern, nonrational history. In contrast to the family-oriented culture of the Middle East, the individual must fend for himself or herself in Western civilization. In conflicts, individuals in Western societies usually turn to an attorney or a therapist. The family is an alien entity, and alienation leads to violence and despair.

For a country emerging from 16 years of civil strife, priorities do not include training for conflict control and reduction. In Lebanon and other Arab societies, conflict resolution techniques are learned and adopted by professional groups such as businessmen or businesswomen, bankers, or engineers. For the rest of the population, conflict control is handled either by state-controlled courts or by traditional means.

In this context, one of the basic criticisms launched against Western conflict resolution techniques is that they are either too mechanistic or based on therapy-oriented formulas. Although Western methods and skills are relevant and useful, they need to be adapted to indigenous realities.

For instance, the role of social workers in family disputes is not the same in Lebanon as it is in the West. In Lebanon, the majority of social workers are women. They are trained in Lebanon's major academic institutions, the state-controlled Lebanese University and the Jesuit-controlled Université Saint-Joseph, and once their degree is completed, they confront the realities of Lebanese society. In conflicts involving couples, they are usually approached by battered wives; husbands, however, often refuse to deal with the social worker. The path to resolution thus goes through the local religious or political za'im, not through the social worker, a typical pattern in patriarchal societies.

Another issue facing social workers attempting to mediate conflicts in Lebanon is child custody matters. In Middle Eastern societies, in the case of divorce, the father is granted custody of the children. In the instances when mothers try to keep their children, the young ones become hostages in a conflict that pits their father's family against their mother.

These examples highlight the problem with applying Western modes of conflict control and reduction in communally-based societies where patriarchy and religious values are paramount. Arab 'citizens' are not citizens in the Western meaning of individuals bound to one another and the state by an agreed-upon interlocking system of rights and duties. Instead, Arabs belong to communities and abide by their rules and rituals. Of course, there are many young professionals and educated men and women who are struggling to establish secular societies based on individual rights and responsibilities and state accountability. But Arab society is still largely traditional.

In large Arab cities, individuals involved in conflicts are more likely than are villagers to resort to the official legal system to settle their disputes. The legal system, however, is clogged and corruption is pervasive. Moreover, the interpretation of the rule of law in sectarian-based societies or societies based on tribal modes of social interaction has a different meaning. The law is usually that of the powerful and the wealthy (politicians and clergy) or heads of village clans or Bedouin tribes.[26]

The rule of law also has to confront the prevalent and powerful influence of patronage and its strong emphasis on asymmetrical power relationships. For example, an individual who has committed a crime can face both the legal justice system and the tribal mode of conflict control and reduction.

This situation underlines the importance of studying closely modes of reconciliation and conflict control in an Arab-Islamic environment. The observer interested in conflict control and reduction in non-Western societies has to look into the rituals that inform individual and community behavior following a crime or any other illegal action.

Among some Middle Easterners, such as the Lebanese, Jordanians, and Palestinians, rituals are used in private modes of conflict control and reduction. Private modes are processes not controlled by the state whereby customary, traditional steps are taken to restore justice. Sometimes, both private and official justice are invoked simultaneously in fostering reconciliation.

One such ritual is the process of *sulh* (settlement) and *musalaha* (reconciliation). According to Islamic law (Shari'a), "the purpose of *sulh* is to end conflict and hostility among believers so that they may conduct their relationships in peace and amity. . . . In Islamic law, sulh is a form of contract (*'aqd*), legally binding on both the individual and community levels."[27] Similar to the private *sulh* between two believers, "the purpose of [public] *sulh* is to suspend fighting between [two parties] and establish peace, called *mawwada* (peace or gentle relationship), for a specific period of time."[28]

The *sulh* ritual, an institutionalized form of conflict management and control, has its origins in tribal and village contexts. "The *sulh* ritual stresses the close link between the psychological and political dimensions of communal life through its recognition that injuries between individuals and groups will fester and expand if not acknowledged, repaired, forgiven and transcended."[29]

"*Sulh* is the best of judgments." This is how the Jordanian Bedouin tribes describe the customary process of settlement and reconciliation. Indeed, given the severity of life conditions in the desert, competing tribes long ago realized that *sulh* is a better alternative to endless cycles of vengeance.

The judicial system in Lebanon does not include sulh as part of the conflict control process, but *sulh* rituals are approved and encouraged in rural areas where state control is not very strong. *Sulh* is used today in the rural areas of the Biqa'a Valley, the Hermel area in eastern Lebanon, and the 'Akkar region of north Lebanon.[30] In Jordan, *sulh* is officially recognized by the Jordanian government as a legally acceptable tradition of the Bedouin tribes. And, in Israel, *sulh* is still used among the Israeli Arabs living in the villages of Galilee.

The Jordanian judge Muhammad Abu-Hassan makes a distinction between public *sulh* and private *sulh*. Public *sulh* is similar to a peace treaty between two countries. It usually takes place as a result of conflicts between two or more tribes which result in death and destruction affecting all the parties involved.[31] In a conflict, each of the tribes involved takes stock of its human and material losses. The tribe with minimum losses compensates the tribe that suffered most, and so on. Tradition has it that stringent conditions are set to settle the tribal conflict definitively. The most famous of these conditions is that the parties in conflict pledge to forget everything that happened and initiate new and friendly relations. The consequences and effects of public *sulh* apply whether the guilty party was identified or was unknown at the time of the *sulh*.

Private *sulh* takes place when both the crime and the guilty party are known. The parties may be of the same tribe or from different tribes. The purpose of private *sulh* is to make sure that revenge will not take place against the family of the perpetrator.

There are two possible final outcomes of the *sulh* process: total *sulh*, or partial or conditional *sulh*. The former type ends all kinds of conflict between the two parties, who decide thenceforth not to hold any grudges against each other. The latter type ends the conflict between the two parties according to conditions agreed upon during the settlement process.

Consider a brief sketch of how the ritual of settlement and reconciliation is used in the Middle East. Following a murder, the family of the murderer, in order to thwart any attempt at blood revenge, calls on a delegation of mediators comprised of village elders and notables, usually called *muslihs* or *jaha* (those who have gained the esteem of the community). The mediators initiate a process of fact-finding, questioning the parties involved. As soon as the family of the guilty party calls for the mediators' intervention, a *hudna* (truce) is declared. The task of the muslihs or jaha is not to judge, punish, or condemn the offending party, "but rather, to preserve the good names of both the families involved and to reaffirm the necessity of ongoing relationships within the community. The *sulh* ritual is not a zero-sum game."[32]

To many practitioners of *sulh* and *musalaha*, the toughest cases to settle are usually those involving blood feuds. Sometimes, a blood price is paid to the family of the victim that usually involves an amount of money set by the mediators. The *diyya* (blood money) or an exchange of goods (sometimes including animals, food, etc.) substitutes for the exchange of death.

The ritual *sulh* process usually ends in a public ceremony of *musalaha* (reconciliation) performed in the village square. The families of both the victim and the guilty party line up on both sides of the road and exchange greetings and accept apologies, especially the aggrieved party.

The *musalaha* ceremony includes four major stages. First comes the act of reconciliation itself, then the two parties shake hands under the supervision of the *muslihs* or *jaha*. Next, the family of the murderer visits the home of the victim to drink a cup of bitter coffee, and finally, the ritual concludes with a meal hosted by the family of the offender. The rituals vary in different places but the basic philosophy is based on *sulh* (settlement), *musalaha* (reconciliation), *musafaha* (hand-shaking), and *mumalaha* ("partaking of salt and bread—that is, breaking bread together).[33]

The Quran is a very important source to understand modes of conflict control and reconciliation in Arab-Islamic societies. The holy book of Islam calls for equity in cases of revenge and for forgiveness in cases of apology and "remission." In the first chapter of the Quran, the Prophet Muhammad describes the extent and limits of punishment (*qisas*) and retribution:

> O ye who believe!
> The law of equality
> Is prescribed to you
> In cases of murder:
> The free for the free,
> The slave for the slave,
> The woman for the woman.
> But if any remission
> Is made by the brother
> Of the slain, then grant
> Any reasonable demand,
> And compensate him
> With handsome gratitude.
> This is a concession
> And a Mercy
> From your Lord[34]

Many of the ethnoreligious conflicts that have emerged over the past ten years are based on centuries-old feelings of victimization and powerlessness. Considering the role of power in persuading enemies to settle and resolve their conflicts is crucial for the success or failure of reconciliation efforts. If conflict control and reduction is to succeed in the new global political order, diplomats, policy-makers, and practitioners must first rethink how power is perceived and used.

According to the political philosopher Hannah Arendt, true power has nothing to do with guns, muscles, threats, or dictators:

> [P]ower is what keeps the public realm, the potential space of appearance between [people] acting and speaking, in existence. . . . Power is always . . . a power potential and not an unchangeable, measurable and reliable entity like force or strength. While strength is the natural quality of an individual seen in isolation, power springs up between people when they act together and vanishes the moment they disperse. Because of this particularity, which power shares with all potentialities that can only be actualized but never fully materialized, power is to an astonishing degree independent of material factors, either of numbers or means.[35]

Empowering victims to help them overcome painful legacies from the past can take place through transformative reconciliation rituals such as *sulh* and *musalaha*. "Such rituals readjust individuals and communities to changing aspects of their life-worlds, thereby enabling them to complete difficult and troubling transitions as individuals and as members of a society."[36]

At the conclusion of the 1994 conference in Lebanon, some participants suggested adapting the ritual of *sulh* in order to facilitate acknowledgment, apology, and forgiveness at the national, not just communal, level in postwar Lebanon. Ghassan Mokheibar, a prominent Lebanese attorney who has written about traditional reconciliation rituals in Lebanon, has stated that modified processes of *sulh* and *musalaha* could play a similar role to that of truth and reconciliation commissions in Latin America and South Africa.

The importance of Arab-Islamic rituals for conflict resolution lies in their communal nature. The problem confronting Western approaches is that the conceptual category of the individual does not have the same validity and importance in the Middle East as it does in Western cultures. In the Middle East, the individual is enmeshed within his or her own group, sect, tribe, or millet. Religion continues to play a crucial role in individual and collective lives.

These and other fundamental features of Middle East society must be taken into consideration when implementing peace processes in the region. Arab states are constructed differently from Western nation-states: the concept of national 'reconciliation' must occur within entities that were artificially created after World War II. Further, power in Middle Eastern societies is usually concentrated at the top of the hierarchy, whether in the village *za'im* or government leaders (presidents, kings, military autocrats). Given the absence of participatory democracy and the pervasiveness of autocratic rule, the population at large cannot be convinced of the desirability of reconciliation unless tangible benefits ensue.

The history of Israeli-Egyptian and Israeli-Palestinian agreements is not encouraging as far as the transformative power of reconciliation is concerned. To the extent that peace has been achieved in these circumstances, it has resulted from military persuasion and economic enticement. At the popular grassroots level, peace is perceived as a deal imposed by a superpower's need to stabilize a region of the world whose culture and values are unfathomable except through an Orientalist perspective.

Returning to Hannah Arendt's definition of power, collective empowerment of the community ought to be undertaken in urban, rural, and remote areas alike in coordination with religious and clan leaders, who can pass along a feeling of empowerment to their communities. As long as Palestinians, Egyptians, Lebanese, Jordanians, Syrians, and other Arabs perceive that the peace process is being imposed on them without addressing age-old grievances, the harder reconciliation with Israel will be. The ritual of *sulh* and *musalaha* offers an example to follow and adapt.

NOTES

1. See Muhammad Abu-Nimer, "Conflict Resolution in an Islamic Context: Some Conceptual Questions," *Peace and Change*, Vol. 21, No.1 (January 1996), pp. 22–40.

2. Many of the Lebanese quoted in this article were participants in the 1994 conference on "Acknowledgment, Forgiveness and Reconciliation: Lessons from Lebanon."

3. The author was introduced to conflict resolution and trained to teach and apply its skills by Dr. Merle Lefkoff, an experienced facilitator based in New Mexico.

4. This worldview is in line with a utilitarian philosophy that pervades intellectual debates in the United States.

5. For further details, see Paul Salem, "A Critique of Western Conflict Resolution from a non-Western Perspective," in Paul Salem (ed.), *Conflict Resolution in the Arab World* (Beirut: American University of Beirut, 1997).

6. Western processes of conflict resolution range across a continuum that includes situations in which parties have most control (communication, collaboration, and negotiation) to situations where parties have least control (mediation and arbitration).

7. Laura Nader, "Conflict: Anthropological Aspects," in David L. Sills, ed. *International Encyclopedia of the Social Sciences*, Vol. 3 and 4 (New York: The MacMillan Co. and The Free Press, 1968), p. 236.

8. For further discussion of victimization and its central role in the perpetuation of conflicts, see Joseph V. Montville, "Psychoanalytic Enlightenment and the Greening of Diplomacy," in Vamik D. Volkan, Joseph V. Montville, and Demetrius A. Julius (eds), *The Psychodynamics of International Relations*, Vol. 2 (Lexington, Mass.: Lexington Books, 1991).

9. See Abraham H. Maslow, *Motivation and Personality, 3rd ed.* (New York and London: Harper and Row, 1987).

10. In his influential book *Getting to Yes*, Roger Fisher writes that interest-based negotiation has four basic elements: 1) separate the people from the problem; 2) focus on interests, not positions; 3) invent options for mutual gain; and 4) insist on using objective criteria. For further details, see Roger Fisher and William Ury, *Getting to Yes: Negotiating Agreement Without Giving In*, 2nd ed. (New York: Penguin Books, 1991).

11. The author, together with his wife, Laurie E. King-Irani, organized the conference in Lebanon. Funded in part by the U.S. Institute of Peace, this conference was the first organized discussion of the applicability and relevance of acknowledgment, forgiveness, and reconciliation to conflicts in Lebanon and the Middle East.

12. These comments can be found in George Emile Irani, "Acknowledgment, Forgiveness, and Reconciliation in Conflict Resolution: Perspectives from Lebanon," in George E. Irani and Laurie E. King-Irani (eds.), *Lessons from Lebanon* (forthcoming).

13. As of this writing, only one warlord, Dr. Samir Geagea, head of the Maronite Christian-dominated militia of the "Lebanese Forces" (now dissolved), has been put on trial and is serving a life sentence in jail.

14. Michael Meeker, *Literature and Violence in North Arabia* (Cambridge: Cambridge University Press, 1979), p. 7.

15. For further details see Laurie E. King-Irani, "Kinship, Class and Ethnicity: Strategies for Survival in the Contemporary Middle East," in Deborah Gerner (ed.), *Understanding the Contemporary Middle East* (Boulder: Lynne Rienner Publishers, 1999).

16. A thorough, groundbreaking analysis on the role patriarchy plays in the Middle East can be found in Hisham Sharabi, *Neopatriarchy: A Theory of Distorted Change in Arab Society* (New York: Oxford University Press, 1988).

17. Ibid.

18. For a thorough analysis of Egyptian politics and Arab politics in general, see the work of the Lebanese-American scholar Fouad Ajami, *The Arab Predicament: Arab Political Thought and Practice Since 1967* (Cambridge, MA: Cambridge University Press, 1981).

19. In Iraq, Saddam Hussein and his family, from the Sunni Muslim village of Takrit in north-central Iraq, have dominated Iraqi politics since the early 1970s. The same applies to Syria, where President Bashar al-Assad's minority Alawi community holds all reins of power. Saddam Hussein is grooming his son to take over power as Hafiz al-Assad did in Syria.

20. See George Irani, *The Papacy and the Middle East: The Role of the Holy See in the Arab-Israeli Conflict* (Notre Dame: University of Notre Dame Press, 1989).

21. Regarding the legal status of non-Muslim minorities, see Antoine Fattal, *Le Statut Legal des Non-Musulmans en Pays d'Islam* (Beirut: Imprimerie Catholique, 1958).

22. Michael C. Hudson, *Arab Politics: The Search for Legitimacy* (New Haven: Yale University Press, 1997), p. 58.

23. Bassam Tibi, "The Simultaneity of the Unsimultaneous: Old Tribes and Imposed Nation-States in the Modern Middle East," in Philip S. Khoury and Joseph Kostiner (eds.), *Tribes and State Formation in the Middle East* (Berkeley: University of California Pres, 1990), pp. 147–149.

24. See Hazem al-Ameen, "Beirut: The Arab Women's Tribunal Symbolized in an Angry Body," Al-Hayat, March 6, 1998, p. 24.

25. Anthony Giddens, *Modernity and Self-Identity: Self and Society in the Modern Age* (Palo Alto: Stanford University Press, 1991), p. 204.

26. For an excellent analysis of the legal system in the Arab world, see Nathan J. Brown, *The Rule of Law in the Arab World* (Cambridge: Cambridge University Press, 1997).

27. M. Khadduri, "Sulh," in C. E. Bosworth, E. van Donzel, W. P. Heinrichs, and G. Lecomte, *The Encyclopedia of Islam, Volume IX* (Leiden, Holland: Brill, 1997), pp. 845–846.

28. Ibid.

29. Laurie E. King-Irani, "Rituals of Reconciliation and Processes of Empowerment in Post-War Lebanon," in I. William Zartman (ed.), *Traditional Cures for Modern Conflicts: African Conflict Medicine* (Boulder: Lynne Rienner Publishers, 1999).

30. For further details see Nizar Hamzeh, "The Role of Hizbullah in Conflict Management Within Lebanon's Shia Community," in Paul Salem (ed.), 1997, op. cit. pp. 93–118.

31. For further details on Jordanian bedouin rituals of reconciliation, see Mohammad Abu-Hassan, *Turath al-Badu al-Qada'i (Bedouin Customary Law)* (Amman, Jordan: Manshurat Da'irat al-Thaqafa wa al-Funun, 1987), pp. 257–259.

32. King-Irani, op. cit.

33. For further details on the basic principles of sulh as applied in the Galilee, see Elias J. Jabbour, *SULHA: Palestinian Traditional Peacemaking Process* (Shefar'am, Israel: House of Hope Publications, 1996).

34. Surah 1:178 in *The Holy Qur'an, Text, Translation and Commentary,* Abdullah Yusuf 'Ali *New Revised Edition.* (Brentwood, Md: Amana Corporation, 1989).

35. Hannah Arendt, *The Human Condition* (Chicago: The University of Chicago Press, 1958), pp. 200–201.

36. King-Irani, op. cit.

12

Liberal Islam

Prospects and Challenges

Charles Kurzman

Although the focus of research and public perception in the West has been on radical Islamic thought and movements, many Muslims adhere to principles that could be described collectively as "liberal Islam." This term refers to interpretations of Islam that have a special concern regarding such issues as democracy, separating religion from political involvement, women's rights, freedom of thought, and promoting human progress. In each case, the argument is that both Muslims and religious piety itself would benefit from reforms and a more open society.[1] These attitudes parallel those of liberalism in other cultures and also of liberal movements in various religious faiths.

It is quite possible that these tendencies will grow more important in the future, perhaps even coming to be the dominant orientation in the years to come. Such a trend could happen because of local factors, modernization and development in Islamic societies, and reasons similar to those that brought about such an evolution in the West.

Liberalism in the Islamic world and liberalism in the West may share common elements, but they are not exactly the same thing. They may both support multireligious coexistence, for example, but go about it in different ways. Within the Islamic discourse, there are three main tropes that I call:

- the "liberal *Shari'a*"
- the "silent *Shari'a*"
- the "interpreted *Shari'a*"

Shari'a is the body of Islamic guidance and precedent that has been handed down from the time of the Prophet Muhammad in seventh-century Arabia.

The 'liberal *Shari'a*' argues that the revelations of the Quran and the practices of the Prophet command Muslims to follow liberal positions. For example, Ali Bulac from Turkey quotes Sura 109, Verse 6 of the Quran: "To you your religion, to me my religion." He goes into great detail describing the "Medina Document," a treaty signed by the Prophet Muhammad with the Jewish tribes of Medina in the first moments of the Islamic era:

> The urgent problem of the day was to end the conflicts and to find a formulation for the co-existence of all sides according to the principles of justice and righteousness. In this respect, the Document is epochal . . . A righteous and just, law-respecting ideal project aiming for true peace and stability among people cannot but be based on a contract among different groups (religious, legal, philosophical, political etc.). . . . This is a rich diversity within unity, or a real pluralism.

Chandra Muzaffar from Malaysia quotes Sura 49, Verse 13: "O mankind! We created you from a single pair of a male and a female, and made you into nations and tribes, that ye may know each other, not that ye may despise each other." The Indian Ali Asghar Engineer quotes Sura 2, Verse 256: "There is no compulsion in religion."[2] Muhammad Talbi from Tunisia quotes Sura 5, Verse 48: "To each among you, have We prescribed a Law and an Open Way. And if God had enforced His Will, He would have made of you all one people." Hostile and discriminatory forms of inter-religious relations, according to this trope, are un-Islamic. In the words of Subhi Mahmassani of Lebanon: "There can be no discrimination based on religion in an Islamic system."

The second trope, the 'silent *Shari'a*,' holds that coexistence is not required by the *Shari'a*, but is allowed. This trope argues that the *Shari'a* is silent on certain topics—not because divine revelation was incomplete or faulty, but because the revelation intentionally left certain issues for humans to choose.

For example, Humayun Kabir from India argues that the precedent of the early period of Islam does not apply automatically to later periods:

> The situation changed as the Muslim empire spread rapidly through large areas of Asia and many different peoples were brought within its fold. Many practical problems arose and Muslim political thinking had to find a place for non-Muslim subjects in a Muslim State . . . [In India, today, for example,]

Muslims have condemned compulsion in religion and admitted that different religions must be given due respect.

Syed Vahiduddin, also from India, quotes the same Quranic verse as Muhammad Talbi: "In a pluralistic and multi-religious society one cannot do better than to ponder on the Quranic vision of human conflicts: To every one of you we have appointed a right way and open path. If Allah had willed, He would have made you one community. . . ." (Sura 5, Verse 48) But Vahiduddin interprets this verse within the context of the changing needs of an evolving Islamic community: the late twentieth century, he writes, was a period when Muslims were "tempted to take an extremely static view of religion. Their pre-occupation with issues which are not of capital importance has made them uncompromising not only in inter-religious dialogue but also in inter-Islamic dialogue."

Similarly, Abdurrahman Wahid of Indonesia, former leader of the world's largest Islamic organization and former president of Indonesia, calls the 1945 Indonesian constitution better suited than an exclusively Islamic state for the particularly multicultural setting of contemporary Indonesia. "[T]here is a need for steps to be taken to resist the deterioration of relations between the different religions and faiths in Indonesia," he writes, and the first of these steps is the defense of democratic freedoms: "First of all, efforts to restore the attitude of mutual respect among people from different faiths should be based on the fundamental legal principles of freedom of speech (even for very small minority groups), the rule of law and equality before the constitution."[3]

The first trope of liberal Islam holds that the *Shari'a* requires democracy, and the second trope holds that the *Shari'a* allows democracy. But there is a third trope that takes issue with each of the first two. This trope is 'interpreted Islam.' In the words of the Iranian 'Abdul-Karim Soroush, "Religion is divine, but its interpretation is thoroughly human and this-worldly":

> The text does not stand alone, it does not carry its own meaning on its shoul-
> ders, it needs to be situated in a context, it is theory-laden, its interpretation is
> in flux, and presuppositions are as actively at work here as elsewhere in the
> field of understanding. Religious texts are no exception. Therefore their inter-
> pretation is subject to expansion and contraction according to the assump-
> tions preceding them and/or the questions enquiring them. . . . We look at
> revelation in the mirror of interpretation, much as a devout scientist looks at
> creation in the mirror of nature . . . [so that] the way for religious democracy
> and the transcendental unity of religions, which are predicated on religious
> pluralism, will have been paved.

Farid Esack from South Africa cites the words of 'Ali ibn Abi Talib, fourth caliph and son-in-law of the Prophet: "this is the Quran, written in straight lines, between two boards [of its binding]; it does not speak with a tongue; it needs interpreters and interpreters are people." Esack translates this into contemporary terms: "Every interpreter enters the process of interpretation with some pre-understanding of the questions addressed by the text—even of its silences—and brings with him or her certain conceptions as presuppositions of his or her exegesis." Esack's pre-understandings emerge from the multireligious struggle against apartheid in South Africa. He argues that this commitment resonates with the spirit of early Islam, when an "emerging theology of religious pluralism was intrinsically wedded to one of liberation."[4]

Similarly, the Egyptian Hassan Hanafi wrote:

> There is no one interpretation of a text, but there are many interpretations given the difference in understanding between various interpreters. An interpretation of a text is essentially pluralistic. The text is only a vehicle for human interests and even passions . . . The conflict of interpretation is essentially a socio-political conflict, not a theoretical one. Theory indeed is only an epistemological cover-up. Each interpretation expresses the socio-political commitment of the interpreter.

Amina Wadud-Muhsin from the United States argues in a similar vein that "when one individual reader with a particular world-view and specific prior text [the language and cultural context in which the text is read] asserts that his or her reading is the only possible or permissible one, it prevents readers in different contexts from coming to terms with their own relationship to the text."

Abdallahi An-Na'im from Sudan said: "There is no such thing as the only possible or valid understanding of the Quran, or conception of Islam, since each is informed by the individual and collective orientation of Muslims . . ."[5]

This third trope suggests that religious diversity is inevitable, not just among religious communities but within Islam itself.

Few, if any, of the authors quoted above have read one another's work, despite the fact that they were all born in the first half of the twentieth century. These liberal positions appear to be emerging independently throughout the Islamic world. This simultaneous appearance is due to three historic shifts of the past several decades.

Widespread higher education has broken the traditional religious institutions' monopoly on religious scholarship. Millions of autodidacts now have access to texts and commentaries, such as nonclerics with secular educations: engineers such as Muhammad Shahrur from Syria and Mehdi Bazargan from Iran; philosophers such as Muhammad Arkun from Algeria (and France) and Tunisian Rachid Ghannushi; and sociologists such as 'Ali Shari'ati of Iran and Chandra Muzaffar from Malaysia.

For example, Fatima Mernissi from Morocco, trained in sociology rather than theology, examined the *hadith* (tradition of the Prophet): "Those who entrust their affairs to a woman will never know prosperity!" Consulting a variety of ancient sources, she discovered that the *hadith* was attributed to Abu Bakra (died circa 671)—born a slave, liberated by the Prophet Muhammad, who rose to high social position in the city of Basra. He is the only source for this *hadith*, and he reported it 25 years after the Prophet's death. Mernissi suggests that this *hadith*, though included in Muhammad ibn Ismail al-Bukhari's collection of traditions, *Al-Salih* (The Authentic), and widely cited in the Islamic world, is suspect for two reasons.

First, when placed in context, Abu Bakra's relation of the *hadith* seems self-serving. He was trying to save his life after the Battle of the Camel (December 656), when, to quote Mernissi, "all those who had not chosen to join 'Ali's clan had to justify their action. This can explain why a man like Abu Bakra needed to recall opportune traditions, his record being far from satisfactory, as he had refused to take part in the civil war . . . [Although] many of the Companions and inhabitants of Basra chose neutrality in the conflict, only Abu Bakra justified it by the fact that one of the parties was a woman." (pp. 116–117)

Second, Abu Bakra had once been flogged for giving false testimony in an early court case. According to the rules of hadith scholarship laid out by Imam Malik ibn Anas (710–796 AD), one of the founders of the science of hadith studies, lying disqualifies a source from being counted as a reliable transmitter of hadith. "If one follows the principles of Malik for *fiqh* [Islamic jurisprudence], Abu Bakra must be rejected as a source of *hadith* by every good, well-informed Malikite Muslim." (p. 119)

Thus, in the world of CD-ROMs and global Internet access, anyone literate in Arabic with a personal computer, like Mernissi, can investigate the sources of Islamic law and question the reigning interpretations.

International communication technologies—radio, television, telephones, and the Internet—as well as newspapers and international trade, are bringing educated people from around the world into ever closer contact. The ideals of Western liberalism, like other Western notions such as nationalism, have entered people's homes around the world. People in Gabon, West Africa, for example, watched the fall of communism in Eastern Europe and started demanding democracy themselves, prompting that country's dictator to comment derisively on the "wind from the east [that is, the communist Eastern bloc] that is shaking the coconut trees."[6]

Another example was when Nurcholish Madjid from Indonesia defended freedom of thought by quoting the famous U.S. judge Oliver Wendell Holmes (1809–1894): "The ultimate good desired is better reached by free trade in ideas—that the best test of truth is the power of thought to get itself accepted [in the] competition of the market . . ." Madjid goes on to say:

> Among the freedoms of the individual, the freedom[s] to think and to express opinions are the most valuable. We must have a firm conviction that all ideas

and forms of thought, however strange they may sound, should be accorded means of expression. It is by no means rare that such ideas and thoughts, initially regarded as generally wrong, are [later] found to be right . . . Furthermore, in the confrontation of ideas and thoughts, even error can be of considerable benefit, because it will induce truth to express itself and grow as a strong force. Perhaps it was not entirely small talk when our Prophet said that differences of opinion among his *umma* [community] were a mercy [from God].

A further example of how technology is inducing change in the Islamic world is the tremendous Internet activity surrounding the arrest of former Malaysian deputy prime minister Anwar Ibrahim, whose trajectory from youthful Islamist militant to liberal reformist coincided with his increasing use of quotations from William Shakespeare and other crosscultural sources. Ibrahim's political career began with a communalist Islamism that scapegoated Chinese Malaysians. In recent years, Ibrahim has become an outspoken proponent of multireligious coexistence, both in Malaysia and at the global level:

> The experience of contemporary Islam in Southeast Asia has much to contribute not only to Muslims in other regions but possibly also to the world at large. This is due to the fact that the devout Southeast Asian Muslim practices his religion in the context of a truly multicultural world. Especially in Malaysia, a Muslim is never unaware of the presence of people of other faiths; as friends, colleagues, collaborators, partners or even competitors.[7]

Supporters of Ibrahim's reform movement contributed to international communication through Web sites such as Anwar Online <http://members.tripod. com/~Anwar_Ibrahim>, Anwar Ibrahim One <http://www.anwaribrahim1.com>, Gerakan Reformasi <http://members.xoom.com/Gerakan>, ADIL <http://members. easyspace.com/reformasi>, Reformasi Dot Com (<http://www.reformasi. com>, quoting poetry by Rabindranath Tagore), and Ibrahim's wife's official Web site, <http://www.anwaribrahim.org>.

Some of these sites registered hundreds of thousands of visitors in two or three months. One flashing pro-Ibrahim Web site noted: "Welcome to J's Reformasi Online, the site of the oppressed and depressed!! In the name of Allah, most gracious, most merciful."

Some countries, such as Saudi Arabia and Iran, have tried to block out foreign ideas precisely because they fear these sorts of intercultural interactions. But blocking foreign ideas, to quote U.S. President Woodrow Wilson out of context, "is like using a broom to stop a vast flood."[8] Few countries will be able to keep up this level of sweeping for long.

A third factor in the rise of liberal Islam is the failure of alternative ideologies. In particular, there appears to be a growing sense that Islamic regimes have not lived up to their promise. The Sudan and Pakistan, for example, have proved to be no less corrupt after the Islamicization of their governments than before. Taliban rule in Afghanistan, it seems fair to generalize, horrified most Muslims.[9]

The number one disappointment for "fundamentalist" Muslims, however, is Iran. The Iranian revolution of 1979 raised tremendous hopes among Islamists in Malaysia, Africa, and throughout the Islamic world. Iran was to be the show-piece of the Islamist movement. For the first time since the seventh century, a truly Islamic society was to be constructed. It has been painful for these people to find that dream unfulfilled.

There are many examples of this painful disillusionment and the liberal outcome that resulted. Consider 'Abdul-Karim Soroush, a controversial figure who wholeheartedly favored the Islamic Republic in the early years. Soroush participated actively in the revolutionary reorganization of the universities in Iran, which involved getting rid of many fine professors in the name of ideologi-cal purity. Yet by the mid-1980s, even this staunch supporter of the Islamic republic had started to distance himself from official committees on which he had served. Within a few years, he came to realize that the Islamic Republic was not ushering in a new era of justice and righteousness. Soroush started to criti-cize the government and began to call for a reinterpretation of Islamic law and for academic and intellectual freedoms that his university reorganization had disregarded in the early 1980s. These themes, along with his impressive erudi-tion and his talent for public speaking, made Soroush one of the most popular public speakers in Iran in the early 1990s. He spoke at mosques and universities and on the radio, always to big audiences. Naturally, the Iranian government found his words threatening, and Soroush has since been barred from speaking publicly in Iran. He now speaks outside Iran, when he is allowed to travel, address-ing international audiences, mainly in Europe and North America, stressing the commonality of his views with Western interpretations of religion. But the pain of Soroush's break with the Islamic Republic and his disillusionment are apparently so great that he literally cannot deal with his own former hopes and aspirations. In interviews, Soroush denies that he was a supporter of the cultural revolution in Iran or that he was active in the reorganization of the universities.[10] The Islamic Republic in Iran appears not only to be generating liberal ideas, but also may even be erasing the memory of those who once professed Islamist ideals.

Although there are Muslims who find common ground with Western liberals, liberal Islam is not without its detractors. Some claim that liberal Islam is inau-thentic, that it is a creation of the West and does not reflect "true" Islamic traditions. "Authenticity movements" have been increasing globally over the past quarter-century, from religious movements such as Islamism or the B. J. P. Hindu nationalist party in India, to ethnic phenomena such as the tribal hos-tilities that have resulted in gruesome massacres in central Africa. The emphasis on authenticity is not limited to the Islamic world.

One of the crucial characteristics of this renewed interest in authenticity is the idea that one can take a culture and draw a box around it; that a culture can be defined as a discrete entity, separate from other cultures, with well-defined boundaries. In reality, these boundaries are rarely so precise. In Uzbekistan, for example, the government insists that the Now Ruz New Year's celebration was invented in Central Asia, not in Iran—as if cultural practices would be less valuable if they were imported. But of course, claiming to have created the event contributes to Uzbek national pride and identity.

The flip side of this increasing need for cultural ownership is a flurry of criticisms against things or people for not being authentic enough. Because liberal Islam shares concerns with Western liberalism, critics claim, it must not be a valid interpretation of the religion—if X is Western, it cannot be Islamic. This binary opposition ignores the tremendous history of cultural borrowings and influences that have permeated the supposed border over the centuries.

If the first charge is that liberal Islam is inauthentic, and therefore somehow wrong, the second charge argues that liberal Islam should not be tolerated whether or not it is wrong. For example, Gai Eaton, a British Muslim, calls liberal Muslims "Uncle Toms."[11] ("Uncle Tom" is a derisive term used by African-Americans to describe a black person who is grotesquely servile to whites.) In essence, Eaton is calling liberal concerns treasonous to the cause of Islam. Not only are these concerns wrong, according to Eaton's way of thinking, but right or wrong, raising these concerns publicly weakens the Islamic world in its struggle with the West. It is like a team sport, where each side demands loyalty from its members and sees any internal critique, any self-critique, as aiding and abetting the other team.

In Iran, for example, the feeling of being besieged by foreign, especially American, hostility is so strong that in order to survive, politicians must prove that they are not "soft" on the "Great Satan."[12] Iranian politicians who wish to negotiate with the West, or to raise concerns about democracy, human rights, or other issues, are immediately labeled by their political opponents as "soft on Satan." This pattern is so common and so damaging to liberal concerns that even reformists engage in liberal-bashing in order to ward off criticism. Iran's president, Muhammad Khatami, is a case in point. Khatami may be more of a politician than a theologian, but his campaign in 1997 adopted liberal positions on civil society, rule of law, and freedom of speech that inspired reformists in Iran and elsewhere in the Islamic world, while making him vulnerable to charges of cultural treason. Possibly to preempt such charges, Khatami interspersed his liberal campaign themes with attacks on some liberal oppositionists, accusing them of having "fallen in the lap of foreigners," of not being a legitimate political party, and of not coming "from inside society."[13]

Western ignorance poses yet another challenge for liberal Islam. For centuries, the West has constructed an image of Islam as 'the Other,' identifying Islam with its most exotic elements. Islamic faith has been equated with fanaticism, as in Voltaire's *Mahomet, or Fanaticism* (1745). Islamic political authority has been equated with despotism, as in Montesquieu's intentionally redundant phrase "Oriental despotism." And Islamic tradition has been equated with backwardness and primitiveness, as in Ernest Renan's inaugural lecture at the Collége de France (1862):

> Islam is the complete negation of Europe . . . Islam is the disdain of science, the suppression of civil society; it is the appalling simplicity of the Semitic spirit, restricting the human mind, closing it to all delicate ideas, to all refined sentiment, to all rational research, in order to keep it facing an eternal tautology: God is God.[14]

Aside from bias, Western policy must better understand the distinctions within Islamic movements. An example is the recent history of Algeria. The Front de Salvation Islamique (FIS) was divided into liberal and radical factions. During the elections of late 1991 and early 1992, the liberal wing was in the ascendant; its leaders were setting the group's policy, its candidates were running for office, and it stood a great chance of actually coming to power. 'Abbasi Madani, the leader of the liberal faction, made a number of statements aimed at calming the fears of Algerians and Westerners about the intentions of the FIS, such as: "Pluralism is a guarantee of cultural wealth, and diversity is needed for development. We are Muslims, but we are not Islam itself . . . We do not monopolize religion. Democracy as we understand it means pluralism, choice, and freedom."[15] The FIS had won 81 percent of the first-round elections in December 1991 and was poised to do equally well in the second round in early January 1992 when the Algerian military, supported by France and the United States, canceled the elections, banned the FIS, and arrested its leaders. The result was that the liberals within the Islamic movement were thoroughly discredited for having proposed an effort to win within the rules of democracy. The radical wing prevailed and even murdered liberal Islamic activists who objected to terrorism, such as Muhammad Sa'id and Abd al-Razak Redjam, who were killed in 1995. The Western inability to believe that there might be such a thing as liberal Islam proved a self-fulfilling prophecy.

There is a growing number of Muslims who share common concerns with Western liberalism, one of which is peaceful multireligious coexistence. There are three Islamic approaches in this context which, while still very much minority views, seem to be growing. In the 'liberal *Shari'a*' school, Islamic scholars base their arguments on injunctions in the Quran and on precedents from the early years of Islam. Using an argument that might be called the 'silent *Shari'a*,' Islamic scholars argue that the *Shari'a* does not speak about certain topics—not because the revelation is incomplete or imperfect, but because these matters have been intentionally left to human invention. The third approach is the 'interpreted *Shari'a*,' where Islamic scholars argue that the revelation is divine, but interpretation is human and fallible and inevitably plural.

These liberal approaches to multireligious coexistence have been stimulated by three historic shifts of the past quarter century: the rise of secular higher education in the Islamic world, which has broken the monopoly of the seminaries over religious discourse; the growth of international communications, which has made educated Muslims more aware than ever of the norms and institutions of the West; and the failure of Islamic regimes to deliver an attractive alternative.

These liberal approaches face serious challenges, including accusations of treason and inauthenticity, and a Western ignorance about the existence and importance of this internal Islamic debate.

NOTES

1. This paper draws and expands on my anthology, *Liberal Islam: A Source-Book* (New York: Oxford University Press, 1988). All quotations not otherwise cited refer to this work.

2. Ali Asghar Engineer, "The Hindu-Muslim Problem," in *Islam and Liberation Theology* (New Delhi: Sterling Publishers, 1990), p. 209.

3. Abdurrahman Wahid, "Religious Tolerance in a Plural Society," in Damien Kingsbury and Greg Barton (eds.), *Difference and Tolerance: Human Rights Issues in Southeast Asia* (Geelong, Australia: Deakin University Press, 1994), p. 42.

4. Farid Esack, *Qur'an, Liberation, and Pluralism* (Oxford: Oneworld, 1997), pp. 50, 179.

5. Abdullahi An-Na'im, "Toward an Islamic Hermeneutics for Human Rights," in Abdullahi A. Na'im, Jerald D. Gort, Henry M. Vroom (eds.), *Human Rights and Religious Values: An Uneasy Relationship?* (Amsterdam: Editions Rodopi; Grand Rapids: William B. Eerdmans Publishing Company, 1995), p. 233.

6. Samuel Decalo, "The Process, Prospects, and Constraints of Democratization in Africa," *African Affairs*, Vol. 91, 1992, p. 7.

7. Anwar Ibrahim, "The Need for Civilizational Dialogue" (Washington, D.C.: Center for Muslim-Christian Understanding, Georgetown University, Occasional Papers Series, 1995), p. 4.

8. Arno J. Mayer, *Politics and Diplomacy of Peacemaking: Containment and Counterrevolution at Versailles, 1918–1919* (New York: Alfred A. Knopf, 1967), p. 602.

9. Aslam Abdullah, "Shaving Is His Protest Against Coercion," *Los Angeles Times*, May 10, 1997.

10. See the Web site devoted to Soroush's thought, <http://www.seraj.org>, and "Intellectual Autobiography: An Interview," in *Reason, Freedom, and Democracy in Islam: Essential Writings of Abdolkarim Soroush*, translated by Mahmoud Sadri and Ahmad Sadri (forthcoming).

11. Gai Eaton, *Islam and the Destiny of Man* (Albany: State University of New York Press, New York, 1985), p. 12.

12. Charles Kurzman, "Soft on Satan: Challenges for Iranian-U.S. Rapprochement," *Middle East Policy*, Vol. 6, No. 1, June 1998, pp. 63–72.

13. *Salaam* (Tehran, Iran), May 6, 1997.

14. Ernest Renan, *Oeuvres Completes* (Paris: Calmann-Livy, 1947), Vol. 2, p. 333.

15. Daniel Brumberg, "Islam, Elections, and Reform in Algeria," *Journal of Democracy*, Vol. 2, No. 1, Winter 1991, p. 64.

13

Inside the Islamic Reformation

Dale F. Eickelman

Like the printing press in sixteenth-century Europe, the combination of mass education and mass communications is transforming the Muslim-majority world, a broad geographical crescent stretching from North Africa through Central Asia, the Indian subcontinent, and the Indonesian archipelago. In unprecedentedly large numbers, the faithful—whether in the vast cosmopolitan city of Istanbul, the suburbs of Paris, or in the remote oases of Oman's mountainous interior—are examining and debating the fundamentals of Muslim belief and practice in ways that their less self-conscious predecessors in the faith would never have imagined.

Buzzwords such as "fundamentalism" and catchy phrases such as Samuel Huntington's "West versus Rest" or Daniel Lerner's "Mecca or mechanization" are of little use in understanding this transformation. They obscure or even distort the immense spiritual and intellectual ferment taking place today among the world's nearly one billion Muslims, reducing it in most cases to a fanatical rejection of everything modern, liberal, or progressive. To be sure, such fanaticism—not exclusive to Muslim majority societies—plays a part in what is happening, but it is far from the whole story.

A far more important element is the unprecedented access that ordinary people now have to sources of information and knowledge about religion and other aspects of their society. Quite simply, in country after country, government officials, traditional religious scholars, and officially sanctioned preachers are finding it very hard to monopolize the tools of literate culture. The days have gone when governments and religious authorities can control what their people know and what they think.

What distinguishes the present era from prior ones is the large numbers of believers engaged in the 'reconstruction' of religion, community, and society. In an earlier era, political or religious leaders would prescribe, and others were supposed to follow. Today, the major impetus for change in religious and political values comes from below. In France, this has meant an identity shift from being Muslim in France to being French Muslim. In Turkey, it means that an increasing number of Turks, especially those of the younger generation, see themselves as European and Muslim at the same time. And some Iranians argue that the major transformations of the Iranian revolution occurred not in 1978–1979 but with the coming of age of a new generation of Iranians who were not even born at the time of the revolution. These transformations include a greater sense of autonomy for both women and men and the emergence of a public sphere in which politics and religion are subtly intertwined, and not always in ways anticipated by Iran's formal religious leaders.

If 'modernity' is defined as the emergence of new kinds of public space, including kinds not imagined by preceding generations, then developments in France, Turkey, Iran, Indonesia, and elsewhere suggest that we are living through an era of profound social transformation for the Muslim-majority world.

Distinctive to the modern era is that discourse and debate about Muslim tradition involves people on a mass scale. It also necessarily involves an awareness of other Muslim and non-Muslim traditions. Mass education and mass communications in the modern world facilitate an awareness of the new and unconventional. In changing the style and scale of possible discourse, they reconfigure the nature of religious thought and action, create new forms of public space, and encourage debate over meaning.

Mass education and mass communications are important in all contemporary world religions. However, the full effects of mass education, especially higher education, began to be felt in much of the Muslim world only since the mid-twentieth century and in many countries considerably later. In country after country—including Morocco, Egypt, Turkey, and Indonesia—educational opportunities have dramatically expanded at all levels. Even where adult illiteracy rates in the general populace remain high, as in rural Egypt and Morocco, there is now a critical mass of educated people able to read, think for themselves, and react to religious and political authorities rather than just listen to them. Women's access to education still lags behind that of men, although the gap is rapidly closing in many countries.

Both mass education and mass communications, particularly the proliferation of media and the means by which people communicate, have had a profound effect on how people think about religion and politics throughout the Muslim world. Multiple means of communication make the unilateral control of information and opinion much more difficult than it was in prior eras and foster, albeit inadvertently, a civil society of dissent. We are still in the early stages of understanding how different media—including print, television, radio, cassettes, and music—influence groups and individuals, encouraging unity in some contexts and fragmentation in others, but a few salient features may be sketched.

At the "high" end of this transformation is the rise to significance of books such as *al-Kitab wa-l-Qur'an* [The Book and the Quran] (1990), written by the Syrian civil engineer Muhammad Shahrur. This book has sold tens of thousands of copies throughout the Arab world in spite of the fact that its circulation has been banned or discouraged in many places. Its success could not have been imagined before there were large numbers of people able to read it and understand its advocacy of the need to reinterpret ideas of religious authority and tradition and apply Islamic precepts to contemporary society. On issues ranging from the role of women in society to rekindling a "creative interaction" with non-Muslim philosophies, Shahrur argues that Muslims should reinterpret sacred texts and apply them to contemporary social and moral issues.

Shahrur is not alone in attacking both conventional religious wisdom and the intolerant certainties of religious radicals and in arguing instead for a constant and open re-interpretation of how sacred texts apply to social and political life. Another Syrian thinker, the secularist Sadiq Jalal al-'Azm, debated Shaykh Yusif al-Qaradawi, a conservative religious intellectual, on Qatar's al-Jazira Satellite TV in May 1997. For the first time in the memory of many viewers, the religious conservative came across as the weaker, more defensive voice. Al-Jazira is a new phenomenon in Arab language broadcasting because its talk shows, such as "The Opposite Direction," feature live discussions on such sensitive issues as women's role in society, Palestinian refugees, sanctions on Iraq, and democracy and human rights in the Arab world.

Such discussions are unlikely to be rebroadcast on state-controlled television in most Arab nations, where programming on religious and political themes is generally cautious. Nevertheless, satellite technology and videotape render traditional censorship ineffective. Tapes of al-Jazira broadcasts circulate from hand to hand in Morocco, Oman, Syria, Egypt, and elsewhere. Al-Jazira shows that people across the Arab world, just like their counterparts elsewhere in the Muslim-majority world, want open discussion of the issues that affect their lives, and that new communications technologies make it impossible for governments and established religious authorities to stop them.

Other voices also advocate reform. Fethullah Gulen, Turkey's answer to media-savvy American evangelist Billy Graham, appeals to a mass audience. In televised chat shows, interviews, and occasional sermons, Gulen speaks about Islam and science, democracy, modernity, religious and ideological tolerance, the importance of education, and current events.

Religious movements such as Turkey's Risale-i Nur appeal increasingly to religious moderates, and in stressing the links between Islam, reason, science, and modernity, and the lack of inherent conflict between 'East' and 'West,' they promote education at all levels, and appeal to a growing number of educated Turks. Iranian, Indonesian, and Malaysian moderates make similar arguments advocating religious and political toleration and pluralism.

As a result of direct and broad access to the printed, broadcast, and taped word, more and more Muslims take it upon themselves to interpret the textual sources—classical or modern—of Islam. Much has been made of the opening up of the economies of many Muslim countries, allowing 'market forces' to reshape economies, no matter how painful the consequences in the short run. In a similar way, intellectual market forces support some forms of religious innovation and activity over others. In Bangladesh, women's romance novels, once a popular secular specialty, now have their Islamic counterparts, making it difficult to distinguish between 'Muslim' romance novels and 'secular' ones.

The result is a collapse of earlier, hierarchical notions of religious authority based on claims to the mastery of fixed bodies of religious texts. Even when there are state-appointed religious authorities—as in Oman, Saudi Arabia, Iran, and Egypt—there no longer is any guarantee that their word will be heeded, or even that they themselves will follow the lead of the regime. No one group or type of leader in contemporary Muslim societies possesses a monopoly on the management of the sacred.

Without fanfare, the notion that Islam should be the subject of dialogue and civil debate is gaining ground. This new sense of public space is shaped by increasingly open contests over the use of the symbolic language of Islam. Increasingly, discussions in newspapers, on the Internet, on smuggled cassettes, and on television cross-cut and overlap, contributing to a common public space.

New and accessible modes of communication have made these contests increasingly global, so that even local issues take on transnational dimensions. The combination of new media and new contributors to religious and political debates fosters awareness on the part of all actors of the diverse ways in which Islam and Islamic values can be created. It feeds into new senses of a public space that is discursive, performative, and participative, and not confined to formal institutions recognized by state authorities.

Two cautions are in order. The first is that an expanding public sphere need not necessarily indicate more favorable prospects for democracy, any more than civil society necessarily entails democracy. Authoritarian regimes are compatible with an expanding public sphere, although an expanded public sphere offers wider avenues for awareness of competing and alternate forms of religious and political authority. Nor does civil society necessarily entail democracy, although it is a precondition for democracy.

Publicly shared ideas of community, identity, and leadership take new shapes in such engagements, even as many communities and authorities claim an unchanged continuity with the past. Mass education, so important in the development of nationalism in an earlier era, and a proliferation of media and means of communication have multiplied the possibilities for creating communities and networks among them, dissolving prior barriers of space and distance, and opening new grounds for interaction and mutual recognition.

14

Islamist Movements in the Middle East

A Survey and Balance Sheet

Barry Rubin

More than two decades after Iran's 1979 Islamist revolution, radical 'fundamentalist' forces in the Middle East have achieved two great victories and suffered two major defeats. These four factors give a clear sense of these movements'— and thus also the region's—present and future situation.

The first great victory is that the Iranian regime has survived. Yet this achievement is seriously undermined by popular dissatisfaction with the regime's performance. A movement led by President Muhammad Khatami has challenged the policies intended to produce an all-embracing Islamic state, though it continues to favor such a structure in a more moderate form.

The second big triumph has been that revolutionary Islamist doctrine and groups have become the principal opposition force throughout the region. In virtually every country, there are organized forces that challenge the current rulers.

At the same time, however, these movements have suffered even more impressive setbacks. First, the spread of upheaval has been far less than its advocates hoped and opponents feared. Radical Islamist groups did not find it easy to seize power where they did, and today their prospects for doing so anywhere else in the Middle East are not good.

The other problem is that popular support for these movements has been limited among Muslims and even among those who are pious. There are many good reasons for Islamist movements' relatively low level of mass support or success. These factors include traditional Islam's rejection of radical Islamism, nationalism's appeal, and incumbent regimes' clever mix of repression and cooptation aimed against these groups.

Radical Islamists claimed, in effect, that they were 'fundamentalists' because they were returning to the historic essence and proper interpretation of Islam. In practice, though, these forces more truly represented an attempt to reinterpret Islam—at least as it was generally practiced—by means of modern ideas and new perspectives. The refusal of most Muslims to accept this claim lies at the root of the movement's failures to gain hegemony in the region.

A three-part definition of the movement's key premises is useful here:

1. Islam is the answer to the problems of Muslims' society, country, and region. The relative weakness of Muslims and of Arab societies compared to the West, their slow or stagnant economic development, the failure to destroy Israel, domestic and inter-Arab disunity, inequality and injustice, and other such problems have been due to the failure to implement Islam properly.

Many Muslims would agree with the first sentence but they would find other sources of doctrine or causes of the current situation equally or more acceptable. For example, very large numbers of Muslims embrace Arab (or Turkish) nationalism and other political ideologies. A majority of Muslims are more likely to attribute the failures of modern times to a need for economic progress, more democracy, Arab unity, regional peace, or many other factors.

The virtually single-factor explanation of shortcomings, grievances and solutions marks the radical Islamist groups. A Western analogy might be that while there were many liberals and social democrats, intellectuals and workers who accepted elements of Marxist arguments—demands for social justice, strong trade unions, and a redistribution of economic power, etc.—far fewer were able to accept the narrow (deterministic, monistic) views of that doctrine to such an extent that they were prepared to join communist parties.

2. Implementing Islam and resolving the huge problems of the people and countries require the seizure and holding of power by radical Islamist groups, and not by any other type of government or political leadership. The best-known, though hardly sole, proponent and architect of this premise was Iran's Ayatollah Ruhollah Khomeini, though not all radical Islamists echo his view that Islamic clerics should be the rulers.

Indeed, in many Arab countries, and also in Iran, the leading clergymen favor conservative Islamic views rather than radical Islamist ones. These traditional doctrines involve accepting the existing rulers, at least as long as they are Muslims, and a division of authority between state and religion. They also discourage the use of violence against other Muslims.

In contrast, the radicals interpret the need for Islam to be in full and direct political power as a core value of Islam. Any view of Islam that does not accept this tenet is illegitimate. In historical terms, the problem here is that Islam existed for many centuries with the domination of the completely opposite idea: A ruler should be properly pious but the state need not be ruled and shaped by Islam. While there have been many exceptions, Islam has usually adopted tolerance and pluralism, at least toward its own adherents.

The radicals claim they are returning to the religion's origins in the seventh century (hence, returning to fundamentals), but in fact theirs is a deviant, even heretical, viewpoint. It must be stressed that this approach is simply not accepted by the majority of Muslims, nor even by the majority of clerics. Even in Iran, there were and are many respected senior clerics who reject Khomeini's views. Indeed, those who reject 'fundamentalism' are often more respected and have better scholarly credentials than those who embrace it.

This factor is an enormous problem for the radicals, who often face an uphill battle to gain or enlarge a base of popular support. A Western analogy here would be that while communist movements claimed to speak on behalf of large social groups—workers, oppressed nations and groups, progressive thinkers—these people usually rejected that purported leadership.

3. The only proper interpretation of Islam is the one offered by a specific political group and its leaders. This premise also poses a serious problem. For if the majority does not accept the doctrine as a whole, even more people will not agree with the details of a given group's ideology, program, tactics, and strategy. While some revolutionary groups draw on one or more respected Islamic clerics, they are often small and marginal groups. And of course one man's respected cleric may be another man's charlatan or heretic.

Several additional consequences arise from this premise. Such movements are almost inherently intolerant because they claim to speak with the voice of God, while their opponents' views can only be explained as heretical or even satanic. But intolerance can inhibit growth; it turns the majority of Muslims into enemies whose ideas and worship are wrong. Moreover, since there is only one correct line, the radicals often quarrel among themselves. There is rarely room in any organization for more than one charismatic leader. Factions and splits are inevitable, thus weakening the movement and sometimes leading to infighting.

The claims of the radical Islamist groups also pose a huge problem for Muslim citizens. If the revolutionaries' brand of Islam is valid, then their own personal versions are wrong, despite the fact that they and their ancestors have lived within that framework for their entire lives. In this way, Muslims can see the radicals' struggle as an attack on them rather than as a battle on their behalf. Government propaganda often builds very successfully on this theme.

As political actors, revolutionary Islamist groups face a series of difficult problems.

Because religious doctrine is at the core of their ideology, Sunni and Shi'ite Muslim radicals find it difficult—though not always impossible—to cooperate.

In some countries, Iran's ethnically Persian and religiously Shi'ite identities are real barriers to attracting Arab and Sunni followers to a doctrine often identified with its revolution. At the same time, Iran's visible failures and internal problems can also discredit the idea that an Islamist revolution would solve all problems. The fact that Islamists deny these factors does not make them any less real.

As was so long true in Arab nationalist groups, handling foreign sponsorship or interference can be a very difficult and divisive challenge for a revolutionary organization. To cite one example, there are about six different factions of (Palestinian) Islamic Jihad each with different sponsorship (Iranian, Syrian, and Libyan). Afghanistan offers similar examples. Some groups became the surrogates or pawns of regimes, whose rulers need not be radical Islamists themselves. The ability of states to offer safe havens, finances, training, military equipment, diplomatic support, and other benefits makes seeking their sponsorship a very tempting proposition for relatively small revolutionary groups.

For example, at a time when Syria was killing and imprisoning Islamist opponents, Iranian interests dictated a strong alliance with Damascus—including massive oil transfers—in order to isolate Iraq. During the 1990–1991 crisis resulting from Iraq's takeover of its neighbor Kuwait, radical Islamists overwhelmingly supported Saddam Hussein, even though he murdered, tortured, and exiled thousands of their colleagues in his own country.

While radical Islamists may decry the existence of separate nation-states, they cannot be ignored. Indeed, Islamist groups often owe their growth and strength to the fact that they are representatives of ethnic or national groups. In Lebanon, Hizballah is essentially a Shi'ite communal party opposing Christian hegemony, a situation that guarantees opposition from the country's other communities. In Syria, the Islamists represent a Sunni majority, the country's traditional rulers, who oppose an essentially non-Muslim (Alawite) government. In Iraq, the movement represents the Shi'ite community against a largely Sunni ruling elite. With the partial exception of the Muslim Brotherhood network—encouraging some cooperation among the Egyptian, Jordanian, Palestinian (Hamas), and Syrian Muslim Brotherhoods—each movement stands mostly on its own in battling a relatively well-financed and well-armed local government.

Similarly, each radical Islamist movement must develop a strategy and tactics appropriate for its individual country with extremely varied environments. Consequently, the groups grow in different directions, set disparate levels of escalation, and find dissimilar responses to their problems.

Finally, governments are often quite sophisticated in using a wide variety of tactics to counter revolutionary Islamists. These measures include expropriating Islamic symbols, co-opting large elements of Islamic institutions, promoting patriotism and Arab nationalism, or unleashing repression. To cite a few examples:

• Saddam Hussein added the phrase "God is great" to Iraq's flag and declared his 1990 invasion of Kuwait a holy war. A decade earlier, he murdered Iraq's leading young radical Shi'ite Islamist cleric and his activist sister.

- Syria's regime—dominated by a non-Muslim minority group—wiped out one of its own biggest cities in 1982, killing between 10,000 and 30,000 people, to eliminate a center of support for the Islamist movement.
- The kings of Jordan, Morocco, and Saudi Arabia possess considerable Islamic credentials of their own. At one politically sensitive moment, the late King Hussein even grew a beard to court this constituency.
- In Egypt, the government controls a huge Islamic sector, ranging from local mosques to the prestigious al-Azhar religious university. Preachers and teachers in Islamic schools are government employees.
- Palestinian Authority Chairman Yasir Arafat created his own satellite Islamist party, assigned Islamist activists who supported him to high posts, and played a clever balancing act between repression and benevolence to keep Hamas in line.
- The Turkish military outmaneuvered the short-lived Welfare Party coalition government in Ankara, forcing Prime Minister Necmettin Erbakan to sign a decree expelling supporters of his own party from the army and ultimately pushing him out of office altogether in 1997.

Aside from questions of ideology, the use of violence is an extremely controversial and sometimes divisive issue. While all radical Islamist movements want to gain power and never relinquish it, there are differences in method, depending on the situation in specific countries and the views of the local leadership. It should be stressed that while small radical Islamist groups employ violence in trying to seize control of several Arab states, the main revolutionary efforts—within Algeria, Egypt, and Lebanon—have steadily declined.

Some radical Islamists have argued that power can be sought by persuasion, using any pluralist openings offered by the system. In addition to elections and propaganda, groups have developed a large variety of grassroots social programs to build a mass base of support by showing their doctrine in action. These efforts include welfare activities and the creation of school systems and youth clubs. Professional associations and student groups can be taken over through institutional elections, even in countries where parliamentary elections are manipulated by the regime. Control of individual mosques and political Islamist preaching is also a useful tactic.

For Islamist politicians, there could be a careerist element in a decision to work inside the system even if an incumbent government will clearly not allow an opposition win. Accepting the role of 'loyal opposition' would keep them out of jail, safeguard their existing wealth, and provide opportunities for additional personal benefits and prestige. In effect, they would gain freedom to operate in exchange for accepting certain limits.

This is not meant to suggest that reformism arises from venal considerations, but such factors can certainly make such a choice more attractive. It can also be a pragmatic response to the failure and relatively limited appeal of armed struggle. Movements that become genuinely reformist try to act as pressure groups to move society toward a more Islamic identity without being able to transform it altogether. It is possible to argue, of course, that this gradualist strategy will eventually arrive at the same result intended by advocates of a revolutionary strategy. Indeed, there is a difference between reformist tactics and a moderation of aims. The movements' opponents often make such an argument, which justifies their ensuring that Islamists never actually take power.

Nevertheless, this trend toward reformist methods that could lead to moderated goals, most clearly true in Turkey and Jordan, could become the dominant trend. But this choice also results in splits, as some militants come to believe that the parent movement has abandoned its original principles. Such was the pattern, for example, in Egypt, where radical groups emerged from the Muslim Brotherhood, whose moderate tactics from the 1970s onward ensured both its survival and its failure to gain power.

There are, indeed, four diverse types of situations for Islamist movements in the Middle East:

1. A highly repressive regime that will kill and imprison radical Islamist activists and ban their movements, as can be seen in Syria, Iraq, and Saudi Arabia. In these cases the government's willingness and ability to apply massive force has crushed Islamist insurgencies.

2. A more flexible regime allows Islamists to operate with a large degree of freedom, establishing and administering a wide range of institutions, but it will not allow them to take power. This is the prevailing situation in Algeria and Egypt where, respectively, a military coup and election rigging have been used to limit the Islamist parties. As a result, large elements among radical Islamist forces take up arms to gain power. These conditions have been the most propitious for the development of a bloody Islamist insurgency, though not necessarily a successful one.

3. The most open regimes, such as those in Jordan, Kuwait, Morocco, Turkey, Israel, and the Palestinian Authority, allow the Islamists a fairer proportion of representation—and in Turkey's case even temporary executive power—while any violent revolutionary forces are dealt with very severely. This situation is made possible by two factors: The government's legitimacy and the system's strength are secure enough that they do not feel endangered by the Islamist forces; and the Islamists themselves are ready to accept the rules of the game because they judge any attempt to seize power would be suicidal.

4. In some places, Islamist forces try to take the place of a nationalist movement in representing an ethnic group that has a distinct confessional characteristic. As noted above, this applies to Hizballah (Lebanese Shi'ite), the Syrian Muslim Brotherhood (Sunni), and Shi'ite groups in Iraq, Saudi Arabia, and Bahrain. These Shi'ite communities are generally geographically concentrated, relatively poor, historically subject to discrimination, and have a disproportionately small amount of political power.

An Islamist group can also be empowered by claiming the job of leading the community against foreign, non-Muslim forces. This was the case with those fighting the Soviets in Afghanistan as well as Lebanese Hizballah and Palestinian Hamas or Islamic Jihad in fighting against Israel. Yet even if they lead a community or direct the fight against infidels, radical Islamist forces are not guaranteed victory. There are always competing—usually nationalist—forces for ethnic loyalties that can usually muster more supporters. Even Hizballah and Hamas, playing on highly popular anti-Israel themes, cannot gain hegemony, respectively, over Amal (the nationalist-oriented Lebanese Shi'ite group) or the Palestinian Authority, which is largely controlled by nationalist Fatah and others from the Palestine Liberation Organization.

The above analysis also indicates the importance and nature of radical Islamist terrorism. Terrorism is not just an insult hurled by the revolutionaries' opponents. It is also a key part of the strategy of some groups. Like those who used similar techniques in Europe a century ago, these radicals believe that bombings and assassinations will delegitimize the government or other enemies and produce a mass uprising. Terrorism also arises from the frustration of groups unable to stage revolutions and increasingly bitter at the masses' refusal to support their cause. The people thus become the enemy.

But there is another way in which terrorism is even more important. By arguing that non-Muslim adversaries have no rights and are enemies of God who should either be driven out or kept out of Muslim territory, the radicals can justify killing any member of a target group—such as Israelis, other communities as in Lebanon, or Western tourists. Such attacks are also designed to raise the revolutionaries' popularity in their own constituency, revenge popular grievances, and show the progress and effectiveness of the organizations involved.

Murdering fellow Muslims is a bigger ideological and practical problem, yet a necessary part of revolutionary armed struggle. Although often contradicted by history—the Iran-Iraq war is a good contemporary example—Muslims are not supposed to wage war on fellow Muslims. The assassination of officials who are Muslims, much less innocent bystanders, often leads to criticism of the radicals as acting improperly in Islamic terms. It brings popular support for government repression. Even suicide bombings against non-Muslims has been criticized by some distinguished clerics as contrary to Islam.

Again, though, it is important to stress that radical Islamist groups have adapted to extremely varied conditions in different countries with distinctive sets of tactics. Three broad categories can be defined, though different organizations may be represented in more than one sector or may change positions over time.

Revolutionaries Revolutionary groups have carried out armed struggle in Algeria, Bahrain, Egypt, Saudi Arabia, Syria, and Iraq to overturn existing governments and create a radical Islamist state. Aside from Algeria, these are all relatively small underground organizations though they have larger circles of supporters. The most repressive states—Syria and Iraq—have had the greatest success in suppressing such insurgencies, which embody grievances barred from expression, much less solution, through other means. It should again be noted that four of these six movements are also representatives of ethnic-national communities: Shi'ite in the case of Bahrain, Saudi Arabia, and Iraq; Sunni in the case of Syria.

In Algeria, the full-scale revolt resulted from the military's refusal to let a broad-based Islamist group, the Islamic Salvation Front (FIS), attain electoral victory. The FIS, then, is a reluctant revolutionary group and many FIS leaders would be happy to achieve a negotiated solution that would give them a share of power. More extreme groups, such as the Armed Islamic Group (GIA), reject any compromise. Ironically, the regime's relative openness earlier may have created a situation in which more moderate Islamist forces were forced into extreme responses.

An interesting comparison can be made to the case in Egypt, where the Muslim Brotherhood is the equivalent of the FIS. The government lets the Brotherhood participate in electoral politics, hold parliamentary seats, and function as a movement. But the permissible lines are clearly set. Periodic repression and vote-rigging remind the Brotherhood that it will be crushed if it seems poised to actually seize power. The violent revolutionaries are much smaller groups that split off from the Brotherhood because they thought it too timid. The radicals also build their own campus or neighborhood groups. As in Algeria, government responses have been largely successful in containing and reducing the relatively smaller and badly divided radical forces.

National Liberationists   Palestinian and Lebanese groups (and those in Afghanistan as well) have had a dual purpose. While they wish to establish an Islamic state among their own people, their first priority has been fighting others. Hamas and Islamic Jihad have launched terrorist attacks on Israel while competing for popular support with the PLO-ruled Palestinian Authority (PA). The PA arrests their activists and refuses them any formal political power, but there is also a strong measure of mutual tolerance in order to prevent a civil war.

Within Lebanon, Hizballah attacked Israel and its allies in southern Lebanon until the Israeli withdrawal in May 2000. Now Hizballah is putting a higher priority on its efforts to gain power within the Shi'ite community and in the country as a whole. The non-Shi'ite communities, the Lebanese government, and Lebanon's Syrian masters totally opposed Hizballah's program for Lebanon even when they tolerated or helped its attacks against Israel. The big question for Hizballah is to what extent it will shift its tactics from armed struggle against Israel or within Lebanon and instead use electoral means to try to achieve its goals.

Thus, while the Islamist groups flourish and are allowed to service their constituencies with various institutions, they are also kept from progressing toward national rule. As long as Islamists accept these limits, the situation can continue. But a serious effort to alter the power balance would lead to civil wars more closely resembling those in the first group discussed above.

Reformists In Egypt, Jordan, Morocco, Kuwait, Turkey, Pakistan, and Israel, the main Islamist forces have eschewed violence and acted as social and parliamentary movements. Operating within the legal system allows them to exert influence and bring about some changes. Equally or more important, this situation allows them to build a vast social and educational apparatus of institutions which creates a community of supporters.

These movements become interest groups within society rather than standing in total opposition outside society with the principal goal of overturning it. The constituency obtains patronage and services from the party. The leadership receives various privileges, including financial benefits, power, and prestige that might be lost if it challenges the government. In turn, the tolerance and benefits that the government allows these groups gives them something to protect. Thus, such institutionalization—even if intended to provide a base for revolutionary activities—could become a restraining force.

But ultimately each movement will have to decide whether to limit itself to this role, for neither the existing governments nor the political systems—including the undemocratic electoral systems—will let the Islamists hold power. This could change in the long run, of course, as different societies develop and if Islamist movements prove their democratic, moderate credentials.

In response, the movements argue that their techniques win followers and provide a springboard for taking power in the future. By appealing to conservative practitioners of a more traditionalist Islam—who oppose or distrust the revolutionary movements—they can dramatically broaden their political base of support. It is also possible or even likely—as has happened with other social and political movements—that they themselves will be transformed into factors that ultimately reinforce rather than subvert the status quo. An ability to live an 'Islamist' lifestyle as an individual is, after all, an alternative to trying to transform an entire society. Moreover, there are many issues to be contested—including struggles over the distribution of the national budget—that fall far short of a struggle to seize state power.

Still, the underlying question is to define these groups' aims. Can they construct a program of changes that would satisfy them within the context of the existing society, or do they still seek its ultimate transition into a very different kind of polity? In short, is their reformism limited only to tactics or does it also embody their goals? This process of rethinking is still going on and, in most cases, has not yet taken hold in the movements, though internal debates and struggles over this issue will probably increase in the future.

The American and French revolutions encouraged a wave of democratic revolutions throughout Europe and elsewhere. The Russian revolution inspired the formation of communist parties that struggled to imitate it for many decades.

The Chinese and Cuban revolutions launched many movements that imitated their strategies in the belief that these victories could be duplicated.

Iran's revolution should be seen in a similar historical perspective. Islamist groups already existed independently—as did parallel movements in the cases of the other revolutions—but were galvanized and strengthened by the seizure of power by their fellows. These organizations provided a response to the failures in their countries of nationalism and other ideologies, the strains of development, shortcomings of existing regimes, pressures of Westernization, and social grievances. They will continue to develop and evolve for some decades to come.

The seizure of power anywhere by an Islamist movement—though this seems unlikely at present—would again inspire imitators. A demographic wave of young people, along with the incumbent regimes' failures and growing socioeconomic pressures, may allow radical Islamist groups to grow in size as well as ability to challenge current rulers. Equally, the lack of real democratic systems that would let Islamists win elections could bring an eventual rejection of moderation.

More likely is a long-run trend toward moderation, producing some Islamist parties with a reformist orientation. There are even signs of such developments in Iran, where moderates and radicals struggle over the regime's orientation. In Turkey, the Islamist party is divided into radical and moderate elements, with the latter realizing the movement can never make much progress until it persuades other Turks that it does not seek to establish an Islamist state.

Islamists could become the equivalent of Christian Democratic parties of Europe or Latin America, or of Israel's Jewish religious parties. In other words, the party would focus on advocacy regarding specific issues and protecting the interests of its supporters or institutions, rather than seeking to transform society as a whole. Party leaders, potential coalition partners, and rivals will all ask whether an Islamist party that did gain power peacefully would also surrender it under democratic conditions.

A trend toward moderation is by no means inevitable. There are strong pressures from Islamist ideology and individual leaders or factions to maintain a hard line. Equally, the fact that employing moderate means is less likely to result in gaining state power also makes this road less attractive. Finally, the momentum of Iran's militant faction and potential regional events is by no means exhausted. Yet the progress of Islamist movements has been far from the triumphal march into power hoped for, and predicted, by the Islamists themselves. Trends toward moderation, while still limited, are stronger than they have been in the past. Of course, the situation will vary according to each country's political culture, situation, and regime.

Perhaps, in the long run, the historical function of Islamist organizations may not be so different from the role religion and social movements have played over the centuries in the West. Such groups formed as responses to the challenges of modernization, nation-building, and the alternative appeals of democracy and dictatorship. Indeed, Islamist movements—despite appearances and their own denials—are part of the broader history of nationalism. Moreover, they oppose what are seen as foreign imports that undermine the tradition and authenticity of their societies. True, they ostensibly stress a primary identity in religious rather than nationalist terms. But in the Middle East, religion is often the main marker of ethnicity.

Ultimately, their choices and institutional structures must be set by a determination of the strategy, tactics, type of society, and variety of political system that would best allow for the expression and preservation of that identity.

Contributors

ALI R. ABOOTALEBI is assistant professor of political science at the University of Wisconsin, Eau Claire. His book, *Islam and Democracy: State-Society Relations in the Developing Countries, 1980–1994* is forthcoming.

BULENT ARAS is assistant professor of international relations at Fatih University, Istanbul. He is author of *The Palestinian-Israeli Peace Process and Turkey* and *The New Geopolitics of Eurasia and Turkey's Position* (forthcoming), and co-editor of *The Oil and Geopolitics in Caspian Sea Region*.

OMER CAHA is associate professor of political science at Fatih University, Istanbul. Widely published on the recent political history of Turkey, his most recent book is on intellectuals and democracy in Turkey.

DALE F. EICKELMAN is Ralph and Richard Lazarus Professor of Anthropology and Human Relations at Dartmouth College. His most recent books include *The Middle East and Central Asia: An Anthropological Approach; New Media in the Muslin World: The Emerging Public Sphere,* co-edited with Jon W. Anderson; and *Muslim Politics,* co-authored with James Piscatori. His contribution to this volume is a revised and updated version of "Inside the Islamic Reformation," *Wilson Quarterly.*

SHAFEEQ N. GHABRA is professor of political science at Kuwait University. He is author of *Kuwait: A Study of the Dynamics of State, Authority and Society* and *Israel and the Arabs: From the Conflict of Issues to the Peace of Interests.* The author would like to thank Kuwait University (research administration) for the grant that made this study possible. An earlier version of this study appeared in *Middle East Policy.*

GEORGE E. IRANI is visiting assistant professor in political science at Washington College. From 1993 to 1997, he was a faculty member at the Lebanese American University (formerly Beirut University College), where he was one of the founders of the Lebanese Conflict Resolution Network (LCRN). In 1997–1998, he was a Jennings Randolph Senior Fellow at the U. S. Institute of Peace. His chapter is based on research he conducted there.

ELY KARMON is a senior research scholar at the International Policy Institute for Counter-Terrorism of the Interdisciplinary Center in Herzliya. He lectures on International Terrorism at the Political Science Department of Haifa University.

CHARLES KURZMAN is assistant professor of sociology at the University of North Carolina and editor of *Liberal Islam: A Source-Book* and *Modernist Islam, 1840–1940: A Source-Book* (forthcoming).

MEIR LITVAK is a senior research associate at the Dayan Center for Middle Eastern and African Studies, Tel Aviv University. He is the author of *Shi'i Scholars of Nineteenth Century Iraq: The 'Ulama' of Najaf and Karbala',* and editor of *Islam and Democracy in the Arab World* (in Hebrew).

BRUCE MADDY-WEITZMAN is a senior research fellow at the Moshe Dayan Center of Middle Eastern and African Studies, Tel Aviv University. He is author of *The Crystallization of the Arab State System, 1945–1954,* editor of the Center's annual *Middle East Contemporary Survey,* and co-editor, with Efraim Inbar, of *Religious Radicalism in the Greater Middle East.*

NILUFER NARLI is associate professor and chair of the sociology department, Marmara University, Turkey. Her publications include "Moderate Against Radical Islamicism in Turkey," *Zeitschrift Fur Turkeistudien*; (with Sinan Dirlik), "Turkiye'nin Siyasi Haritas" (The Political Map of Turkey), *Turkiye Gunlucu*; and "Women and Islam: Female Participation in the Islamicist Movement in Turkey," *Turkish Review of Middle East Studies.*

REUVEN PAZ is director of the Project for the Study of Islamist Movements at the Global Research in International Affairs Center. His works on Palestinian Islamic movements are widely published, including the first two academic articles ever published analyzing Hamas and the Islamic movement in Israel.

BARRY RUBIN is director of the Global Research in International Affairs Center and its Institute for Turkish Studies. He is the editor of the *Middle East Review of International Affairs,* and editor of *Turkish Studies.* A prolific author, his latest book is *The Tragedy of the Middle East.*

EMMANUEL SIVAN is a professor at the Hebrew University. His books include *Radical Islam*; the co-edited *War and Remembrance in the Twentieth Century: Mythes Politiques Arabes;* and *Strong Religion.*

DAVID ZEIDAN received a Ph.D. from the University of London for his thesis "The Resurgence of Religion: A Comparative Study of Selected Themes in Christian and Islamic Fundamentalisms." His publications include "The Copts— Equal, Protected or Persecuted? The Impact of Islamization on Muslim-Christian Relations in Modern Egypt," *Islam and Christian-Muslim Relations*; and "The Alevis of Anatolia," *Middle East Review of International Affairs.*

EYAL ZISSER is a senior research fellow at the Moshe Dayan Center for Middle East and African Studies, and head of the program of Middle Eastern Studies at the Department of Middle Eastern and African History, Tel Aviv University.

Index

Abd al-Rahman, Shaykh Umar, 13, 17, 19
al-Abdallah, Shaykh Sa'ad, 119
al-'Abidin 'Ali, Zayn, 3
Absent Truth, The. *See al-Haqiqah al-Gha'ibah*
Abu Bakra, 195
Abu Hamza, Shaykh, 5
Abu Hassan, Muhammad, 183
Abu Nidal group, 53
Abu Zaid, Muhammad Fuad, 30
Abu Zayd, Nasr, 118
al-'Adl wal-Ihsan (Justice and Charity movement), 74, 75, 76
al-Adwah, Khalidm, 113
Afghanistan, 4, 8, 19, 33, 197, 213
AIS (Islamic Salvation Army), 3, 80, 82, 83
Akademi, 46. *See also* Turkish Islamist movements, publications by
Akgonenc, Dr. Oya, 132
Akinci Yolu, 46. *See also* Turkish Islamist movements, publications by
Akit, 131. *See also* Turkish Islamist movements, publications by
Akman, Nuriye, 143
Akparti (Justice and Development Party), 135
Aksoy, Muammar, 45
Aksu, Abdulkadir, 47, 132
Akyol, Natik, 128
al-Alfi, Hassan, 19
Algeria, 3, 6, 80, 84, 161, 212
    Islamist activities in, 69, 76, 79, 80–85
Algerian Hamas, 80

Algerian Muslim Brotherhood, 6. *See also* Social Movement for Peace
Ben 'Ali, Zayn 'Abidin, 3, 77, 78, 79
Alpay, Sahin, 146
Altan, Mehmet, 150
Altayli, Fatih, 52
Amal movement, 93, 96, 97, 98, 100
American embassies, attacks on, 19
Amin, Hussain Ahmad, 118
Anatolian Lions, 128. *See also* MUSIAD
An-Na'im, Abdallahi, 194
Annan, Kofi, 96
Ansari, Muhamad, 109
al-Aqsa mosque, 28
Arab Child's House, 27
Arafat, Yasir, 211
Arendt, Hannah, 185, 186
Arkun, Muhammad, 118, 194
Arslan, Fathallah, 76
Asghar, Ali, 192
al-Assad, Bashar, 99
al-Assad, Hafiz, 3, 98, 99
Association of Independent Industrialists and Businessmen. *See* MUSIAD
Asya Finans, 146
Aujjar, Mohammed, 75
awareness. *See wa'i*

Ba'ath Party (Iraq), 24, 180
Ba'ath Party (Syria), 24, 180
al-Badir, Sulaiman, 115
Bin Badis, Shaykh Abd al-Hamid, 69
al-Baghdadi, Ahmad, 115–116
Bahrain, 3, 212
Barak, Ehud, 91

Barlas, Mehmet, 150
Barri, Nabih, 93
Bartholomeos, Patriarch, 144
Basesgioglu, Murat, 52
Basri, Driss, 72
Bayramoglu, Ali, 150
Bazargan, Mehdi, 194
Bedouin, 109, 183
Belhadj, 'Ali, 80, 81, 82
Benjedid, Chedli, 80
Benjelloun, Omar, 73
Benkirane, Abdallah, 74
Bethlehem University (prev. Freres College),
    30, 36
Bi-aqlam al-Shabab. See Palestinian Hamas,
    publications by
Bir, Cevik, 56–57
Birand, Mehmet Ali, 150
Bir Zeit University, 30, 33, 36
Boumedienne, Houari, 80
Bourghiba, Habib, 3, 77
Bosnia, 4
Bouteflika, Abd al-'Aziz, 84
Bouyali, Mustafa, 80
Bulac, Ali, 192

Caliphate. *See khilafa*
Cagarici, Irfan, 46
Cakir, Rusen, 149
Candar, Cengiz, 150
Celik, Gulten, 132
Celik, Halil, 53
Ceylan, Hasan Huseyni, 53
Ceysullah, 59
Chamoun, 179
CHP (Republican People's Party), 126, 129
Cicek, Cemil, 131
Ciller, Tansu, 130, 150
Civil society. *See al-mujtama' al-madani*
Coskun, Ali, 132
Cultural Social Society (*jam'iyyat al-
    Thaqafah al-Ijtima'iyah*), 107, 108

da'wa, 2
Da'wa associations, 2
Dayton agreements (1995), 4
Demirel, Suleyman, 49, 58, 126, 127,
    145, 146, 148

Democratic Forum (*al-Manbar al-Dimuqrati*),
    112
Democratic Left Party (DLP), 51, 125,
    130, 133
Democratic Party (DP), 125, 129
dhimmis, 17, 179–180. *See also* Islam,
    Christians and Jews in
Dirani, Mustafa, 100
Djaballah, Shaykh Abdallah, 80
Donmez, Kemal, 52
DSKO. *See* World Shari'a Liberation
    Army

Eaton, Gai, 198
Ecevit, Bulent, 51, 55, 56, 126, 127,
    145, 146, 148
Egypt, 3–4, 6, 110, 160, 161, 173, 211,
    215
Egyptian Jihad, 5, 29
Egyptian Muslim Brotherhood, 5, 7, 11,
    12, 14, 27, 36, 71, 77, 107, 210,
    212, 214
Eickelman, Dale F., 145
EIK-TM. *See* Turkish Fighters of the
    Universal Islamic War of Liberation
EKC-SIM. *See* Universal Brotherhood
    Front—Shari'a Revenge Squad
Erbakan, Necmettin, 41, 46, 47, 49, 50–
    51, 52–53, 56, 125, 127, 131, 135,
    148, 211
Erdis, Salih Izzet (Salih Mirzabeyoglu),
    51
Erdogan, Recep Tayip, 126, 131, 134,
    135, 149
Esack, Farid, 193
Esmerer, Abdurrahman, 128
Ethiopia, 5
Evren, Kenan, 127

al-Faluji, Shaykh 'Imad, 7
Faraj, Abd al-Salam, 14, 17
    Neglected Obligation, The, 13
*al-farida al-gha'ibah. See Neglected Obliga-
    tion* (Faraj), *The*
al-Fasi, 'Allal, 70
Fatah, 34, 35, 53, 213
fatwa (religious legal edict), 17
Faldlallah, Muhammad Husayn, 97, 98

Fatma Gate, 96
Fazilet Party. *See* FP
Fellah, Tariq, 75
fiqh, 15
FIS (Islamic Salvation Front), 6–7, 47, 53, 78, 80–83, 160, 199, 214
FIT. *See* Tunisian Islamic Front
Fighters of the Islamic Revolution (IDAM), 42
FLN (Front de Liberation Nationale), 79, 80
Fountain, The, 145. *See also* Turkish Teachers' Foundation
four schools of Islam, the. *See madhabs*
FP (*as* Virtue Party, *as* Fazilet Party), 50, 51, 53, 57, 126, 129, 132, 134, 135, 148, 149
France, 70, 84, 92, 204
Freres College. *See* Bethlehem University
Front de Liberation Nationale. *See* FLN
fundamentalism, 157–158

Gaza Strip, 23, 24, 25, 27, 37
Gemayel family, 179
al-Ghannushi, Rashid, 9, 77–80, 164, 165, 194
gharb, 69, 70
al-Ghazzali, 159
Gholizadeh, Abbas, 45
GIA (Islamic Salvation Group), 3, 18, 44, 81–84, 214
Giddens, Anthony, 181
God's sovereignty. *See hakimmiyya*
Gokalp, Ziya, 151
Golan Heights, 100
Graham, Billy, 205
Great Eastern Islamic Fighters Front, The. *See* IBDA-C
Green, Jerrold, 167
Guessous, Muhammad, 70
Gul, Abdallah, 47, 132
Gulen, Fethullah, 53, 142–144, 146, 149, 152, 205
    conception of Turkish Islam, 141, 143–144
    opposition to, 147–150
    political influence of, 145

    support to, 144–145, 150
    See also Gulen movement
Gulen movement, 144–146, 150–152.
    See also Journalists' and Writers' Foundation; Turkish Teachers' Foundation; Gulen, Fethullah
Gurses, Emin, 54

HADEP (People's Democracy Party), 129–130
hadith, 15
al-Hajji, Yusef, 106
hakimmiyya (God's sovereignty), 12
Haktanir, Korkmaz, 55
Hama, massacre, 3
Hamas. *See* Palestinian Hamas
al-Haqiqah al-Gha'ibah (The Absent Truth), 36
al-Harakah al-Islamiyyah al-Tulabiyyah (The Islamic Student Movement), 34
Harakat al-Islah wal-Tajdid (Movement for Reform and Renewal), 74
Harakat al-Tawhid wal-Islah (Movement for Unification and Reform), 74
Harb, Muhammad, 29
al-Haroun, Dr. Musaid, 114
King Hassan II, 71, 74
    policies of, 72–73
Hebrew University, 37
Hebron University, 29
Hermassi, Abd al-Baki, 70
High Education Council. *See* YOK
hijra (Muhammad's original flight from Mecca to Medina), 13, 16
Hizballah, 7, 91, 93–95, 97, 99, 101, 210, 212
    Iranian support to, 92, 94, 95, 97, 98, 99, 101
    opposition to, 96–97, 98, 99
    struggle against Israel, 92, 93, 95–96, 99–101, 214
    Syrian support to, 92, 94, 95, 98, 99, 101
    use of violence by, 92, 94
Hizb al-Tahrir al-Islami. *See* Islamic Liberation Party
Huntington, Samuel P., 78, 166, 203

al-Husayni, 27
Hussein, Saddam, 3, 210

IBDA-C (The Great Eastern Islamic
Fighters Front), 44, 52, 53, 59, 133
publications by, 46. *See also* Turkish
Islamist movements, publications by
use of violence by, 45, 46, 51, 52
Ibn Anas, Imam Malik, 195
Ibn Hanbal, 159
Ibn Qatada, Shaykh, 5
Ibn Taymiyya, 15, 19, 159
Ibrahim, Anwar, 196
al-Ibrahim, Hassan, 108
ICCB (Union of Islamic Associations
and Societies), 59
ICM. *See* Islamic Constitutional Move-
ment
IDAM. *See* Fighters of the Islamic
Revolution
IKO. *See* Turkish Islamic Liberation
Army
IKP-C. *See* Islamic Liberation Party
Front
Ilicak, Nazli, 132, 133
IMO. *See* Turkish Islamic Fighters Army
Imset, Ismet, 42, 43, 47
INA. *See* Islamic National Alliance
Independent Islamists, The. *See al-
Islamiyyun al-Mustaqillun*
Intifada, 27, 32, 35, 36, 101
IPA. *See* Islamic Popular Alliance
Iran, 8, 35, 44, 54, 55, 143, 158, 160,
161, 163, 167, 204
Islamic Revolution in, 29, 34, 42, 43,
71, 92, 93, 107, 155, 157, 159,
163, 197, 207
and relations with Turkey, 46–48, 50,
55
support to Hizballah by, 92, 94, 95,
97, 98, 99, 101
support to terrorism by, 44, 47–48,
50, 57
and war with Iraq, 44, 213
Iraq, 179,
and war with Iran, 44, 213
and war with Kuwait, 110, 210, 213

Islam, 155, 161, 180, 208–209
Christians and Jews in, 17, 179–180.
See also dhimmis
civil society in, 157, 163
and democracy, 155, 157, 160, 162,
164, 166, 167
doctrine of, 155, 158, 162
See also 'ulama; Shari'a
Islamic Action, 45, 46
Islamic Action Front. *See* Jordanian
Muslim Brotherhood
Islamic Constitutional Movement (ICM),
111, 113, 115, 117
Islamic Group, The (*al-Jama'ah al-
Islamiyyah*), 34
Islamic information centers, 26
Islamic Jihad Squadrons (*Saraya al-Jihad
al-Islami*), 35
Islamic Jihad Squadrons Jerusalem/the
temple (*Saraya al-Jihad al-Islami
Bait al-Maqdes*), 35
Islamic Liberation Party (*Hizb al-Tahrir
al-Islami*), 24, 42
Islamic Liberation Party Front (IKP-C),
42
Islamic Movement (*Islami Hareket*), The,
42, 43, 45, 52, 59–60
Islamic National Alliance (INA), 111
Islamic People's Command, 131
Islamic Popular Alliance (IPA), 111
Islamic Resistance (*Islami Direnis*). *See*
Islamic Movement (*Islami Hareket*)
Islamic Salvation Army. *See* AIS
Islamic Salvation Front. *See* FIS
Islamic Salvation Group. *See* GIA
Islamic Social Reform Society (*al-Islah al-
Ijtima'i*), 106, 107, 108, 111
Islamic Student Movement, The. *See al-
Harakah al-Islamiyyah al-Tulabiyyah*
Islamic University of Gaza, 25, 28, 31,
33, 34, 35, 36
Islamist movements, 1–4, 6, 8, 9, 12,
41, 76, 78, 94, 100, 160, 207, 208,
211–217
activities of, 2, 4, 5, 6, 28, 75, 142
ideology of, 4, 44, 156, 157, 160, 166
and Israel, 28, 33, 34, 36, 49, 53,

56–57, 92, 93, 95–96, 99–101, 213–215
opposition to, 3, 6
publications by, 27–29, 43, 46
use of violence by, 3, 18, 45, 49, 213
Islamist Welfare Party. *See* RP
al-Islamiyyun al-Mustaqillun (The Independent Islamists), 34
al-Israa' wal-Mi'raj, 28
Israel, 4, 12, 24, 25, 37, 163, 177, 212
  Hizballah's struggle against, 92, 93, 95–96, 99–101, 214
  and Islamist movements, 28, 33, 34, 36, 49, 53, 56–57, 92, 93, 95–96, 99–101, 213–215
  relations with Lebanon, 29, 91, 92, 95, 96, 98, 101, 214
  relations with Syria, 95, 99, 100, 101
  relations with Turkey, 49, 53, 56–57
Israeli-Palestinian conflict, 100, 161
itjihad (legal reinterpretation), 8, 15
'Iz al-Din Ibrahim, Dr. *See* al-Shqaqi, Dr. Fathi
'Iz al-Din al-Qassam Brigades, 34

jahiliyya (pagan ignorance), 12, 15
Jalal al-'Azm, Sadiq, 205
al-Jama'ah al-Islamiyyah (Palestinian). *See* Islamic Group, The
al-Jama'at al-Islamiyya (Radical Islamic societies), 7, 11, 12, 19, 160
jama'at. *See* al-Jama'at al-Islamiyya
Jamaat-i Islami, 159
Jama'at al-Jihad or al-Jihad (Society of Struggle), 12, 14–16
  use of violence by, 13, 17–19
Japanese Red Army, 53
al-Jaza'ira, 83, 205
Jerusalem, 23, 25
jihad, 12, 17, 33
Jordan, 3, 4, 173, 177, 211, 212, 215
Jordanian Communist Party, 24
Jordanian Muslim Brotherhood, (Islamic Action Front), 7, 27, 32, 210
Journalists' and Writers' Foundation, 145, 150. *See also* Gulen movement
JP (Justice Party), 126–127, 129

Jumblatt family, 179
Justice Party. *See* JP
Justice and Charity movement. *See* al-'Adl wal-Ihsan
Justice and Development Party. *See* Akparti

Kabir, Humayun, 192
Kabir, Rabah, 82
Kadiris, 59
Kamhi, Jak, 45
Karaday, Ismail Hakk, 148
Karamanoglu, Altan, 53
Karimov, Islam, 53
Kazan, Sevket, 131
Khamene'i, Ayatollah Ali, 44, 53, 57, 98, 158
kharijis, 19
Khatami, Muhammad, 57, 133, 158, 198, 207
Khatib, Abd al-Karim, 74
khilafa (Caliphate), 14, 15, 19, 35
Khomeini, Ayatollah Ruhollah, 34, 43, 44, 80, 84, 97, 158, 208
al-Khorafi, Jassem, 119
Kilic, Altemur, 150
al-Kindari, Jamal, 114
Kirca, Ali, 46
Kislali, Ahmet Taner, 51, 52
al-Kitab wal Quran (Shahrur), 118, 205
Kubba, Laith, 167
Kutlar, Onat, 45, 46
Kurdistan Workers' Party. *See* PKK
Kurds, 129, 130, 132, 133
Kutan, Recai, 131, 133, 149
Kuwait, 3, 105, 106, 109, 110, 118, 120, 121, 160, 164, 215
  application of Shari'a in, 111–112, 114, 117, 119
  and conflict with Iraq, 110, 210
  relations with the United States, 110, 116
Kuwait University, 107, 109, 113–114, 120
Kuwaiti Islamic movements, 109, 111
  political of activities of, 107–108, 112–115
  revival of, 105, 107, 117

Kuwaiti Muslim Brotherhood, 107, 108, 111, 117

bin Ladin, Osama, 19
Lapidot, Anat, 42
League of the Islamic Future. *See Rabitat al-Mustaqbal al-Islami*
Lebanese American University, 176
Lebanese University, 182
Lebanese Hizballah, 53
Lebanon, 4, 92, 106, 160, 173, 177, 179, 182
    Maronite-Sunni community in, 93, 94, 98, 181
    and relations with Israel, 29, 91, 92, 95, 96, 98, 101, 214
    Shi'ite community in, 91–93, 94, 95
    Western culture and, 176, 177
legal reinterpretation. *See itjihad*
Lerner, Daniel, 203
Libya, 3

Madani, Dr. 'Abbasi, 80, 81, 82, 199
madhhabs (the four schools of Islam), 15
al-Madhkur, Khalid, 117
Madjid, Nurcholish, 195–196
Mahcupyan, Etyen, 150
mahdi, 11, 18
Mahmassani, Subhi, 192
majlis al-shura, 13
Makovsky, Alan, 56, 58
Malatya (Islamic Youth), 61, 133
Mandela, Nelson, 176
al-Manbar al-Dimuqrati. See Democratic Forum
March 1991, revolt of, 3
Markaba, 100
Mashriq, 69, 70
Mawdudi, Abul A'la, 159
Mawdudi, Mawlana, 77
Mernissi, Fatima, 70–71, 194–195
Merzaq, Madani, 82, 83
MGK. *See* NSC
MHP. *See* Nationalist Movement Party
MIA (Mouvement Islamique Armé), 81
Milliyet, 55
Mirzabeyoglu, Salih. *See* Erdis, Salih Izzet

MIT. *See* Turkish National Intelligence Organization.
Morocco, 3, 4, 6, 69, 70, 75, 211, 215
    Islamist activities in, 73, 75, 76
Motherland Party, 129
Mouvement Islamique Armé. *See* MIA
Mouvement Populaire Democratique et Constitutionnel. *See* MPDC
Movement for Reform and Renewal. *See Harakat al-Islah wal-Tajdid*
Movement for Unification and Reform. *See Harakat al-Tawhid wal-Islah*
MPDC (Mouvement Populaire Democratique et Constitutionnel), 74
Mu'awad, Rene, 94
Mubarak, Hosni, 3, 5, 47
mudawwana (Moroccan personal status law), 72, 76
mufassala kamila (total separation), 16
King Muhammad VI, 71, 72, 73, 75
Muhammad's original flight from Mecca to Medina. *See hijra*
mujaddid, 11
mujahidin, 19
al-Mujtama, 117
al-mujtama' al-madani (civil society), 78, 157, 163, 165
al-Mukhtar al-Islami. See Islamist movements, publications by
Mumcu, Ugur, 45, 47, 48, 49
al-Muntalaq, 30, 31. *See also* Palestinian Islamic groups, publications by
musalaha, 174, 183–186. *See also Shari'a*
MUSIAD (Association of Independent Industrialists and Businessmen), 128
Muslim Youth Association, 29
Mustafa, Shukri, 13
al-Mutawa, Abdallah, 111, 118
al-Mutayri, Mufaraj Nahar, 113
al-Muti, Abd al-Karim, 74, 75
Muzzaffar, Chandra, 192, 194
Mzali, Muhammad, 78

Nader, Laura, 174–175
al-Nahda movement, 7, 9, 77, 80, 164
Nahnah, Shaykh Mahfoud, 6, 80

al-Najah university, 30, 32, 34, 36
Nakshibendis, 59, 126
Naksibendi, Bahaeddin, 146
NAP (National Action Party), 126–127
Nasrallah, Hasan, 94, 96, 100, 101
Nasser, 11
National Action Party. *See* NAP
National Order Party. *See* NOP
National Palestinian Council, 29
National Salvation Party. *See* NSP
National Union of Kuwaiti Students, 119
National View, 53
National Youth Foundation, 59
Nationalist Movement Party (MHP), 43,
    51, 129
Neglected Obligation, The (Faraj), 13
Neo-Destour party, 9
New Jihad Group, The (Vanguards of
    the Conquest), 18
al-Nidaa. See Palestinian Hamas,
    publications by
NOP (National Order Party), 125–126
November 17 Organization, 53
NSC (National Security Council), 44, 49,
    50, 58, 128, 131, 134, 135, 147
NSP (National Salvation Party), 41,
    126–127, 129
al-Nur. See Palestinian Islamic Jihad,
    publications by
al-Nur al-Ilahi. See Palestinian Islamic
    Jihad, publications by
al-Nur al-Rabbani. See Palestinian Islamic
    Jihad, publications by
Nur movement, 141, 142, 161, 205
Nurcu movement. *See Nur* movement
Nurcus, 126
Nursi, Said, 141, 142, 143, 162
    Risale-i-Nur, 142

Objektif, 43, 46. *See also* Turkish Islamist
    movements, publications by
Ocalan, Abdullah, 53, 54, 55, 58, 133
Ocalan, Osman, 55
Oman, 164, 203
One Minute of Darkness for Enlighten-
    ment protest, 131. *See also* Turkey,
    political discontent in

Orientalists, 155
Ottoman Empire, 142, 180
Ozal, Turgut, 46, 47, 128, 129, 143
Ozdag, Umit, 54
Ozdalga, Elisabeth, 146
Ozkaragoz, Mehmet, 144
Ozdemir, Hasan, 52
Ozkok, Ertugrul, 51
Ozturk, Prof. Yasar Nuri, 52

pagan ignorance. *See jahiliyya*
Pakistan, 3, 5, 215
Paladin Howitzer crisis, 116
Palestine, 33, 36
Palestinian Authority, 36, 37, 214
Palestinian Communist Party, 29, 31
Palestinian Hamas (Palestinian Muslim
    Brotherhood), 4, 7, 23, 24, 27, 28,
    33, 35–36, 47, 160, 210, 213
    and activities in universities, 29–31
    publications by, 29, 32
    social activities of, 26–28
    use of violence by, 26
Palestinian Islamic groups, 23, 27, 28,
    30, 32, 34
    activities of, 28, 29, 33
    publications by, 30, 31, *See also al-*
        Muntalaq; al-Nidaa
Palestinian Islamic Jihad 23, 26, 27, 28,
    33, 34, 44, 101, 210, 213, 214
    publications by, 29, 34, 35
    use of violence by, 35
Palestinian Liberation Organization. *See* PLO
Palestinian Muslim Brotherhood. *See*
    Palestinian Hamas
Palestinian society, 24–26, 36, 37
Pan-Arabism, 1, 70
Parti de la Justice et du Developpement.
    See PJD
Party of the Blissfulness. *See* Saadet Party
People's Democracy Party. *See* HADEP
People's Liberation Army of Kurdistan, 53
PJD (Parti de la Justice et du Developpement),
    74
PKK (Kurdistan Workers' Party), 42, 46,
    47–49, 50, 55, 56
    use of violence by, 52, 53

PLO (Palestinian Liberation Organization), 25, 26, 27, 28, 33, 36, 213
PMMC Report (Prime Minister's Monitoring Council), 58
Protestant Ethics of Capitalism, The (Weber) 151–152

Qadhafi, Muammar, 3, 131
al-Qaradawi, Shaykh Yusuf, 5, 205
al-Qasim, Na'im, 94, 100
Qutb, Sayyid, 11–12, 34, 77, 82, 159

Rabitat al-Mustaqbal al-Islami (League of the Islamic Future), 74
Ra'd, Muhammad, 101
Radical Islamic movements. *See* Islamist movements.
Radical Islamic societies. *See* al-Jama'at al-Islamiyya
Rahman, Fazlur, 159
Rahmet Group, 54
Rassemblement National Democratique. *See* RND
Redjam, Abd al-Razak, 199
Refah Party, 148, 149
Religious legal edict. *See fatwa*
Renan, Ernest, 199
Republican People's Party. *See* CHP
Resalat, 56
Revivalist. *See salafi*
al-Risalah. See Palestinian Hamas, publications by
Risale-i-Nur (Nursi), 142
RND (Rassemblement National Democratique), 82
Rosefsky Wickham, Carrie, 163
RP (Islamist Welfare Party), 41, 47, 48–49, 50, 53, 57, 126, 127, 130, 131, 132, 211
al-Rube'i, Ahmad, 114

Saadet Party (Party of the Blissfulness), 134
al-Sa'adoun, Ahmad, 116
Sabah, 106
al-Sabah, Shaykh Sabah al-Ahmad, 119
al-Sabah, Shaykh Sa'ud Nasser, 116

Sadat, 12, 13, 29
al-Sadiq al-Nayhum, 118
al-Sadr, Musa, 93, 97
Sa'id, Muhammad, 199
al-Salaf organization, 107, 108, 111
salafi, 14, 24, 69, 71, 83
Salam family, 179
Salvation from Hell group, 18
Santillana, 160
Saraya al-Jihad al-Islami. See Islamic Jihad Squadrons
Saraya al-Jihad al-Islami Bait al-Maqdes. See Islamic Jihad Squadrons Jerusalem/the temple
Saudi Arabia, 12, 24, 42, 71, 111, 143, 160, 164, 206, 211
Savasir, Iskender, 150
Sawt al-Haqq Wal-Quwah Wal-Hurriyah. See Palestinian Hamas, publications by
Sayari, Sabri, 42
September 1980 military coup, 41, 43, 127
September 11, 2001, attacks of, 19, 121
Sezer, Ahmet Necdet, 149
Shaba'a Farms, 100, 101
Shabiba (lijan al-shabibah lil-'amal al-ijtima'i, youth committees for social work), 31
al-Shabiba al-Islamiyya, 74, 75
al-Shafi'i, 159
Shafiq, Munir, 8
Shahrur, Muhammad, 118, 194, 205
  Al-Kitab wal Quran, 118, 205
al-Shqaqi, Dr. Fathi (pseud. Dr. 'Iz al-Din Ibrahim), 29, 44
Shari'a (Islamic law), 5, 14, 15, 19–20, 80, 109, 111, 142, 143, 158, 159, 161, 192, 199, 200. *See also* Islam; *sulh* ritual; *musalaha*
al-Shatti, Dr. Isma'il, 117
al-Shawayyib, Fahid Abd al-Rahman, 111
al-Shihab. See Palestinian Hamas, publications by
Shu'ayb, 'Alya, 115
shura, 8, 77, 159
Siddiqui, Kalim, 43

Sidky, 'Atef, 19
Sizinti, 145. See also Turkish Teachers'
    Foundation
SLA (South Lebanese Army), 96
SMC (Supreme Military Council), 49
Social Movement for Peace, 6
Society of Muslims. See Takfir wal-Hijra
Society of the Rebirth of Islamic Tradi-
    tion, 111
Society of Struggle. See al-Jama'at al-
    Jihad
El-Sohl, 179
Soroush, Abdul Karim, 164, 165, 193,
    197
South Lebanese Army. See SLA
Soviet Union, 2, 42
Sudan, 2, 8, 160, 161, 167
Suez Canal, 3
Sufi tradition, 141–142, 152
sulh ritual, 174, 183–186. See also
    Shari'a
Sunna, 14
Syria, 3, 33, 58, 110, 160, 177, 179,
    211
    relations with Israel, 95, 99, 100, 101
    support to Hizballah by, 92, 94, 95,
    98, 99, 101
Syrian Muslim Brotherhood, 53, 210,
    212

Tabligh, 74
Ta'if Agreement, 93, 94, 98
Tajammu al'Islah party, 7
takfir (unbelief), 12, 13
Takfir wal-Hijra or al-Takfir (Society of
    Muslims), 13, 15, 17–18
    ideology of, 12, 14–16, 19
    recruitment by, 13–14,
    use of violence by, 18, 19
Talbi, Muhammad, 192, 193
Taleqani, Ayatollah, 158, 162
Taliban, 160
talqin, 5
al-Tamimi, Shaykh As'ad, 35
taqnin al-Shari'a, 7
Taraf, 46. See also IBDA-C, publications
    by; Turkish Islamist movements,

publications by
tawaghit (idols), 15
Tehvid, 43, 46. See also publications by ·
    Turkish Islamist movements
Tekdal, Ahmet, 53
Ten-member consultation committee. See
    majlis al-shura
Territories, the. See Gaza Strip; West Bank
THKP-C. See Turkish People's Liberation
    Party Front
Tibi, Bassam, 180
TIKB. See Turkish Islamic Liberation
    Union
TIK-C. See Turkish Islamic Liberation
    Front
Total separation. See mufassala kamila
Tozy, Mohamed, 74
True Path Party, 129, 130
TSIK. See Turkish Shari'a Revenge
    Commandos
al-Tufayli, Shaykh Subhi, 97, 98
Tunc, Abd al-'Aziz, 55
Tunisia, 3, 6, 69, 70, 74, 76–77, 79
Tunisian Islamic Front (FIT), 7
al-Turabi, Hasan, 8, 71, 80, 162
Turkes, Alpaslan, 126, 127
Turkey, 3, 7, 41, 47, 51–52, 125–127,
    163, 204, 212, 215
    conflict between Sunnis and Alevis in,
    127, 129 130, 144
    political discontent in, 127, 130, 131.
    See also One Minute of Darkness
    for Enlightenment protest
    and relations with Iran, 46–48, 50, 55
    and relations with Israel, 49, 53, 56–
    57
    socioeconomic situation in, 125, 127,
    128, 130, 133, 134
Turkish Businessmen's and Industrialists'
    Association. See TUSIAD
Turkish Fighters of the Universal Islamic
    War of Liberation (EIK-TM), 42
Turkish Hizballah, 42, 43, 44, 47, 52,
    54, 59, 60, 133
    use of violence by, 45–46, 51, 53
Turkish Islamic Fighters Army (IMO),
    42

Turkish Islamic Jihad, 42, 44, 45
Turkish Islamic Liberation Army (IKO), 42
Turkish Islamic Liberation Front (TIK-C), 42
Turkish Islamist movements, 41, 42, 48, 50, 125, 126, 129, 132, 134
  ideology of, 44, 127–128
  influence of Iran on, 133–134
  publications by, 43, 46, 131
  use of violence by, 45, 49
  See also CHP (Republican People's Party); Democratic Left Part (DLP); Democratic Party (DP); Fighters of the Islamic Revolution (IDAM); FP (Fazilet Party); IBDA-C (The Great Eastern Islamic Fighters Front); ICCB (Union of Islamic Associations and Societies); Islamic Action; Islamic Liberation Party; The Islamic Movement; Nationalist Movement Party (MHP); NOP (National Order Party); NSP (National Salvation Party), PKK (Kurdistan Workers' Party); RP (Islamist Welfare Party); Turkish Fighters of the Universal Islamic War of Liberation (EIK-TM); Turkish Hizballah; Turkish Islamic Fighters Army (IMO); Turkish Islamic Liberation Army (IKO); Turkish Islamic Liberation Front (TIK-C); Turkish Islamic Liberation Union (TIKB); Turkish National Intelligence Organization (MIT); Turkish People's Liberation Party Front (THKP-C); Turkish Shari'a Revenge Commandos (TSIK); Universal Brotherhood Front—Shari'a Revenge Squad (EKC-SIM); World Shari'a Liberation Army (DSKO)
Turkish Islamic Liberation Union (TIKB), 42
Turkish-Islamic Synthesis, 41–42, 46, 49, 57
Turkish National Intelligence Organization (MIT), 42

Turkish People's Liberation Party Front (THKP-C), 59
Turkish Shari'a Revenge Commandos (TSIK), 42
Turkish Teachers' Foundation, 145. See also Gulen movement; Fountain, the; Sizinti; Yeni Umit
TUSIAD (Turkish Businessmen's and Industrialists' Association), 128

'Ubayd, Abd al-Karim, 100
'ulama, 155, 156, 159, 162, 166
  role in Islam of, 157–158
  See also Islam
umma, 5, 14, 71, 159
unbelief. See takfir
Union of Islamic Associations and Societies. See ICCB
Union Socialiste des Forces Populaires (USFP), 72, 74
United Arab Emirates, 110
United States, 84, 92, 173–176
  relations with Kuwait, 110, 116
Universal Brotherhood Front—Shari'a Revenge Squad (EKC-SIM), 42
Université Saint-Joseph, 182
UN Resolution 425, 100
USFP. See Union Socialiste des Forces Populaires
al-'Uthman, Layla, 116

Vahiduddin, Syed, 193
Vanguards of the Conquest. See New Jihad Group, The
Velioglu, Huseyni, 55
Virtue Party. See FP
Voice of Truth, Power and Freedom (Sawt al-Haqq Wal-Quwah Wal-Hurriyah). See Palestinian Hamas, publications by

Wadi al-Anjil, 3
Wadud-Muhsin, Amina, 194
Wahabi, 24
Wahid, Abdurrahman, 193
wa'i (awareness), 28
Waqf, 23, 24, 27
Wasat party, 7, 9

Wendell Holmes, Oliver, 195
West Bank, 23, 24, 25, 27, 36, 37
Western conflict-resolution model of, 173–174, 175, 182
Wilson, Woodrow, 196
World Trade Center, first bombing of, 19
World Shari'a Liberation Army (DSKO), 42
Wright, Robin, 158

Yalcin, Hasan, 53
Yarar, Erol, 128
Yasin, Shaykh Abd al-Salam, 74, 75, 76
al-Yasin, Shaykh Jasim Muhalhal, 111
Yasin, Nadia, 76
Yassin, Shaykh Ahmad, 30
Yazdi, Ibrahim, 158, 161
Yemen, 3, 4, 7
Yeni Safak, 131. See also Turkish Islamist movements, publications by
Yeni Umit, 145. See also Turkish Teachers' Foundation

Yeryuzu, 43, 46. See also Turkish Islamist movements, publications by
Yesevi, Ahmed, 146
Yildiz (Islamic Youth), 60
Yilmaz, Sevki, 53
YOK (High Education Council), 147
Youssoufi, Abd al-Rahmane, 72, 73, 75
Youth committees for social work (lijan al-shabibah lil-'amal al-ijtima'i). See Shabiba
Yuksel, Nuh Mete, 53

al-Zammur, 'Abbud, 18
al-Zamzami, Fqih, 74
Zartman, I. W., 71
al-Zawahiri, Dr. Ayman, 18
Zeituni, Jamal, 83
Zeroual, Liamine, 82, 84
Ziyad, Abd al-Ilah, 75
Zoubri, 'Antar, 83
Zubaidi, Sami, 48